Consciousness and Matter

Consciousness and Matter

Mind, Brain, and Cosmos in the Dialogue
between Science and Theology

Edited by
KIRILL KOPEIKIN
& ALEXEI V. NESTERUK

☙PICKWICK *Publications* • Eugene, Oregon

CONSCIOUSNESS AND MATTER
Mind, Brain, and Cosmos in the Dialogue between Science and Theology

Copyright © 2024 Wipf and Stock Publishers. All rights reserved. Except for brief quotations in critical publications or reviews, no part of this book may be reproduced in any manner without prior written permission from the publisher. Write: Permissions, Wipf and Stock Publishers, 199 W. 8th Ave., Suite 3, Eugene, OR 97401.

Pickwick Publications
An Imprint of Wipf and Stock Publishers
199 W. 8th Ave., Suite 3
Eugene, OR 97401

www.wipfandstock.com

PAPERBACK ISBN: 978-1-6667-7699-7
HARDCOVER ISBN: 978-1-6667-7700-0
EBOOK ISBN: 978-1-6667-7701-7

Cataloguing-in-Publication data:

Names: Kopeikin, Kirill [editor]. | Nesteruk, Alexei V., 1957– [editor].

Title: Consciousness and matter : mind, brain, and cosmos in the dialogue between science and theology / Kirill Kopeikin and Alexei V. Nesteruk.

Description: Eugene, OR: Pickwick Publications, 2024 | Includes bibliographical references and index.

Identifiers: ISBN 978-1-6667-7699-7 (paperback) | ISBN 978-1-6667-7700-0 (hardcover) | ISBN 978-1-6667-7701-7 (ebook)

Subjects: LCSH: Religion and science. | Religion—Philosophy. | Philosophy of mind. | Soul—Christianity. | Theological anthropology. | Cognitive science.

Classification: BT702 K67 2024 (print) | BT702 (ebook)

All Scripture quotations are from the King's James Version.

Disclaimer

This publication has been implemented within the framework of the Project "Science & Orthodoxy around the World," which was made possible through the support of a grant from the Templeton World Charity Foundation, Inc. The opinions expressed in this publication are those of the authors and do not necessarily reflect the views of the Project or the Templeton World Charity Foundation, Inc.

Contents

Notes on Contributors ix
Illustrations xiii
Preface xv
Acknowledgements xxxiii

1. Once Again about the Brain and Semiosis:
Can Neural Networks Make Their Point? 1
    Tatyana Chernigovskaya

2. Brain, Mind, and Soul in the Context
of the Dialogue between Science and Religion 12
    Dmitry Kiryanov

3. We Are More Than Our Brains:
In Search of the Subjective Beginning 28
    Alexander Kaplan

4. Liquid Light as a Model of Matter-Consciousness Dualism 38
    Alexey Kavokin

5. The "Hard Problem" of Consciousness Elucidated Cosmologically:
The Saturated Phenomenality of the Universe versus Its Object-Like
Constitution 45
    Alexei V. Nesteruk

6. The Biblical Thesis of the Creation of the World *ex nihilo*, the
Heisenberg Cut, Quantum Blindness, and the Ψ-*chism* of the
Universe—A Final Solution to the Hard Problem of Consciousness 85
    Kirill Kopeikin

7. Theology and Thermodynamics of Life and Mind:
The Legacy of Nikolai Kobozev (1903–74) 120
    Sergey Krivovichev

8. Neuroethics, Quantum Physics, and Theology 133
 Oleg Reznik and Kirill Kopeikin

9. Seed and Law: Neuroscience and Virtue Ethics in Christian Anthropology 160
 Walker Trimble

Index of Names 225

Notes on Contributors

EDITORS

Kirill Kopeikin holds PhD in Physics and Mathematics, as well as in Theology. He is a visiting researcher at the National Hellenic Research Foundation (Greece) on leave from his position of associate professor at St. Petersburg Theological Academy and St. Petersburg State University (Russia). Being a member of the European Society for the Study of Science and Theology (ESSAT) he directed for many years the interdisciplinary "Science and Theology" seminar, as well as co-chaired the "Science and Theology" section at the annual "Nativity Readings" International conference. His research interests include the relationships between matter and consciousness, fundamental physics and theology, biblical hermeneutics and natural theology. Selected publications: *Stairway to Heaven* (2009), *What Is Reality? Reflecting on the Work of Erwin Schrödinger* (2014).

Alexei V. Nesteruk is a visiting lecturer at the University of Portsmouth, UK. He holds PhD in Physics and Mathematics, and DSc in Philosophy. His main interests are in the field of phenomenological (transcendental) philosophy and cosmology, as well as in the dialogue between cosmology and Eastern Orthodox theology. Nesteruk writes extensively in the field publishing four books in English, three books in Russian, and three books in Romanian including: *Light from the East. Theology, Science, and the Eastern Orthodox Tradition* (2003); *The Universe as Communion. Towards a Neo-patristic Synthesis of Theology and Science* (2008); *The Sense of the Universe: The Philosophical Explication of Theological Commitment in Cosmology* (2015); *The Universe in the Image of Imago Dei: The Dialogue between Theology and Science as a Hermeneutics of the Human*

Condition (2022). Together with Christopher Knight, he co-edited the volume: *Orthodox Christianity and Modern Science: Theological, Philosophical, Scientific, and Historical Aspects of the Dialogue* (2021).

CONTRIBUTORS

Tatyana Chernigovskaya, PhD, DSc (Physiology, Linguistics). She is a professor at St. Petersburg State University (Russia) as well as at N. P. Bekhtereva Institute of the Human Brain. She is also Director of Institute for Cognitive Studies at St. Petersburg State University. Member of the Norwegian Academy of Sciences and Letters. Honorary member of the Semiotic Society of Finland. President of the Russian Association for Cognitive Studies (2008–10). Invited lecturer in many European and North American Universities. Major research interests include the cerebral basis for linguistic and cognitive functions, artificial intelligence, language evolution, acquisition and pathology, analytical philosophy. Recent publications include: *The Cheshire Smile of Schrödinger's Cat: Brain, Language, and Consciousness* (2022).

Alexander Kaplan, PhD, DSc. (Neurophysiology, Psychophysiology), professor at Lomonosov Moscow State University (Russia). He is a founding director of Neuro-Computer Interfaces Laboratory. A leading researcher in brain-machine interfaces and applied technology. A visiting professor at RIKEN Brain Science Institute, Japan, and at a number of technological and medical universities in India, South Korea, Germany, and the USA. Current research interests include non-invasive brain-computer interfaces based on EEG, biosignal processing, after stroke rehabilitation based on BCI-training, multi-signal integration for human-machine communication and virtual reality.

Alexey Kavokin, PhD, DSc (Physics), holds a Chair of Nanophysics and Photonics at the University of Southampton (UK). He is a Director of the International Center for Polaritonics at Westlake University, Hangzhou, China. Research interests include quantum physics, condensed matter physics, photonics. Recent co-authored publications include: "Steady State Oscillations of Circular Currents in Concentric Polariton Condensates," *Scientific Reports* 13 (2023); "Split-Ring Polariton Condensates as Macroscopic Two-Level Quantum Systems," *Physical Review Research* 3

(2021); "Excitonic Fine Structure in Emission of Linear Carbon Chains," *Nano Letters* 20 (2020).

Dmitry Kiryanov, PhD (Theology, Philosophy), associate professor at the Tobolsk Theological Seminary (Russia). Research interests include twentieth-century Roman Catholic philosophy and theology, fundamental theology, science and religion and philosophy of religion. Member of the European Society for Study of Science and Theology (ESSSAT), participant in Templeton Foundation Projects such as "The Development of a New Methodology for the Dialogue and Cooperation between Science and Religion in Russia" (2014–15), "Science and Eastern Orthodoxy." Author of more than fifty articles and books. Among them are: *Twentieth-Century Thomist Philosophy* (2009); *Science and Religion in Modern Western Theological Thought* (2016); "Evolution and Orthodox Theology in Russia: An Uneasy Way to Dialogue" in *Orthodox Christianity and Modern Science: Tensions, Ambiguities, Potential* (2019).

Sergey Krivovichev, PhD, DSc (Geology). The member of the Russian Academy of Sciences (RAS), General Director of the Kola Science Center of the RAS. Scientific interests are devoted to mineralogy, crystallography and inorganic material chemistry. President of the International Mineralogical Association (2014-2016), recipient of a number of international awards, including the Schlumberger-Neumann medal of the Mineralogical Association of Great Britain and Ireland and the Dana medal of the Mineralogical Association of America. Foreign member of the Torino Academy of Sciences. Author and editor of ten books on mineralogy and crystallography and two books on science and theology, including the textbook *Orthodoxy and Natural Sciences* (2022).

Oleg Reznik, Doctor of Medicine (PhD). Janelidze Research Institute of Emergency Medicine, St. Petersburg, Northwestern State Medical University, professor. Director of the Transplantology Department of the First St. Petersburg Pavlov State Medical University, member of the American Society of Transplantologists, European Society of Organ Transplantation. Research interests include the study of brain death, which naturally leads to the study of the religious aspects of the problems of consciousness. Editor of *Aporias of Modern Transplantology* (2020).

Walker Trimble, PhD (Philosophy). E-Quadrat Science & Education GmbH (Germany), senior expert. Senior lecturer and assistant professor at St. Petersburg and Herzen Universities (2008–23). Lecturer in translation studies, methodology and cognitive science. Research interests include the theology of creation, theory of information, epistemology and aesthetics. Related publications include: "From Function to Surface: Phenomenology of the Thinking Organ," in *Iranian Yearbook of Phenomenology* (2022); "Epistemic Foraging and the Creative Process," in *Lecture Notes in Networks and Systems* (2021); "Species Specierum': Late Scholastic Eucharistic Theology and the Roots of Posthumanism," in *Proceeds of the Theology Faculty, St. Petersburg Seminary* (2021); "Brains Situated, Active, and Strange: Neurosurgical magnification and physicalism's aesthetic consequences," *Jarbuch Technikphilosophie* (2020).

Illustrations

Figure 1: The relationship between human consciousness and the world presented by stereographic projection. (p. 58)

Figure 2: The "uroboros-like" representation of the radical inseparability of consciousness and the universe explicating the paradox of subjectivity. (p. 62)

Figure 3: Two rows of symbols. (p. 125)

Figure 4: Sagittal cross section of the human brain. (p. 196)

Preface

THE MAIN OBJECTIVE OF the present project on "Consciousness and Matter" is to reassess the current research in the field of interaction/mediation/dialogue between the sciences and theology in the context of the perennial Mind-Body problem. The topic of the project was part of the cross–disciplinary research undertaken by scientists, philosophers, and theologians within the framework of the Project "Science & Orthodoxy around the World" run by the National Hellenic Research Foundation (Athens) from 2019 to 2023. The project and this publication contribute to the academic activity in the field of science and religion with a particular accent on the contribution of Eastern Orthodox theology to this dialogue, as well as to the venues of advancement of theology given the recent breakthroughs in quantum physics, physiology, medical sciences and philosophy.

As the history of science testifies, many of the revolutions that have radically changed our concepts of the world have coincided with great social cataclysms. Indeed, the formation of classical physics, according to Galileo, began during the Thirty Years' War (1618–48), which shook the foundations of the former world order, and completed the transition from the Middle Ages to the Modern period. The result of this war led to the new Westphalian system of international relations, which was based on principles of state sovereignty (a kind of equivalent of the "principle of inertia") and the balance of power (a kind of analogue of Newton's soon-formulated Third Law). The dynamic laws introduced at that time by Galileo Galilei (1564–1643) differed radically from the description of the static, hierarchically ordered world that existed before. They described not self-existent, self-essential being, but the dynamics of being—the movement of some elements of the universe relative to others—in other words, the relativity of being. This represented a fundamentally new version of ontology. Based on the concept of dynamic laws, Isaac Newton (1642–1727) created a universal system of physics: the *Philosophiæ Naturalis Principia Mathematica* (1687), which revolutionized science by formulating the fundamental laws that pertain to the entire universe. In the following year, 1688, the English Parliament adopted a code of civil rights: *An Act Declaring the Rights and Liberties of the Subject and Settling the Succession of the Crown*. This granted legislative approval for laws that even the royal powers were compelled to obey. The "Bill of Rights" was the legal result of the Civil War, which had broken out in 1640 in England, and the Glorious Revolution that followed it—events that the famous historian of the Victorian era, Thomas Babington Macaulay (1800–1859), considered the central event of English history. The immediate consequence of the Glorious Revolution was the Industrial Revolution. The Great Industrial Revolution, which began in Great Britain, covered the countries of Europe and the new United States of America. In just a few generations, it transformed an agrarian society into an industrial one and led to the establishment of capitalism as the dominant world economic order.

As the nineteenth century drew to a close, classical physics solidified, asserting itself as a comprehensive portrayal of the laws governing the non-living aspects of nature. Within its confines, classical physics established the foundation for a materialistic perspective that viewed the Universe as an assembly of material particles, meticulously adhering to deterministic laws, while existing in an unchanging space and time framework. It is noteworthy that even Newton himself did not wholly align with this Newtonian mindset; the materialistic interpretation did not fully resonate with him. Recognizing that the intricacies of life and the essence of the soul couldn't be solely explained through mechanical interactions, he devoted considerable time to theological contemplation and alchemical exploration, seeking elusive signs of God's presence in the natural world. Despite his persistent efforts, Newton never succeeded in uncovering this profound connection. As he kept his theological and alchemical pursuits concealed, his posthumous legacy painted him as a prominent materialist thinker, erroneously attributing him as the architect of an atheistic mechanistic representation of the world, devoid of humanity. This misinterpretation propagated the notion that the materialistic viewpoint was the exclusive valid perspective. In the realm of classical physics, both space and time remain impervious to the influence of the matter they encompass or the shifts in reference frames. For Newton, space was the "sensorium of God"—*Sensorium Dei*—a medium through which the Creator perceived the entirety of the Universe.

In the early decades of the twentieth century, the emergence of the theory of relativity and quantum mechanics brought about a profound transformation in our understanding of the universe. This transformative shift subsequently triggered a revolutionary wave of technological advancements. For many, the intricate pursuits of intellectual elites engaged in scrutinizing the standard model of elementary particles, investigating the Higgs boson's properties at the Large Hadron Collider, or delving into the mysteries of Dark Matter in the universe, may appear distant and abstract. These endeavors seem removed not only from their immediate concerns but also from any tangible practicality.

In stark contrast, the very devices that intertwine with our daily lives—mobile phones, navigational systems, televisions, flat-screen monitors, computers, laser printers, and the expansive realm of the Internet—owe their existence to the principles of quantum mechanics and the theory of relativity. Yet, it is these principles that have paved the way for the functionalities of our cherished gadgets. These monumental breakthroughs have not only propelled the development of nuclear weaponry and nuclear reactors but have also given birth to semiconductor chips, lasers, and the sprawling domain of high-tech microelectronics—an industry that, by present estimations, constitutes a substantial portion of the global economy.

The exploration in the realm of atomic and subatomic particles, along with the pioneering creation of transformative technologies in the early twentieth century, earned the label "first quantum revolution." It's notable that the scientific revolution of the twentieth century unfolded amidst a complete rupture with the prevailing system of social relations. This shift was starkly evidenced by monumental events such as the World War 1 (1914–18), the Russian February and October Revolutions (1917), the German November Revolution (1918), and the disintegration of four empires: Russian, Austro-Hungarian, Ottoman, and German.

Renowned historian of science, Paul Forman, in his seminal work *Weimar Culture, Causality and Quantum Theory, 1918–1927: Adaptation of German Physicists and Mathematicians to an Unfriendly Intellectual Milieu*, of 1971, contends that the distinct post-war milieu of the Weimar Republic—permeated with irrationalism and mysticism—played a pivotal role in dismantling many previously seen as unshakable presuppositions of classical science. Particularly noteworthy was the substitution of the Laplacean determinism, a cornerstone of classical physics, with indeterminism intrinsic to quantum mechanics.

As the Second World War concluded, it bore witness to the unleashing of the atomic bomb (in 1945) and the subsequent creation of the thermonuclear bomb (in 1952). The core principle of the latter is based on the conversion of mass into energy ($E = mc^2$). Despite substantial changes in the picture of the world, materialism as a philosophical outlook persevered as the bedrock of the natural sciences and the corresponding worldview.

In the twenty-first century, according to the insights of numerous experts, humanity is on the edge of what has been tentatively termed the "second quantum revolution." Our endeavors are now centered on mastering the manipulation of individual quantum entities: the orchestration of transistors at the atomic scale and the control of singular photons, among other notable achievements.

This second quantum revolution implies the promise of entering a new era of information technologies. It seeks to bring forth cutting-edge devices for quantum cryptography, quantum computing, and quantum sensors. Moreover, it aspires to deepen our comprehension of the intricate nature of the human psyche and bring us closer to the creation of artificial intelligence. This revolutionary pursuit is a global endeavor, with nearly all advanced nations engaged in its exploration. The United States has ratified the "National Quantum Initiative Act," while the European Union has embarked on the expansive research and innovation endeavor "Quantum Flagship." Not to be outdone, China, India, and Russia have also entered the race, marking a collective pursuit of quantum advancements.

Forecasts from experts underscore the transformative potential of this "second quantum revolution," envisaging profound metamorphoses across the realms of science, industry, and society at large. According to Nicolas Gisin, a prominent figure within the field, the conceptual revolution taking place today completely overturns our previous pictures of nature and will doubtlessly give rise to a range of new technologies that will simply look like magic.

However, there is a problem. Claiming advances related to the "second quantum revolution" in technological applications, the very nature of quantum theory remains mysteriously concealed from those who use it. According to the American physicist Sean Carroll, "even physicists don't understand quantum mechanics. Worse, they don't seem to want to understand it." This is the title of his September 7, 2019, *The New York Times* essay based on his book *Something Deeply Hidden: Quantum Worlds and the Emergence of Spacetime*. Carroll's words may seem like a dramatic exaggeration, but surveys conducted over the last decade indicate that, even among professionals, there is no consensus as to the foundations and interpretation of quantum physics. Physicists know how to apply quantum mechanics, but they are far from certain about what ontological reality is behind the mathematics of quantum physics and its operational success. What exactly does quantum theory describe? Although almost 100 years have passed since the formation of quantum theory, there is still no complete clarity despite many different interpretations of the mathematical apparatus used have been proposed. If one reflects upon such a situation, it seems to be at least strange. This is the kind of situation one might expect from the human sciences that, *ab initio*, assume the plurality of different interpretations, but this is not what we should expect from the natural sciences which pretend to be descriptive and not just hermeneutical. This kind of uncertainty in approaching the sense of nature reflects de facto that condition of human consciousness as it approaches the limits of its own comprehension. In a way, such a variety and uncertainty of views about nature reflects the essence of the human condition as not fully known by man.

It seems that today we are approaching not just a technological, but also a socio-political "revolution"—this is evidenced by the current social, political, ecological and demographic situation. Humanity became a hostage of the scientific progress and its actual orientation on the world is closely related to the capacity to have access and to exploit natural resources. This creates tensions among nations inequally positioned economically and technologically and desiring for a just share of the common good. To the same extent as a political turmoil of the WWII stimulated an incredible advance in the sciences and technologies, the present social, political and economic disequilibrium is to give rise to the further revolution in worldviews, especially in those strategies of survival and preservation of the planet which humanity should adopt. This follows from the unfolding truth that science is not only about developing new technologies and creating more and more complex gadgets simplifying life, but, actually, about explication and preservation of life as such. As Erwin Schrödinger, the Nobel Prize winner and one of the greatest physicists of the twentieth century insisted, the highest aim of science can be formulated in the words of the Delphic Oracle: "Γνῶθι σεαυτόν"—"Know the thyself." The highest aim of science is to help humanity to understand its own sense, its place, and its destiny in the universe. This understanding aims to respond to the perennial questions such as "Who are we? How and why did we end up in this world that brings us so much suffering? What awaits us after death?" All these questions now go together with another pain-staking question of how humanity need to sustain its development in order to survive in view of many glooming predicaments. All such questions are essentially theological because they imply an appeal to that concealed foundation of life in the world which different religions call God. This appeal does not guarantee that humanity will accomplish its way to the truth of the world. Being made in the unknowable God's image, and thus being made incomprehensible for itself, humanity can understand the world only to that extent which was granted to it through the image. Thus the world can only be comprehended in the image of the image.

This leads to the intuition that if the "second quantum revolution" aims to advance the sense of intelligent existence, it is impossible to arrive at this revolution remaining within the old materialist paradigm, asserting the primacy of the inanimate matter. Indeed, no materialism can account to the emergence of the human intelligence. The latter implies not only the study of the physical conditions for the existence of sentient beings, not only the study of some forms of "social" behavior in animals and men, but, first of all, of that personal consciousness which makes possible to articulate the world and create artefacts capable of supporting, advancing, and expanding humanity in the whole of nature. The problem is that most of the natural sciences leave behind the problem of intelligence because in their functioning they already imply this hypostatic intelligence as already given. This is the reason why the second quantum revolution implies not only the study of nature as such, but the very conditions of the possibility of this nature as articulated reality. The latter brings humanity to the necessity of doing research in the field of neuro-biology, psychology, and neuro-philosophy bearing in mind that the ultimate sense of humanity remains hidden in its being created and hence all scientific research contributes to the open ended hermeneutics of the human condition.

Today, the study of the brain and consciousness is one of the primary foci of research. The elucidation of the "hard problem of consciousness" as a split between hypostatic self-givenness (in first-person) and the worldly position among other things (in third-person) is considered to be the main scientific challenge of the twenty-first century. And although the number of laboratories analyzing the workings of the brain is growing constantly, there is still no answer to the question of what consciousness is and how it is related to brain function. In light of the vexing problems of understanding the mechanisms of the brain, the nature of the psyche and artificial intelligence. It seems that materialism as a philosophical orientation and attitude (shaken but still standing after the scientific revolutions of the early twentieth century), must be finally dismissed from the field of consciousness and a new attitude to its study adopted.

How such a change in orientation of research can be achieved? There are two options possible: one is philosophical and the second is also philosophical, but imbued with theology. First, one needs to bring explicitly into the discourse the very presence of consciousness. This entails that the content of scientific experiments and theories must be referred to the very conditions of possibility of these experiments and theories originating in forms of the human subjectivity. In other words, one must be understood that the resulting picture of the world is conditioned by the implicit and explicit presence of humanity in it. The structures of consciousness can be traced through the generative steps of subjectivity in constructing the world. Yet even this shift in attitude does not shed any light on the origin of consciousness as such. This origin can be interpreted, but not explained. The change of the attitude from the natural one to the phenomenological, when the content of the outer reality remains suspended and not ontologized, explicate the sense of what in some refences call the uroboros of consciousness implying that no strict separation between consciousness and its worldly content, that is, mind and body, is possible. In modern terms this is not a trivial repetition of the famous Protagoras's statement on man as a measure of all things, but a clear indication that all new scientific technologies witnessing to the second quantum revolution are humanly constructed, so that the sense of reality is inextricably imbued with the human presence. Technology as the extension of the human body, together with the recent application to the artificial intelligence as learning and synthesizing capacities of the human mind, make it more evident that the sense of reality cannot be separated materialistically as something independent from the presence of an incessant human expansion into the outer visible (empirical) and invisible (intelligible) worlds.

One of the church fathers of the seventh century, St. Maximus the Confessor, talked about the abovementioned as the ongoing incarnation of humanity in the world labelling it with the term "makroanthropops," meaning that the universe is "man at large." Christianity attributes this function of articulating the universe at large, that is, of performing a synthesis of the universe, to man in the Divine Image. Man has a capacity of "enhypostasizing" the world, that is, making it palpable and graspable in the hypostasis (personhood) of humanity. Yet, unlike the sciences and philosophy, theology links this capacity with the archetype of the Logos-Christ in whose hypostasis the world was created. The latter means that the image of the world as it is given to us is that which is "seen" by the Logos himself. In other words, man sees the world though the "eyes" of the Logos-Creator for whom the factual specificity of the created world expresses the volitions and wisdom of the Logos. Can then one claim that the modern scientific advance, including the second quantum revolution and recent breaks in the artificial intelligence technologies witness to the fact that humanity accelerates its grasp of reality by acquiring the "mind" of the Logos himself?

In other words, can one approach the sciences as if their content reflects those creative ideas with respect to the world by God himself? In this perspective a popular phrase that through nature we study the "mind of God" becomes justified. But then the content of the sciences, in particular fundamental physical sciences, can be seen as the unfolding of the activity of that personal agency which "stands" behind the world. Man's study of nature then becomes a form of a dialogue between the hypostatic man and the hypostasis of God, so that the old metaphor of the first book of the Creator and the book of Nature as its second book, receives its new incarnation as the inseparability of the Divine and natural in man himself. Paradoxically, but contemporary science reinstates man to its central place in nature as a mediator between the world and God as the very possibility of knowledge and science. And it is this fact which effectively outdates and dismantles any form of the old-fashioned materialism. The fact that the world is created is confirmed in the modern science exactly through the fact that its incredible complexity and the latter's explicability cannot receive any elucidation in terms of their facticity as given to human consciousness. That is, consciousness itself is beyond any discursive explanation because it itself lies in the foundation of any knowledge. On the one hand, this consciousness is functioning in the conditions of the physical world, on the other hand, this consciousness as the center of disclosure and manifestation of reality, as something which is radically non-local and capable of making an instantaneous synthesis of the universe, has its "origin" unexplainable through physical causality and mysterious in terms of its hypostatic properties.

Quantum mechanics, relativity and cosmology, together with astriobiology, physiology and psychology, all are dependent on the contingent facticity of consciousness. They indirectly contribute to the understanding of its functioning but yet remain silent about its origin and its basic ambivalent presence in the conditions of nature. The hard problem of consciousness as its ambiguous presence in first- and third-person remains a mystery to the same extent as the incarnate God was present in the universe hypostatically and in the human flesh. Gradually, the academic community is coming to the realization of the fact that an effective solution to the problem of consciousness is impossible without the involvement of theological discourse, implying the presence of a personal view of psychic reality "from within." In other words, the biblical and theological non-descriptive account of God-manhood can inspire scientists, philosophers and theologians to rethink their one-sided approaches and to look for a synthetic view of reality which will include consciousness as one of its explicitly articulated parts. This could advance the construction of a new non-materialistic paradigm of the sciences which will allow one to approach the solution of the fundamental problem of matter and consciousness, that is, of the perennial mind-body problem. Ultimately, all the sciences together with the philosophical and theological insights are destined to seek for the understanding of the sense, the place and value of humanity in the universe. This infinite task demands integrity of the human person in withstanding the chaos, unpredictability and uncertainty of its existence. Science, philosophy and theology seem historically capable of sustaining human identity thus producing an open-ended hermeneutics of the human existence.

The pieces in this collection are divided into two radically different starting points: mind and matter from the material brain outward, and upward, and consciousness and matter from the cosmos inward. In other words, one is that which starts from the person, including the flesh of the person, and moves toward consciousness, and that which starts with consciousness and moves toward its relation to the cosmos which has matter within it. The first presumes that, since consciousness is only observed concomitant to brain activity, that is the only place to start. The second presumes that, since only consciousness can embrace the cosmos, and in a sense determine it, consciousness has a fundamental place there. Because all articles touch upon the humanities and theology, they do not hold, in contrast to the dominant views on brain science, that the brain is also where such inquiries *end*. Both starting points are, in varying ways, dualist or at least maintain a strict position in relation to dualism.

All authors are in universal agreement about the virtues of theology to give meaning to human thoughts and actions and the fault of contemporary neuroscience for its reductionism.

Most contributions address a central and oft-noted conundrum, part of David Chalmers's "Hard Problem of Consciousness": how does the material structure of the brain lead to qualitative experience?

The first contribution "Once Again about the Brain and Semiosis: Can Neural Networks Make Their Point?" of Tatyana Chernigovskaya discusses the semiotic aspects of higher human functions and the feasibility and relevance of the search for their neurophysiological mechanisms. The author holds that objective analysis of the structures of neural networks (the most popular approach in neuroscience) is not going to give us an account of the subjective. The chapter accentuates the inadequacy of research and artificial intelligence (AI) modeling in what concerns the human side of reasoning, thinking, and language. One must turn to subjective information to understand subjective experience. This requires that theorists of mind and brain give more credit to the humanities, art, and all the works of human creativity. This implies that the data from humanities and arts need to be included into the discourse of the natural sciences.

Then Dmitry Kiryanov in his chapter "Brain, Mind, and Soul in the Context of the Dialogue between Science and Religion" analyzes modern discussions about the relationship between the brain and consciousness, as well as the associated idea of the human soul. It is shown that the reductionist paradigm that currently dominates neuroscience cannot be considered sufficient to explain human consciousness. Kiryanov addresses the mind-body problem directly by examining one of the more widespread theories of consciousness that regards it as an emergent phenomenon. The emergent approach, which has now become widespread among a number of scientists and philosophers, can pretend to give a some adequate explication of the problem of consciousness. Such a view is welcome in this volume since it can involve mathematical and physical descriptions of emergence for comparison. However, Kiryanov focuses on the feasibility of emergence as a concept from a philosophical and theological perspective. Examining the views of prominent scholars on the topic, he notes that emergent views of reality tend to move away from reductionism and toward forms of monism. It is shown that, despite the value of an emergent understanding of mental processes, an emergence which relies only on material existence merely begs the same question at different analytic and causal levels. Thus such an approach is insufficient and should be supplemented by a theological view of man as a unity of soul and body. Kiryanov concludes that the substance dualism of soul and body still provides a better solution.

A physiologist Alexander Kaplan argues in his chapter "We Are More Than Our Brains: In Search of the Subjective Beginning" that the subjective world of an individual human being is still a problem that resists a natural scientific explanation. He argues that the brain's activity builds a model of the world in which the self inhabits. This model exists like "a projected image that can appear on a screen, over walls, on the ceiling, without losing its integrity." This model can also account for the ability of the brain to build vast, complex, and distant theoretical constructs beyond its biological basis and requirements. This "mental" human environment without "seams and joints" may be an indication of a specifically human need—a cognitive deficit which reconstructs reality beyond the necessity of biological adaptation and leads to the construction of a general picture of the world. Perhaps all our intuitive decisions, creative insights, great discoveries and high art are all the result of introspectively invisible acts of the mental model of the external world, formed in the highly complex neural networks of the human brain.

Then a physicist Alexey Kavokin in his chapter "Liquid Light as a Model of Matter-Consciousness Dualism" argues in favor of a possibility that some physical effects studied since the 1960s, and those which have come under increased interest in the twenty-first century after the experimental demonstration of the Bose-Einstein condensation of polaritons and the superfluidity of polariton condensates, can indirectly provide some insights about how consciousness functions in its physical basis. He suggests that the behavior of quantum-entangled systems such as exiton-polaritons can serve as a toy model (an analogy in the form of a thought experiment) for the action of God's will in the world and the relationship between thought and matter. Surveying studies that show the possible use of quantum effects as information-bearing channels in the brain, Kavokin moves toward the suggestion that similar systems might actually be at work in the functioning of consciousness itself. He then examines cases where quantum systems assume behavior that is both theoretically and actually impossible to predict. In this sense they "decide" upon a course of activity. This is followed by a consideration of the information-bearing capacities of quantum computers, including an examination of "neuromorphic" computing that makes use of exciton-polariton condensates. Light is frequently associated with thought. We say "fast as thought", "thought like lightning," etc. According to the Bible, light appeared at the very beginning of Creation, its appearance preceded the creation of matter. In a modern understanding, quanta of light are the most widespread particles in the Universe. They are responsible for most interactions in physics and, logically, they may be related to communication of Divine will to the material world. From this point of view, strongly coupled light-matter states such as exciton-polaritons may be considered as a toy model for the interaction between consciousness and matter. These directions in research lead the author to conclude that they can serve as a model for the operation of consciousness, free will, and determinism as an expression of Divine will.

The subsequent chapters of this volume deal with mind and matter in more cosmic terms. In his philosophical chapter "The 'Hard Problem' of Consciousness Elucidated Cosmologically: The Saturated Phenomenality of the Universe versus Its Object-Like Constitution," Alexei V. Nesteruk discusses the relevance of cosmological ideas to the explication of the "Hard Problem of Consciousness." Rather than attaching ourselves to mechanisms by which consciousness can be generated by matter, one should first consider the nature of the thinking subject. This subject is a hypostasis that has a particular lived existence and position that places that lived existence in the world. The rational capabilities of that hypostasis allow the person to start from its position and contemplate the whole of existence from the smallest conceivable scale to the largest as the whole of creation itself. Life as an existing being gives the hypostasis a discrete particularity; but from that position the person can direct its intentionality toward the whole of existence. The subject is thus a micro- and macrocosm of discrete being in the world. The object of consciousness embraces the universe at its extremes of greatness and smallness as a continuous surface which amounts to a continuous band, or an uroboros, the mythic serpent biting its tail. What unites this whole is nothing but the conscious hypostasis of the person. Thus the universe is not a flat extension of time and space, but a sphere, torus, or uroboros-like structure determined by the world line of the subject. Essential to this hypostatic particularity is the body of the subject in matter, time, and space. What is the character of this subject's lived existence? The relationship of "I=I" in the subject, and then in its existence in the world is a saturated experience that transcends the subject-object relation and provides the true ground for consciousness in relation to the givenness of the world. The universe is present in the human condition as a saturated phenomenon inseparable from the very existence of the human. It is this phenomenon, to the extent that it cannot be articulated in terms of quantity, quality, modality and relation, that constitutes the "I" in its ambivalent condition of being the center of disclosure and manifestation of the universe and, at the same time, an insignificant organic component of it.

The "hard" problem of consciousness as the split in the experience of existence into first- and third-person reflects this paradoxical position of man and requires its elucidation through an open-ended hermeneutics that is similar to that for the universe as a saturated phenomenon. Hence the hard problem of consciousness can be seen through its endless hermeneutics not as a problem, but as that which incessantly explicates the sense of human existence as given. This concept locates the person in relation to the nature of its species, enhypostasized entities in the world, through the incarnational theology that lies at this term's origins.

The physicist and theologian Kirill Kopeikin in his chapter "The Biblical Thesis of the Creation of the World *ex nihilo*, the Heisenberg Cut, Quantum Blindness, and the Ψ-*chism* of the Universe—a Final Solution to the Hard Problem of Consciousness" moves in similar directions but with a different approach and different sets of materials. Francis Bacon's "Two Books" doctrine is the starting point. If the Book of Nature was written on the grounds of the Divine rationality, it can be interpreted through the biblically understood creation out of nothing, that is, by recognizing that all things are dependent upon God. The physics of fundamental nature has demonstrated that the point at which the observer makes measurements determines the state of the physical system. Kopeikin argues, that the subjective knowledge, obtained through the process of observation in quantum mechanics acquires the features of the objective state, that the quantum system evolves from this state according to the causal evolutionary equations. This means that the act of knowing changes reality: the very knowledge of a system being subjective, coincides with the new observed state of the same system and thus is objective. This implies in turn that that reality which is traditionally treated as "objective," that is, physical, in fact has propensities of being psychic. Considering that God has, through his Logos, created this natural world, the physical world can be treated as the *psychē* of the Creator. This position is compared to a panentheism, whereby God is not all things, but is *in* all things. The Hard Problem of Consciousness is thus reinterpreted by recognizing the psychic, panentheistic nature of Creation.

Then a geological scientist and chemist Sergey Krivovichev in his historical chapter "Theology and Thermodynamics of Life and Mind: The Legacy of Nikolai Kobozev (1903–74)" dwells on the neglected contribution to the interaction between science and religion that came from the Soviet chemist Nikolai Kobozev. The latter argued that an inherent feature of any living organism, non-derivable from any physical structure or property, was its preservation of order against the principle of the Second Law of Thermodynamics (growth of entropy as a measure of chaos and disorder). Kobozev's appeal to "anti-entropy" as a model for the explanation of life differs significantly from Erwin Schrödinger's more influential free energy explanation and, as such, deserves reconsideration. Kobozev's arguments have received some corrections in the intervening years. Data have shown that the maxim "*omne vivum ex vivo*" is violated in the spontaneous generation of complex molecules and the generation of artificial living systems. Kobozev's response to Schrödinger's notion of negative entropy is highly interesting in the light of recent theories in biology, notably the "Free Energy Principle (FEP)" of Karl Friston and approaches that use elements of the Second Law of Thermodynamics for information. Additionally, his notion that optical stereoisomerism is more fundamental than the thermodynamics of atoms is another interesting contribution. In stereoisomeric molecules, the atoms can be exactly the same but their spatial arrangement means they cannot be involved in the same chemical reactions. This is essentially the argument that the form of an object is a fundamental determiner of its nature despite the composition of its parts. This is essentially the same critique of reductionism that other authors in this volume assert by much different means and can be applied to Orthodox notions of irreducible wholeness. Kobozev's views on life and consciousness were closely related to his scientific and religious convictions which limited their influence under the Soviet ideology.

In their joint chapter a medical practitioner Oleg Reznik, together with a physicist and theologian Kirill Kopeikin, discuss ethical questions related to the medical treatment of the brain, consciousness and person in the chapter with the title "Neuroethics, Quantum Physics, and Theology." They consider the problems of neurobiotechnological enhancement from the point of view of neuroethics and so-called "neurotheology." It is argued that a meaningful discussion of ethical problems of human neurotechnological enhancement requires involving quantum physics understood through a biblical theological context. The authors maintain that the term "neurotheology" is speculative and is not fully explicated, whereas understanding the essence of neuroscience and neuroethics requires theology.

The volume is concluded by the chapter of Walker Trimble, "Seed and Law: Neuroscience and Virtue Ethics in Christian Anthropology," touching upon some issues of the so called "neuroethics," a field whose computationalist theoretical roots put it squarely in the rule-based camp that resulted in a twofold conflation. First, biological processes are falsely identified with rules as a type of "process fallacy." This then leads to the assumption that the articulation of the rule in one system, for example, a semiotic one, maps to its articulation in another system, for example, a biochemical one. From a theological perspective, this assumption implies a false teleology that introduces a "pseudo-soul" in the guise of an algorithm. Common statements such as "language is encoded in the genes" and "free will is an illusion of the brain" are party to this error. In a review of a wide range of materials, Trimble argues that a pre-modern concept of the person as agent, one informed by the incarnational theology of the Logos, presumes an ethical relation of the whole person with, and within, the principles of a rationally ordered world. Such a perspective can account for the phenomena of agency, observation, and regularities in ways relevant to ethics and the foundations of positivist science. There are some interesting points of contrast in the papers Trimble and Kaplan. They both note the discovery of "lattice cells" in the brain which form "mental maps" of the organism's surroundings. For Kaplan this means that the rats in question "travel not only or not so much in the physical world, but in the space of the neural networks of their brains." This leads towards his Cartesian conclusion that the brain builds a "model of the world" in which it inhabits. Trimble notes the same research to argue that, since the brain can make mental maps, it is capable of building analogous models of objects in the world and objects in the brain. Yet for most other types of behavior, including, especially, language and abstract thought, the analogies of map and territory that we see in the case of lattice cells do not exist. He arrives at the anti-Cartesian conclusion that there is "no watcher within." Contrasting these positions shows the diversity of views even within one broad theistic tradition, but also the commonality in the sense that both regard the brain as an instrument that acts dynamically with the world.

While the pieces in this collection view matter and consciousness from two very different positions, in many places paths converge. Namely, dualism appears in many forms, classical, Cartesian mind-body dualism in Kaplan and body soul dualism in Kavokin; but most prominently in the dualism between Creator and creation. Yet, the vast distance between Creator and created is seen not as a lamentable void but a space for the work (*energeia*) of the Divine. We dare here to look at material creation as matter imbued with the divine presence. This can, in turn, be read as a creation of multiple worlds, a foundation of physics as the relation between dependent and independent beings (Kopeikin), and a foundation for scientific inquiry (Kopeikin, Trimble). The importance of life as a primary principle is also present (Nesteruk, Trimble). The notion of the hypostasis as a grounding point for the human is also an important element (Nesteruk, Trimble), and here we see that the contribution Orthodox incarnational theology may be able to make to the foundations of science.

A crucial element is also the importance of positioning consciousness and matter at the points where they converge. Modern philosophical thinking is characterized by a transfer from the pursuit of the nature of essences to a pursuit of the relations between bodies (Kopeikin). Essences that derive their nature on the basis of their material objecthood are not well received in this work. Instead of objects, we are called to consider relations, states, and perspectives. Essential to consciousness is its perspective (Krivovichev, Kopeikin and Reznik, Nesteruk). The ability of consciousness to "fly to fancies unknown" is a characteristic that allows it to violate the classical laws of matter and this defines its point of departure, its horizon. A system's starting point is an essential element that defines its intentionality, its capacities and its teleology. It is crucially important that this positioning is true both for material systems, such as the body and brain, and for individual conscious beings. On several occasions the authors in this volume note the theological importance of this particularity, its openness, and its relationship with the theology of the incarnation.

Finally, the mind-body problem is addressed in some papers and it receives interpretation referring to the concept of person as the primary source of disclosure and manifestation of reality. Trimble argues that activity and agency establish both the metaphysical and ethical "boundaries around the person." Breaking up our vision into voxels and our actions into brain activity leads to an artificial fragmentation of agency, which then leads us to argue that agency and the person do not exist. Nesteruk likewise notes that "no scientific effort can discover what has been intended in the very *decision* to enact objectification. *Intentional* acts cannot be subjected to straightforward physical causation and hence no non-existential foundation of science is possible." Kopeikin shows us how the so-called *Heisenberg Cut* requires that a coherent agent be defined somewhere. Perhaps it is in the neurons connected to the retina, perhaps in the equipment the researcher is using, but the cut must be made somewhere. This is the most compelling argument running through this volume. For Trimble, if social evolution is the source of the complexity of the brain, you cannot argue that the person does not exist. For Kopeikin, the implications of the Copenhagen interpretation of quantum physics mean that one cannot argue that there is a strict distinction between matter and consciousness. To determine the real, you have to make the cut somewhere. But the Heisenberg cut, and Nesteruk's cosmological account also show us that distinctions do not have to do with defining words or essences, but defining positions in relationship to the world. One could extend the illustration Kopeikin quotes from John von Neumann that the position of measurement can exist in the mercury of the thermometer, or in the nerves in the retina. That a decision is comprised of a number of biochemical and neural processes does not mean that thought does not take place. One simply must be careful not to idealize where you wish to draw your boundaries—sometimes the body is not enough. Kopeikin writes: "There is a feeling that 'inside' quantum reality there is some kind of analogue of 'inner freedom,' a kind of 'will' of the universe, 'on the surface' that manifests itself when projected onto external measuring instruments." This is also where we see interesting parallels between epistemology and physics. Just as a particular set of brain activity's accounts for the movements and expression of the self, so the action of measurement determines the fact of reality. Both of these states or systems are accounted for by the presence of agency, teleology, and activity.

Whether this project succeeded in elucidating the perennial problem of consciousness and matter, or mind and body, must be decided by the reader, who, we hope, will have no regrets of reading this book.

Acknowledgments

THE EDITORS WANT TO express their gratitude to all contributors for their attention to the project and the time and effort in writing the chapters. On behalf of all contributors, special thanks are to the National Hellenic Research Foundation (NHRF) for supporting logically and technically all stages of this project, in particular to Efthymios Nicolaides, Nikos Livanos, Costas Tampakis, and Ersi Bakou. Many thanks to all participants of the concluding workshop of the SOW project in January 2023 in Athens who directly and indirectly contributed into the discussion of the topics from this volume. The work of editing, polishing, and general setting of the manuscript by Walker Trimble is very much appreciated.

1

Once Again about the Brain and Semiosis

Can Neural Networks Make Their Point?[1]

Tatyana Chernigovskaya

> Leaving point "A," the train is on the flatland.
> Headed to point "B," not yet in sight.
> —Joseph Brodsky

Introduction

THE SCIENCE OF OUR times is faced with existential challenges that demand engagement with philosophical discourse, but that in neuroscience occupy only a strangely peripheral area. When discussing the so-called "*hard*" problems, in particular the long-standing mind-body problem, it has been repeatedly set forth that such issues are differently understood within different fields of knowledge. Furthermore, there are different interpretations that range between the mind-body and psychophysiological aspects of the problem and the question as to whether the scientific

---

1. The following is the English translation of an article that first appeared in *Voprosy filisofii* 6 (2021): 5–13. The author expresses her thanks to A. Efimov and S. Shumsky for their comments on the Russian version.

method itself can address such questions (Lektorskii 2011; Dubrovsky 2011; Alexandrov and Sams 2005; Aleksandrov 2009; Kaplan 2019; Chernigovskaya 2012; 2017; 2020; 2021).

Experimental neuroscience has maintained by default that the matter of understanding consciousness and the spirit is a matter of understanding the properties of neurons and their interactions (Crick and Koch 2007). Of course, not everyone believes this is the case, but it is the view of most of the representatives of the natural sciences. At the other end of the spectrum, for example, John Searle argues that consciousness is irreducible, and this illusion is a reality that natural science cannot accept (Searle 1992). In a survey article Konstantin Anokhin takes pains to specify the *main* problem of the "mind-brain" and the *hard* problem of "consciousness-brain" and then describes what particular tasks must be performed to succeed in arriving at an answer to these problems (Anokhin 2021). This does not negate the paradoxes that the brain is in the world, and the world is in the brain (Lektorskii 2011), and that the external world is constructed from within (Zinchenko 2010). It is impossible not to agree that, within the framework of existing ideas about the work of the brain and with the help of accepted approaches, the main problems cannot be solved. In this article, as in a previous one (Chernigovskaya 2021), I propose to approach this incredibly complex task not only by developing a theory of the cognitome and all related multidisciplinary problems, but also using the "archaeology" of mental principles manifested in semiotic human behavior, in particular, in art.

Eternal questions still require answers from the natural sciences—from physiology and genetics—but also from anthropology and now the sphere of artificial intelligence in its various guises.

I would divide the most urgent topics into four questions:

- Are the natural sciences themselves sufficient to discover the principles and mechanisms by which the brain operates in its higher functions, and not just simple skills comparable to the capabilities of other living beings or artificial intellectual agents?
- Language, consciousness, thinking, qualia—are these unique characteristics of the person? If this can be demonstrated, how could we do so?
- How does this work in the brain and in which brains? Modules, networks and their properties, hypernetworks, connectomes, and cognitomes.

- Can this be reproduced? not only our intellect, but our inner world as well?

A Brave New World . . .

Obviously, this is followed by another question—why? Is it to understand how the brain works (and, as a final answer: for theory)? Is it to understand what is possible in the mental world at all, including the one that we don't know of or that doesn't yet exist? Is it to understand how we can be biologically or technically "improved," to create new people who will be faster, smarter, with a huge memory, those who do everything better than we do now? Is it to make some "Frankenstein" or, even more ambitious, to digitize our mental and emotional world and thereby achieve immortality?

As Boris Groys writes, "For a long time, man was ontologically assigned the middle position between God and animal. At the same time, it seemed more prestigious to stand closer to God and further away from the animal. But the Modern puts the human between an animal and a machine. And in this new context, it seems better to be an animal than a machine" (Groys 2013, 113). Intelligent self-learning programs such as AlphaZero have transcended almost all boundaries: chess, go, shogi, even poker. There were many enthusiastic reviews of the AlphaZero chess matches with the former champion, the StockFish program. AlphaZero's success came from its "deep intuition," going through "only" eighty thousand positions per second (as opposed to StockFish's seventy million), and nevertheless it won. It is believed that AlphaZero played more holistically, subordinating all moves to a single goal, making seemingly ridiculous, and even incorrect moves, if you do not look very far ahead, while forcing the opponent into what is called *Zugzwang*. The program used "artificial intuition" as opposed to rigid iterative logic (Perez 2017). Such a manner of playing is described as "alien." It is not how people do it, and it is not how programs created by people play. The semantic gap between intuition and logic has been overcome, and it looks like a cognitive attack, or even a challenge to civilization, to our ideas of human intellectual capability (see Ushakov 2011). The analysis of the matches that devastated the world's best go players amazed the experts. The victory over Lee Sedol in 2016 and over Ke Jie in 2017 showed much the same thing: people do not make such moves and such strategies never occurred to them (at some points the program may incur losses only to recoup them in following moves). When the disadvantageous moves are being made, the result is evident neither to the human player nor to the observer, so the program's decisions sometimes seem strange; the program may sacrifice one or several stones to gain a tactical advantage—something human players usually do not do (Knight 2017).

So, we are faced with a new cognitive space. Of course, we could say that, if a human brain played go for another couple of thousand years, it might have come up with such strategies. And if it didn't? Does it not follow that neuroscience is essentially continuing to look in the brain only for that which it already knows (an understandable, but short-sighted, aim). I give here these examples of the possibilities of artificial intelligence as I see their parallelism with the appeal to the "archeology" of thinking/consciousness/intuition through art.

We set out to repeat repetitions—to create those who will create worlds along with us, or even instead of us. On the surface, it looks like a student's task: write like Mozart, Dürer, Pushkin; play with a flawless technique at unimaginable speeds (we see this vector in human art as well, until recently it was impossible to imagine such extraordinary heights of speed and technique in instrumental or choreographic arts). Of course, with some progress, programs will do these things "better" than people. If, of course, we reduce art to technology, and remove personality, soul, mind, interpretations, proximate conditions; i.e., the human, all too human.

Co-evolution of Language, Thinking, and the Brain

The main work of the brain is semiosis, and its study has a long biological history (Eco 2000; Hoffmeyer and Kull 2003; Kull 2014; Natochin and Chernigovskaya 2020). Discussions about the relationship between the social and the biological in man have been going on for a long time; and, I must say, with little progress, because there is actually no balanced position (see Kozintsev 2013a, 2013b; Panov 2017). Umberto Eco in his book *Kant and the Platypus* discusses the origins of semiosis and asks the most pressing questions: Why do we use signs? How reliable and stable are the connections between them and what they mean? What makes us express ourselves at all (*What makes u stalk?*) in either a philological onto-genetic sense? (Eco 2000). It is impossible not to recall profound Pierce's discovery that such a correlation is based on attention to the object, and not to all its features, but only to those relevant to a particular situation or convention (Pierce 1980). In an interesting way, this is similar to the cognitive role of photography (Nurkova 2020). This, of course, leads to an even more general problem of the origin of language and even the need for definitions—understanding what we mean when we say "language"—with the whole panoply of options from the structural to the functional (Deacon 2013). In this sense the views of the biologist and the poet strikingly converge: T. Deacon remarks on the co-evolution of language and the brain and insists that "language occupied the brain" (Deacon 2013, 289). Joseph Brodsky in his Nobel Lecture formulates this no less starkly: "The poet, I wish to repeat, is language's means for existence—or, as my beloved Auden said, he is the one by whom it lives. . . . One who writes a poem writes it because the language prompts, or simply dictates, the next line. One who writes a poem writes it because the language prompts, or simply dictates, the next line. Beginning a poem, the poet as a rule doesn't know the way it's going to come out. . . . The one who writes a poem writes it above all because verse writing is an extraordinary accelerator of consciousness, of thinking, of comprehending the universe" (Brodsky 2002, 764–65). And elsewhere: "with language you anatomize your experience" (Brodsky 2002, 724).

The idea of recreating worlds is not new. A person is his brain, and he does not only process information that enters him through the senses: he also creates worlds that have never been there before, the brain—and, with some limitations of scale, not only the human brain—is a semiotic device that generates sign systems, and this is a serious obstacle to transferring information about the brain and animal behavior on humans (Uexküll 1922; Uexküll 1970; Knyazeva 2015; Zolyan et al. 2020). Meanings are more important than algorithms, and because of the complexity of their production and decoding, they require huge energy costs. When mastering a language, a small child learns large quantities of information each day (mostly lexical semantics). For language development it is clear that meanings are more important than the syntax that allows language to become structured and, of course, is specific to humans (Mollica and Piantadosi 2019). Research in the field of language origins and evolution is directly related to researchers' fundamental approaches. These are reduced to the opposition of structure and functions and the search for special zones in the human brain that are distinguished from those of closely related species (Deacon 2004; Pylkkänen 2019; Neubauer et al. 2020). These are, especially, human genetic mechanisms and their prerequisites (Clark and Grundstein 2000; Heide et al. 2020). We know that in our brain there are connections linking the anterior and lateral temporal divisions with the frontal lobes, forming the so-called *uncinate fasciculus*, a hook-shaped mass characteristic only of the human brain, although it has evolutionary prerequisites (Balezeau et al. 2020). This structure has to do with ventral language flow, which provides the processing of the semantic aspects of the language. Results form neuroscience have illustrated which characteristics of the connectome ensure the functioning of the most complex structure of the mental lexicon, allowing you to retain different layers of memory, to distinguish reality from hallucinations, and the like (Hugdahl 2002; Davtian and Chernigovskaya 2003; Kireev et al. 2015).

Yes, a person generates meanings with his brain, but the result cannot be achieved by one individual: meaning is always at the intersection of the creator and the recipient, it is always a dialogue, and success depends on such interaction, the ability to understand an interlocutor, which is possible only with a comparable cultural and intellectual base (Kitayama 2002; Alexandrov and Sams 2005). Consciousness cannot develop "in the dark" not only in the sense of the concepts of Chalmers and Nagel, but also in the context of Mamardashvili and Pyatigorsky, who spoke *about the terrible work of thought taking place at the limit of the humanly possible, the exertion of all forces, in the context of culture, and society* (Mamardashvili 2002; Pyatigorsky 2004). Sergei Kapitsa emphasized that "humanity is a nonlinear, highly interactive system, encompassed by cultural, intellectual interaction" (Kapitsa 2000). Lotman repeatedly wrote about textual polysemanticism, about the self-growing logos, because the text knows more than the author (Lotman 1992). Meanings are born in dialogue, from the dialogue of cultures to the dialogue of different types of thinking inside the brain itself (Lotman 1984; Chernihiv and Deglin 1984; Kitayama 2002; Arutyunova and Alexandrov 2019). The instability of meanings dependant on a changing context, on the relationship of the signified and the signifier—something with its own social and personal significance (Tulchinsky 2019; Zolyan et al. 2020)—is a very relevant topic of discussion, especially with an eye to artificial intelligence. To understand the complexity of meaning, you need training. This dynamic of constantly changing priorities, and hence textual interpretation, can be experimentally determined by registering the process of "textual scanning" with different cognitive strategies using eye-tracking techniques (Chernihiv et al. 2018; Petrova et al. 2020).

Archaeology or Anatomy?

The natural sciences are looking for answers to the main questions of humanity with "microscopes and telescopes," but meanings will not be found in this way, and meanings are what we need. Meanings are more important than structures. The archaeology of civilization is more important than measuring objects, including in the brain itself. Moreover, there are no stable objects there at all, but there are multidimensional clouds simultaneously embedded in each other and in themselves, according to a mathematics of the brain to us as yet unknown. At the pinnacle of evolution, the human brain has reached incredible heights in the evolution of particular functions, having developed the languages of mathematics, music, the arts, poetry. It is useless to anatomize these functions (Chernihiv 2021). Art shows us what our world is like. The world of humanity. But these languages are not imitations, but a "probing" of the world, they are mental and emotional efforts to comprehend it. As Joseph Brodsky felt, a *simple thought, alas, scares the sight of convolutions*, and then, *there are fragments of old arias hanging in the air*.

Outside the context of cultural discourse itself, it is often underestimated that extraordinary advances in what would be called cognitive science have been made by methods that would be regarded as completely unscientific (Lehrer 2008; Shelepin 2017). In art the brain shows what it can do as a cognitive instrument. It can use beams of light to highlight focal points, as in Baroque painting, it can play with "non-existent" combinations, as in surrealism, it can attempt to describe the world with geometric forms, it can abandon form altogether, or can use only forms as "innate ideas" and abstractions, or it can compress all forms and colors into a black square. And this is only in the visual arts. It can play with time in music and poetry, with gravity and space in ballet and architecture. The brain seems to test the strength of the laws of nature, including those that have not yet been discovered. Styles in art open the register of working with meanings to an attentive observer.

Complex Simplicity

The more I think about whether we are going the right direction by trying to understand what a person is, to what extent biology determines culture and vice versa, to what extent increasingly complex modern technologies are determinative of success on this path, the more clearly is the sense that drawing, even sound, the arts, and not the formula, shine through. What the brilliant Gia Kancheli called "complex simplicity" is becoming clearer and clearer. The roads of art and science suddenly began to converge. Art is compressed time. Compressed thought. Let's stop. Let's think about it.

Bibliography

Aleksandrov, Yuri I. 2009. "From the Theory of Functional Systems to Systemic Psychophysiology." In *Psikhologiia segodnia: Teoriia, obrazovanie i praktika*, edited by Anatoliy L. Zhuravlev et al., 13–56. Moscow: Institut Psikhologii RAN.

Alexandrov, Yuri I., and Mikko E. Sams. 2005. "Emotion and Consciousness: Ends of a Continuum." *Cognitive Brain Research* 25(2): 387–405.

Anohin, Konstantin V. 2021. "Cognitom: In Search of Fundamental Neuroscientific Theory of Consciousness." *Zhurnal vysshei nervnoi deiatel'nosti* 71(1): 39–71.

Arutiunova, Karina R., and Yuri I. Aleksandrov. 2019. *Moral and Subjective Experience*. Moscow: Institut Psikhologii RAN.

Balezeau, Fabien, et al. 2020. "Primate Auditory Prototype in the Evolution of the Arcuate Fasciculus." *Nature Neuroscience* 23(5): 611–14. https://doi.org/10.1038/s41593-020-0623-9.

Barulin, Alexander N. (2000/2002). *Foundations of Semiotics: Signs, Sign, System, Communication. Pt. 1*. Moscow: Sport and Culture.

Bickerton, Derek. 2009. *Adam's Tongue: How Humans Made Language, How Language Made Humans*. New York: Hill and Wang.

Brodsky, Joseph. 2002. *Essays*. Yekaterinburg: U-Faktoriia.

Burlak, Svetlana A. 2011. *The Origins of Language: Facts, Research, Hypotheses*. Moscow: Astrel.

Cartmill, Erica A., et al. 2014. "The Evolution of Language." In *Proceedings of the 10th International Conference (EVOLANG10) Vienna, 14–17 April 2014*, 479–81. Vienna: World Scientific.

Chalmers, David J. 1996. *The Conscious Mind: In Search of a Fundamental Theory*. Oxford: Oxford University Press.

Chernigovskaya, Tatiana V. 2004. "Homo Loquens: Evolution of Cerebral Functions and Language." *Zhurnal Evolyutsionnoi Biokhimii i Fiziologii* 40(5): 400–406.

———. 2012. "Languages of Mind: Who Reads the Texts of Neural Networks." In *Chelovek v mire znaniia: v chest' 80-letiia akad. V. A. Lektorskogo*, edited by T. G. Shchedrina et al., 403–15. Moscow: ROSSPEN.

———. 2017. *The Cheshire Smile of Schrödinger's Cat: Language and Mind*. Moscow: Yazyk Slavianskoi Kultury.

———. 2020. "Biology, Environment, and Culture: From Animal Communication to Human Language and Cognition." *Vestnik Sankt-Peterburgskogo universiteta. Filosofiia i konfliktologiia* 36(1): 157–70.

———. 2021. "Neuroscience's Search for Meaning: Brain as the Baroque?" *Voprosy filosofii* 1: 17–26.

Chernigovskaya, Tatyana V., and Vadim L. Deglin. 1984. "The Problem of Internal Dialogism (A Neurophysiological Study of Linguistic Competence)." *Struktura dialoga kak printsip raboty semioticheskogo mekhanizma, Trudy po znakovym sistemam* 17: 48–67.

Chernigovskaya, Tatiana V., et al. 2018. *The Look of Schrodinger's Cat: Eye Movement Registration in Psycholinguistic Studies*. St. Petersburg: St. Petersburg University Press.

Clark, William R., and Michael Grundstein. 2000. *Are We Hardwired? The Role of Genes in Human Behaviour*. Oxford: Oxford University Press.

Crick, Francis, and Christof Koch. 2007. "A Neurobiological Framework for Consciousness." In *The Blackwell Companion to Consciousness*, edited by Max Velmans and Susan Schneider, 567–79. Oxford: Blackwell.

Davtian, Stepan, and Tatyana Chernigovskaya. 2003. "Psychiatry in Free Fall: In Pursuit of a Semiotic Foothold." *Sign Systems Studies* 31(2): 533–46.

Deacon, Terrence W. 2004. "Monkey Homologues of Language Areas: Computing the Ambiguities." *Trends in Cognitive Sciences* 8(7): 288–90.

———. 2013. *Incomplete Nature: How Mind Emerged from Matter*. New York: Norton & Company.

Dubrovskii, David I. 2011. "Relevant Problems of Intersubjectivity." In *Estestvennyi i iskusstvennyi intellekt* edited by David I. Dubrovskii and Vladislav A. Lektorskii, 129–48. Moscow: Kanon.

Dunbar, Robin. 2020. *How Many Friends Does One Person Need? Dunbar's Number and Other Evolutionary Quirks*. Cambridge: Harvard University Press.

Eco, Umberto. 2000. *Kant and the Platypus: Essays on Language and Cognition*. New York: Harcourt Brace.

Fitch, Tecumseh W. 2010. *The Evolution of Language*. New York: Cambridge University Press.

Groys, Boris E. 2013. *Under the Gaze of Theory*. Moscow: Ad Marginem.

Heide, Michael, et al. 2020. "Human-Specific *ARHGAP11B* Increases Size and Folding of Primate Neocortex in Fetal Marmoset." *Science* 369(6503): 546–50.

Hoffmeyer, Jasper, and Kalevi Kull. 2003. "Baldwin and Biosemiotics: What Intelligence Is For." In *Evolution and Learning: The Baldwin Effect Reconsidered* edited by Bruce H. Weber and David Depew, 253–72. Cambridge: MIT Press.

Hugdahl, Kenneth. 2002. *Experimental Methods in Neuropsychology*. New York: Kluwer Academic.

Kapitsa, Sergei P. 2000. "Russia's Demographic Present and Demographic Future." http://nikitskyclub.ru/?p=3224.

Kaplan, Alexander Y. 2019. "We Are More Than Our Brains: In Search of a Subjective Beginning." *Trudy kafedry bogosloviya Sankt-Peterburgskoj Duhovnoj Akademii. Teologiya i sovremennye issledovaniya soznaniya* 2(4): 25–34.

Kireev, Maxim et al. 2015. "Changes in Functional Connectivity within the Fronto-Temporal Brain Network Induced by Regular and Irregular Russian Verb Production." *Frontiers in Human Neuroscience* 9(36): 193–220.

Kitayama, Shinobu. 2002. "Culture and Basic Psychological Processes—Toward a System of Culture: Comment on Oyserman et al." *Psychological Bulletin* 128: 89–96.
Knight, Will. 2017. "A Stronger Alpha Go Defeats the World's Number One Player." *MIT Technology Review*, May 23, 2017.
Knyazeva, Elena N. 2015. "The Concept of 'Umwelt' by Jakob Von Uexküll and Its Significance for Modern Epistemology." *Voprosy filosofii* 5: 30–43.
Kozincev, Alexander G. 2013a. "Zoosemiotics and Glottogenesis." *Antropologicheskii forum* 19: 326–59.
———. 2013b. "Origin and Early History of the Species Homo Sapiens: New Biological Data." In *Fundamental'nye problemy arkheologii, antropologii, etno-grafii Evrazii (k 70-letiiu akad. A. P. Derevianko)*, edited by Vyacheslav V. Molodin and Michael V. Shun'kov, 538–54. Novosibirsk: Institute of Archeology and Ethnography of the Siberian Branch of the Russian Academy of Sciences.
Kull, Kalevi. 2014. "Towards a Theory of Evolution of Semiotic Systems." *Chinese Semiotic Studies* 10(3): 485–95.
Lehrer, Jonah. 2008. *Proust Was a Neuroscientist*. New York: HMH.
Lektorskii, Vladislav A. 2010. "I." In *The New Philosophical Encyclopedia*, edited by V. S. Stepin et al., 4:497–502. Moscow: Mysl'.
———. 2011. "Studies of Intellectual Processes in Modern Cognitive Science: Philosophical Problems." In *Estestvennyi iiskusstvennyi intellekt*, edited by David I. Dubrovskii and Vladislav A. Lektorskii, 3–16. Moscow: Kanon.
Lotman, Yuri M. 1984. "On the Semiosphere." In *Structure dialoga kak printsip raboty semioticheskogo mekhanizma: Trudy po znakovym sistemam*, edited by Yuri M. Lotman, 17:5–23. Tartu: Tartu Ülikool.
———. 1992. "Brain-Text-Culture-Artificial Intelligence." In *Izbrannye stat'I*, edited by Yu. Lotman, 1:25–33. Aleksandra: Tallin.
Mamardashvili, Merab K. 2002. "Cartesian Mediatations." In *Filosofskie chteniia*, 225–367. St. Petersburg: Azbuka-Klassika.
Mollica, Francis, and Steven T. Piantadosi. 2019. "Humans Store about 1.5 Megabytes of Information during Language Acquisition." *Royal Society Open Science* 6(3): 181393. https://doi.org/10.1098/rsos.181393.
Natochin, Yuri, and Tatiana Chernigovskaya. 2020. "From Archebiosis to Evolution of Organisms and Informational Systems." *Biological Communications* 65(3): 215–27.
Neubauer, Simon, et al. 2020. "Evolution of Brain Lateralization: A Shared Hominid Pattern of Endocranial Asymmentry Is Much More Variable Than in Great Apes." *Science advances* 6(7): 1–11.
Nurkova, Veronika V. 2020. *The Psychology of Photography: Cultural and Historical Analysis*. Moscow: Yurait.
Panov, Eugune N. 2017. *Man—Creator and Destroyer: Evolution of Behavior and Social Organization*. Moscow: IaSK.
Perez, Carlos E. 2017. "AlphaZero: How Intuition Demolished Logic." *Medium*, December 11. https://medium.com/intuitionmachine/alphazero-how-intuition-demolished-logic-66a4841e6810.
Petrova, Tatiana E. et al. 2020. "An Eye-Tracking Study of Sketch Processing: Evidence from Russian." *Frontiers in Psychology* 11: 297.
Pierce, Charles S. 1980. *Semiotics*. Turin: Einaudi.

Pyatigorsky, Alexander M. 2004. *Continuous Conversation*. St. Petersburg: Azbuka-klassika.
Pylkkänen, Liina. 2019. "The Neural Basis of Combinatory Syntax and Semantics." *Science* 366: 62–66.
Searle, John R. 1992. *The Rediscovery of the Mind*. Cambridge: MIT Press.
Shelepin, Yuri E. 2017. *Introduction to Neuroiconics*. St. Petersburg: Troitskiy most.
Tulchinsky, Grigory L. 2019. *The Body of Freedom: Responsibility and the Embodiment of Meaning: Philosophical and Semiotic Analysis*. St. Petersburg: Aletheia.
Uexküll, Jakob von. 1922. "Wie sehenwir die Natur und wiesiehtsiesichselber?" *Die Naturwissenschaften* 10(12): 265–81.
Uexküll, Kriszat G. von. 1970. *Streifzugedurch die Umwelten von Tieren und Menschen*. Frankfurt: Fischer.
Ushakov, Dmitry V. 2011. *Psychology of Intelligence and Giftedness*. Moscow: Institute of Psychology of the Russian Academy of Education.
Zinchenko, Vladimir P. 2010. *Consciousness and the Creative Act*. Moscow: Iazyki slavianskikh kultur.
Zolyan, Suren T., et al. 2020. "Meaning in Life and Meaning in the Text." *Slovo.ru: baltijskij accent* 11(1): 7–33.
Zorina, Zoya A., and Anna A. Smirnova. 2006. *What Did the "Talking" Monkeys Talk About: Are Higher Animals Capable of Operating with Symbols?* Moscow: Iazyki slavianskikh kultur.

2

Brain, Mind, and Soul in the Context of the Dialogue between Science and Religion

Dmitry Kiryanov

Introduction

IN THE MODERN WORLD, the dialogue between science and theology covers a wide range of problems and issues that relate to the evolution of the universe, life and man, the origin of religion, morality, and all aspects of human culture. The challenges that modern science poses to the traditional Christian understanding of these questions require serious critical analysis. The success that the natural sciences have demonstrated in explaining nature cannot fail to impress, and the technologies that we make use of clearly demonstrate the effectiveness and practical significance of the knowledge that humanity has acquired.

The methodological approach that has been given the name "critical realism" has become dominant in the long-term dialogue between science and theology. This approach regards scientific theories as preliminary while still being relevant to the reality they account for. For example, the physicist John Polkinghorne drew the analogy between scientific theories and maps in the atlas, which have different scales and details. Each map represents a certain model of reality, but not reality itself, which is always something richer in its capacities (see Kiryanov 2021). Polkinghorne notes that "epistemology and ontology are distinct from each other, but the strategy of realism is to use the former as a source for reasonable motivations in favor of ideas regarding the latter" (Polkinghorne 1996, 4). A critically realistic approach, according to philosopher Roy Bhaskar, should take into account the stratified nature of reality, since without "the concept of stratification, science would be presented as a kind of historical accident lacking any internal rationality" (Bhaskar 1989, 71). Relying on Bhaskar's critical realism, the Anglican theologian Alister McGrath takes precisely this characteristic of critical realism as important for the dialogue between science and theology since it enables a true defense of the independence of the theological method from that of the other sciences. While agreeing with Polkinghorne that "epistemology and ontology are inextricably linked" (McGrath 2004, 90), McGrath nevertheless warns that the bottom-up approach chosen by many researchers in the field of science and theology is insufficient because it is reality that determines the means of cognition, and not the reverse. When using such concepts as "nature," "the real," "naturalism" we imply a certain ontology *a priori*: "We don't just 'see' nature, we see it in a certain way" (McGrath 2002, 44). If we consider nature as an autonomous entity independent of any external reality of essences, we will not even try to seek an understanding of nature at levels other than that available to observation and experiment. McGrath stresses that naturalism "imposes an embargo on the transcendent without offering any scientific justification for doing so" (McGrath 2001, 130). McGrath's line of argument becomes especially important because it lays bare the need to take into account the layered, or stratified, nature of reality both in understanding the nature of the universe and also of humanity.

Consciousness as Understood by the Reductionist Paradigm

When the problem of explaining consciousness is discussed in the modern dialogue between science and theology, the first question brought to the fore is that of reductionism. As early as 1974 the biologist Francisco Ayala (Ayala 1974, 8–9) noted the difference between the three types of reductionism that scientists adhere to in practice. Methodological reductionism is an inevitable element of scientific activity as a strategy for studying the whole through division into component parts. However methodological reductionism by no means implies that it is impossible to talk about any entities that go beyond the scope of scientific description. A tougher position is epistemological reduction, which assumes that laws and theories of higher levels of complexity can be derived from lower ones. Ontological reductionism is the most extreme position that asserts the reality of only the most fundamental objects, such as elementary particles, and assumes that objects of higher levels of organization and complexity are nothing more than just atoms and particles. This approach is especially characteristic of modern neuroscience, in which empiricism, physicalism, reductionism and determinism are the dominant philosophical positions. It is not surprising that the vast majority of scientists working in this field are convinced that in the end, not only all the processes of consciousness, but also the subjective world of a person will sooner or later be explained through the physico-chemical processes of the brain. For example, the discoverer of DNA Francis Crick writes: "You, your joys and your sorrows, your memory and your ambitions, your sense of personal identity and free will are, in fact, nothing more than the behavior of a huge ensemble of nerve cells and related molecules" (Crick 1994, 3). The problem associated with this statement is that there is no reason in extreme reductionism to arbitrarily stop at nerve cells and related molecules, one should go all the way to the subatomic level of quarks, electrons, and, possibly, superstrings. But can Francis Crick be sure that our joys and sorrows can be explained by some scientific theory at the level of microparticles or superstrings? This can be called the paradox of incomplete reduction. Stopping at nerve cells or even molecules, Francis Crick by default recognizes that these levels of organization are not reduced completely to the quarks and superstrings that would be the real causal actors in the exchange. Moreover, as noted by cosmologist George Ellis, "there is no reason to deny the reality of the causal forces of your joys and your sorrows (the emotional system) or your memory" (Ellis 2016, 375). That is why the evolutionary biologist Theodosius Dobzhansky calls this approach "unreasonable reductionism": "Most biologists . . . are reductionists to the extent that we view life as a very complex, very special and very incredible pattern of physical and chemical processes. For me, this is 'reasonable' reductionism. But should we go further and insist that biology should be reduced to chemistry in such a way that biological laws and regularities could be deduced from what we have learned from processes associated with biochemistry? This, I think, is 'unreasonable' reductionism" (Dobzhansky 1974, 1). However, reductionism, despite its methodological effectiveness, is insufficient even for biology. Thus, biologist Martinez Hewlett emphasizes: "Modern biology with its very reductionist approach cannot answer the question (of life), because the properties of the molecules that make up a living system do not predict life as such. I think the answer lies in the form of 'meta-biology'—asking big questions that biology itself is not capable of considering" (Stoeger 2002, 146).

In our days, neuroscience has taken up the banner of reductionism. The discoveries of modern neuroscientists who correlate certain areas or systems of the brain with specific cognitive functions would seem to support this approach. However, not all scientists and philosophers agree with such an extreme position. The reaction to extreme reductionism was the development of a research direction within the framework of the dialogue of science and theology, emphasizing, on the one hand, the fundamental nature of physico-chemical processes as the basis for the emergence of complex cognitive functions and, on the other hand, the development of arguments in favor of the thesis of the irreducibility of consciousness to physico-chemical processes. Among such approaches can be found the non-reductive physicalism of Nancey Murphy, the emergent monism Phillip Clayton and George Ellis, and Polkinghorne's two-dimensional monism. It should be noted that these authors insist on the denial of the substantial dualism of soul and body. The main reason for the rejection of substantial dualism is the impossibility of combining it with modern scientific ideas. The appropriateness of rejecting such a view shall be discussed below.

Non-reductive Physicalism and Emergent Monism

In her publications, the theologian and philosopher of science Nancey Murphy defends an approach that she calls a non-reductive physicalist view of human nature. The essence of this view is that a person is a psychosomatic unity, both a biological organism and a responsible ego. By itself, such a position does not raise any questions until Murphy explicitly declares that her position differs from reductive materialism and dualism of soul and body. The main question posed by Murphy is the following: "If mental events are internally related to neural events, how can it be that the content of mental events is not guided by the laws of neurobiology?

If neurobiological determinism is true, then it should follow that there is no free will, that moral responsibility is in danger, and, indeed, our conversation about the role of reason in any intellectual discipline is meaningless" (Murphy 2002, 148). The question is posed correctly, but then what can Murphy mean by "non-reductive physicalism"? Is this not a contradiction in terms? Murphy explains that by "physicalism," she means that mental states are a consequence of the activity of a neural network, however by itself this does not mean that mental states can be fully explained in terms of neural processes. Thus this type of physicalism should be called non-deductive. Murphy seeks to emphasize that, despite the fact that states of consciousness are conditioned by the lowest level of organization, the brain's neural state, the content of mental states can have a downward causal effect on the brain and its states. To explain this, Murphy uses Donald Campbell's idea of descending causality in relation to the evolutionary process (Campbell 1974, 179–87). John Ellis notes that today descending causality can be demonstrated through computer simulations of complex systems (Ellis 2016, 18), and thus emergence can no longer be taken as mere philosophy. The concept of descending causality is essential if you want to explain the fact that you have the ability to read a book in English or some other language. This fact is due to the fact that your neural connections were adapted to understand this language as you interacted with the society around you. Thus, brain activity implies a complex interaction of descending and ascending causes.

Murphy maintains that the phrase "non-reductive physicalism" is synonymous with "emergent monism" but is preferable because "emergence" as a term is ambiguous. Clayton and Ellis, however, hold that this term expresses a level of organization in various levels of complexity in nature. The term emergence at once means that higher levels of order arise from lower ones and also that, at a certain stage, "the agents studied become so highly individualized that it is already debatable whether their actions can be explicable on the basis of underlying laws" (Clayton and Knapp 2011, 80). Thus there is continuity of development in the order of the natural world; but also this line of development at certain stages leads to the appearance of a degree of organization that has holistic properties and so is irreducible to lower levels.

Such an approach has the advantage of acknowledging the positive significance of research in the field of neurobiology for understanding brain function and human behavior and includes such an understanding in the general framework of the evolution of life on earth. It also focuses attention on the fundamental non-reducibility of consciousness and its functions for lower levels of organization. At the same time, physicalist approaches raise the question: how far can physicalism go without denying the factors necessary for religious faith? Clayton admits that "physicalists deny the existence of God solely on the grounds that ontological physicalism presupposes the existence of only physical objects" (Clayton 2002, 184). Clayton identifies several possible approaches that characterize the possible relationship between theology and brain science. Thus, physicalists are convinced that the human person will eventually be fully explained in neurobiological terms, which makes theology utterly superfluous. This judgment is called the sufficiency thesis. Opposed to this is the thesis of insufficiency, which Clayton adheres to, since "being a person means something that, in principle, is beyond the limits of neurobiology" (Clayton 2002, 188). At the same time, Clayton admits that, while he maintains insufficiency himself, the dispute between these two theses is not scientific but purely philosophical. As a thesis it is quite compatible with the belief in the explanatory power of neuroscience. Polkinghorne agrees with this view and remarks that "the reduction of thought exclusively to the physical states of neural networks is not a conclusion from neuroscience, but a metaphysical position imposed on the scientific discipline" (Polkinghorne 2011, 28–29). The problematic of such a complete reduction was demonstrated by John B. S. Haldane in his famous judgment: "If I believe that my beliefs are simply the product of neurons, then I have no reason to trust that my beliefs are true—therefore, I have no reason to believe that my beliefs are simply the product of neurones" (Verschuuren 2017, 155).

Clayton, Murphy, and Ellis allow that neurobiology recognizes consciousness as being associated with neural activity. Yet this emergent property is a high-level feature of neurons that is not reducible to them because of the profound and complex sets of relations within the physical, social and intellectual environment. Neuroscientists attempt to find and account for the neural correlates of consciousness. They consider that they have found such a correlate when they eliminate the obvious contrast between neuroscientific representations and descriptions of conscious experience in the first person. Here we are then faced with the "hard problem of consciousness." Philosopher David Chalmers notes that scientists, as a rule, may be able to solve the "soft problems of consciousness" related to reactions to stimuli, attention, memory, behavioral control, etc. However, the really difficult problem of consciousness is the problem of experience. Being a proponent of strong emergence, Chalmers gives a clear example of why neuroscience cannot solve the Hard Problem of Consciousness: "A scientist who is colorblind can gain complete physical knowledge about the brain and its functions; and yet he cannot deduce from here what it means to have a conscious experience of red colors" (Chalmers 2006, 246). Clayton also believes that subjective experience cannot be explained by neuroscience, because "one can fully know the structures and functions of some experience, and yet not know what it means to have such an experience" (Clayton 2004, 122). He gives an example that demonstrates the inadequacy of the theories of the identity of consciousness and the brain: "Suppose, in principle, you can know exactly what neural processes occur when Michael is asked to define the concept of 'justice' and give an answer. Yet these events will never be identical to his definition of justice" (Clayton 2002, 192). The problem is that a complex experience cannot exist divided among many objects, such as neurons. The paradox is that, on the one hand, understanding cannot be denied as an indisputable fact of our life, and on the other hand, this understanding, as noted by William Hasker, "cannot be either a single neuron or a group of neurons, such as a brain, and cannot be any material object at all" (Hasker 2011, 208).

Our subjective or internal experience of mental functions, together with our understanding of them and ourselves as a single center of consciousness, requires an explanation that transcends the purely physical functioning of the brain, even if we reasonably assume that all these functions are related to the brain and to a certain extent depend on it. It is no surprise that Jerry Fodor puts the problem so acutely: "No one has the slightest idea how something material could be conscious. No one even knows what it must be like to have even the slightest idea of how something material could be conscious. This is a big part of the philosophy of consciousness" (Clayton 2004, 122–23). Thus, some form of dualism is almost inevitable. It is not surprising that to a certain extent dualism continues to persist even in the approach of Murphy and Clayton, despite the fact that Clayton calls his approach "emergent monism" and categorically rejects the dualism of soul and body. Clayton sees monism in the fact that "there is only one physical system, and no energy is introduced into this system through some spiritual substance external to it" (Clayton 2002, 196). Note that this very judgment does not contradict in any way that a person is a unity of soul and body. The immaterial soul is not external in relation to the body because the person is a unity of body and soul. At the same time, Clayton quite clearly emphasizes the dualism of properties, saying that the language of physics and personality only partially overlap. He rightly notes that "the disputes between physicalist and non-physicalist views on personality are related not only to science, but to what actually or really or definitively exists" (Clayton 2002, 198). While one can agree with Clayton that the mental depends upon, but is not reducible to, the physical, the emergent approach can be taken as a necessary but insufficient, approach to a theological understanding of human personality. One can scarcely agree with Clayton that the introduction of the substance of the soul (i.e., in its proper theological understanding) must result in the rejection of any debate on the matter. Such a judgment is similar to the view that the introduction of the concept of God should lead to the rejection of any discourse between science and theology. A different problem with emergent monism, according to the philosopher Robin Collins, is that the introduction of emergent properties or structures is insufficient in itself, since "it simply moves the problem one level back to the laws that determine when emergent properties or structures arise" (Collins 2011, 232).

The Soul in the Context of the Dialogue between Science and Theology

However, the main problem of non-reductive physicalism, or emergent monism, is that these approaches ignore theological devotion, the importance of which we emphasized at the very onset. Answers to questions about nature essentially depend on what our view of nature is, and what kinds of answers we can get based on such a view. This also fully applies to the idea of the person. Christian theological anthropology has always emphasized the presence of the human soul as an active human principle. Moreover, Christian eschatology assumes that the soul continues to exist after the death of the body and exists separately from it until the universal resurrection. An emergent consciousness that appears from physiochemical processes is clearly not a sufficient understanding of human nature in the eyes of theology. John Polkinghorne does not accept Murphy and Clayton's approach because he believes that it is vague and leads to the fact that matter becomes the causal basis of reason. As noted by William Hasker, the Christian doctrine of the resurrection of the dead suggests that "the conscious mind is an ontologically distinct entity from the physical brain" (Hasker 2011, 216). Therefore, Hasker calls his approach "emergent dualism," and Polkinghorne "two-dimensional monism." From the point of view of the latter, the soul appears to be "an information-bearing model, expressing the continuity of a living personality and organizing matter" (Polkinghorne 2002, 106). However, the problem with this understanding is that this informational model, which arises in the human as a result of evolution, exhibits, according to Polkinghorne independent activity. That is to say, it differs from the usual input of information into the system. It is no surprise that Ward then queries Polkinghorne with the reasonable question as to whether he regards the soul as substantial? It is obvious that ordinary information always exists on a specific medium and is "connected with a physical structure so much that when this structure is destroyed, it also collapses" (Ward 2012, 133). To avoid such a conclusion, Polkinghorne postulates that this information sample has internal activity. Ward rightly points out this contradiction in Polkinghorne's view, which could easily be eliminated if the latter did not *a priori* refuse to understand the psychosomatic unity of man in the form in which it is presented in traditional Christian theology and in Descartes (Ward 2012, 135). This becomes even more obvious when Polkinghorne talks about the eschatological future. The resurrection is conceived by Polkinghorne as a change of all created things in accordance with the new laws that God introduces into the universe. At the same time, two aspects stand out in this transformation: the continuous and the discontinuous. On the one hand, the history and development of this world with its laws are interrupted, on the other hand, the eschatological future assumes that the previously existing world is transformed into a new state. When Polkinghorne talks about an informational pattern, he believes that this pattern can be transferred by God into a new form of corporeality. To explain the possibility of such a transfer, Polkinghorne uses the metaphor of the soul as "software" and the body as "hardware." Such a metaphor allows us to imagine the possibility of transferring software or an "information-bearing model" into a new physical environment of the transformed world. However, the metaphor of the "active informational sample" itself makes sense only when we move away from two-dimensional monism and assert that psychosomatic unity should be understood precisely as the unity of the human soul and body.

In this regard, a question naturally arises. If, for example, according to Barbour and others (Barbour 2002, 253), the existence of the soul cannot be proven or disproven by science, then what objective reasons do philosophers and theologians involved in the debate have to reject dualism? As noted by William Stoeger, "from the point of view of science and modern philosophy, [the soul] is seen as utterly useless, although I cannot see that it somehow contradicts the natural sciences" (Stoeger 2002, 144). Stoeger believes that we can expand the emergent description if we reflect on what we mean by the very concept of the laws of nature. Stoeger distinguishes two understandings of the laws of nature:

1. how we know, understand and model the laws,
2. how they really function in reality, which is more than what we know, understand and are adequately modeling. (Stoeger 2002, 144)

Neuroscience, within the framework of its approaches, can study the laws of nature in the first sense and approach the second to a certain extent. In this first meaning, the description of emergence proposed by Clayton and Ellis can be taken as a working model. At the same time, even these emergent models do not answer the question: how can something that cannot be empirically observed, like consciousness, be just a combination of brain states whose nature is observable? Stoeger believes that the answer is that "consciousness is not 'just a combination' of brain states, but rather involves a complex evolving pattern of brain states, constituted in some very specific way by certain relationships, including those that we need to discover and understand" (Stoeger 2002, 144). Thus, those correlates of consciousness that are available to science represent a subgroup of the laws of nature that are potentially cognizable by the natural sciences. The soul in this sense can be thought of as a complete network of relationships that exist in reality. Thus, if we consider nature as a creation of God, then this understanding assumes that the laws of nature as they function in reality express God's relationship with stratified reality in its entirety. With regard to the soul and consciousness, this suggests that the laws of nature as they function in reality presuppose the entire spectrum of relationships, including neural connections, interaction with the entire human body, its emergence and development, as well as a relationship with higher levels of reality that are in themselves inaccessible to scientific research. Stoeger notes that the concept of the soul "presupposes its connection with the Foundation of its being" (Stoeger 2002, 137).

Philosophical objections to the concept of the soul, as a rule, are connected with the criticism of the substantial dualism of René Descartes, who, according to the traditional representation of Cartesianism, opposed the thinking substance (*res cogitans*) to the extended substance (*res extensa*). In philosophy, this view has been called the "homunculus error" (Verschuuren 2017, 159). However, this understanding of dualism is actually a simplification of Descartes' approach to the problem, since the latter shared the traditional Christian idea of man as a unity of soul and body: "Nature also teaches me that I am not only present in my body, as a sailor is present on a ship, but there are these feelings—pain, hunger, thirst, and the like—I am in the most intimate sense connected with my body and, as it were, mixed with it, thus forming a kind of unity with it" (Descartes 1994, 65). The theologian Keith Ward believes that the accusation of dualism against Descartes' is one of the most common misconceptions in the history of philosophy. Ward writes: "Cartesian dualism, in fact, is the doctrine that the body and mind are different in appearance, but essentially integrated and connected to form one being, man" (Ward 2012, 129). The philosopher of religion Charles Taliaferro also admits that materialists such as Daniel Dennett portray dualism in a caricature form, considering the personality as a tiny subject in the theater that is in the head. Taliaferro writes: "When you see me writing, you don't see a soul controlling a body, you see an embodied personality. Dualism is better considered along integral lines. In healthy conditions, mind and body, mental and physical function as a unity. But in other conditions, in case of death, for example, the body may disappear, but if the personality is larger than the body, death may not mean the end of the personality or soul" (Taliaferro 2011, 40). In this perspective, it seems quite possible to investigate the hypothesis of the soul, which, according to philosophers Mark Baker and Stewart Goetz, "can function as a hypothesis in the sense that it is an integral part of a complex theory about the true nature of people . . . and its connection with the observations of empirical data should be real and irreducible, but that connection can be complex and indirect" (Baker and Goetz 2011, 14). Another objection that is often raised against the acceptance of the concept of an immaterial soul is that it is not observable through scientific methods. However, as Hans Halvorson points out, "Postulating an unobservable structure behind phenomena is a common strategy of theoretical science, its justification stems from the fact that it explains empirical facts that would otherwise be mysterious" (Halvorson 2011, 159).

The Orthodox theologian Christopher Knight holds that science makes it quite possible to successfully study the functions of the soul that today relate to consciousness and reason. Recognizing the advantages of emergent approaches and their criticism of reductionism, Knight considers their main disadvantage to be that they reject the possibility that emergent qualities, such as thinking, free will, etc., "might have some kind of reality outside the body" (Knight 2018, 154). He rightly notes that, since the beginning of the eighteenth century, the term soul has been replaced in scientific discourse by the concepts of mind or consciousness, but the identification of the soul with mind and consciousness is not correct. Knight considers another important drawback of the emergentist approach the desire to fully substantiate the emergence of consciousness and mind from the lower levels of the organization of matter, ignoring an important aspect of the Christian understanding that "matter has its origin in the mind of God" (Knight 2019, 152), since all nature, as we have already noted, should be considered as creation.

Based on what we know today about brain functions, about the connection of thinking and consciousness with neural activity, and also based on the understanding of the irreducibility of consciousness to neural correlates, Collins proposes a "two-dimensional model of the soul" (Collins 2011, 234). The soul has subjective properties or qualia, which are non-reducible, as well as non-subjective properties that can be described by mathematical laws. Such a two-dimensional model of the soul makes it possible to describe mental activity in scientific terms, and at the same time emphasize that there is something in a person that is not reduced and cannot be represented by scientific description. Collins believes that the postulation of the dualism of entities, although it is a metaphysical position, comes from an understanding of the kind of explanation sought by science itself—the description of known phenomena in the most elegant fashion. According to Collins, "the introduction of a new entity, the soul, which has subjective and non-subjective properties, can potentially provide a fairly simple representation of the observed correlations between brain states and subjective states" (Collins 2011, 246). From Collins' point of view, the non-subjective properties of the soul have nothing to do with consciousness and can be described by mathematical laws, while the subjective properties of the soul are not available for such a description.

Collins' approach is consistent with Orthodox anthropology. In the Orthodox theological tradition, human nature is the unity of the bodily and spiritual principles. Thus St. Maximus Confessor repeatedly emphasizes that a "complete person is a body [capable of being] an instrument [co]united with a rational soul" (Maximus 2020, 272). The body, according to St. Maximus, is an instrument of the soul, and the soul accommodates the body, being entirely present in each of its parts. At the same time, the very idea of the soul presupposes the presence of aspects in it that can be described through interaction with the body, as well as those aspects that are non-reducible and express the soul's attitude to God. Thus, the Orthodox theologian Fr. Dmitriu Stăniloae emphasizes that "the spiritual breath of God produces the ontological spiritual breath of man, namely, the spiritual soul, which has its roots in the biological organism and is in conscious dialogue with God and with other people" (Stăniloae 2000, 85). This emphasis on the unity of man excludes any form of substantial dualism in which man is regarded simply as a spirit or soul. Rather, a person is an embodied spirit or an animated being in which the soul manifests itself through the body, and the body has its foundations in the soul. The Orthodox understanding of the soul presupposes that it has various aspects or abilities, some of which may well be explained by its close connection with the bodily nature of man, and the other part, on the contrary, is irreducible. Relying on the works of St. Gregory of Nyssa, Knight focuses on the theological concept of the mind (νοῦς) as the highest cognitive ability of a person on the way to God, expressed in direct intuitive knowledge of the divine, which should be distinguished from rational knowledge (διάνοια), associated with the existence of a person in the world after the fall and conditioned by his biological nature. Knight notes: "If a coherent understanding of faith is to be developed, something is needed that provides a non-reductionist connection between it and other aspects of human psychology" (Knight 2019, 147). Thus, cognitive sciences and brain sciences are quite capable of studying processes related to human rationality, human volitional behavior and the emotional world, but are limited in understanding the highest cognitive ability—the mind (νοῦς), which according to the thought of St. John of Damascus "is not different in comparison with [the soul], but is the purest part of it (for as the eye is in the body, so is the mind in the soul)" (John of Damascus 2002). Fr Dumitru Stăniloae emphasizes the eschatological significance of the mind when he writes: "After the mind is freed from all things and representations of this world, it will know God in a direct intuitive way" (Stăniloae 2000, 74). This understanding gives an important meaning to the eschatological perspective, in which, in Polkinghorne's sense, the "information-bearing model" is not just transferred to a new "box," remaining essentially unchanged, but is transformed and transfigured into a new state. Knight points out that the metaphor of "software" and "hardware" that Polkinghorne uses today has become inadequate both from a scientific and theological point of view, since "what we call reason is conditioned by the physical substrate from which it arises" (Knight 2019, 159). This means that those aspects of the mind that are conditioned by the relationship with the brain and the human body are part of our present physicality, which will not necessarily be transferred to the world to come after the resurrection: "the resurrected mind will be associated with a new situation and will inevitably differ from our earthly mind" (Knight 2019, 159). The cognitive abilities of the soul after the resurrection will not be connected with διάνοια, but with the νοῦς, the "eye of the soul," which gives a direct intuitive knowledge of God, since the nature of man's transformation into a new state is indicated in the Holy Scriptures as a vision of God "face to face" (1 Cor 13:12).

Conclusion

Summing up the above, we can draw the following conclusions. Ontological reductionism is a metaphysical position that is not a necessary precondition for the practice of science. The dialogue between theology and science cannot be carried out from some theologically neutral abstract position. It must presuppose an understanding of nature as divine creation. The currently available data from cognitive research and neuroscience allow us to reasonably talk about the presence of emergent properties, such as mind and consciousness. These phenomena are not reducible to brain functions. Such emergent properties can be divided into two categories: those properties that arise as a new level of organization from physico-chemical and biological structures, i.e., emergent properties, and those that are associated with the existence of a soul or nous that determines the person's relationship to God. Constructive interaction between Christian theology and modern human sciences is possible without the need for a radical revision of the traditional Christian teaching about man and the elimination of the concept of the soul.

Bibliography

Ayala, Francisco J. 1974. "Introduction." In *Studies in the Philosophy of Biology: Reduction and Related Problems*, edited by Francisco J. Ayala and Theodosius Dobzhansky, vii–xvi. Berkeley: University of California Press.

Baker, Mark, and Steward Goetz, eds. 2011. *The Soul Hypothesis: Investigations into the Existence of the Soul*. New York: Continuum.

Barbour, Ian G. 2002. "Neuroscience, Artificial Intelligence, and Human Nature—Theological and Philosophical Reflections." In *Neuroscience and the Person: Scientific Perspectives on Divine Action*, edited by Robert John Russell et al., 249–81. Vatican City: Vatican Observatory Foundation.

Bhaskar, Roy. 1989. *Reclaiming Reality: A Critical Introduction to Contemporary Philosophy*. London: Verso.

Campbell, Donald T. 1974. "'Downward Causation' in Hierarchically Organized Biological Systems." In *Studies in the Philosophy of Biology: Reduction and Related Problems*, edited by Francisco J. Ayala and Theodosius Dobzhansky, 179–87. Berkeley: University of California Press.

Chalmers, David. 2006. "Strong and Weak Emergence." *The Re-emergence of Emergence: The Emergentist Hypothesis from Science to Religion*, edited by Philip Clayton and Paul Davies, 244–57. Oxford: Oxford University Press.

Clayton, Philip. 2002. "Neuroscience, the Person, and God: An Emergentist Account." In *Neuroscience and the Person: Scientific Perspectives on Divine Action*, edited by Robert John Russell et al., 181–215. Vatican City: Vatican Observatory Foundation.

———. 2004. *Mind and Emergence: From Quantum to Consciousness*. Oxford: Oxford University Press.

Clayton, Philip, and Steven Knapp. 2011. *Predicaments of Beliefs: Science, Philosophy, and Faith*. Oxford: Oxford University Press.

Collins, Robin. 2011. "A Scientific Case for the Soul." In *The Soul Hypothesis: Investigations into the Existence of the Soul*, edited by Mark Baker and Stewart Goetz, 222–46. New York: Continuum.

Crick, Francis. 1994. *Astonishing Hypothesis: The Scientific Search for the Soul*. New York: Scribner's Sons.

Descartes, René. 1994. "Reflections on First Philosophy." In *Collected Works in Two Volumes*, translated by S. Ya. Sheinman-Topshtein et al., 2:1–73. Moscow: Mysl.'

Dobzhansky, Theodosius. 1974. "Introductory Remarks." *Studies in the Philosophy of Biology: Reduction and Related Problems*, edited by Francisco J. Ayala and Theodosius Dobzhansky, 1–2. Berkeley: University of California Press.

Ellis, George. 2016. *How Can Physics Underlie Mind: Top-Down Causation in the Human Context*. Berlin: Springer.

Halvorson, Hans. 2011. "The Measure of All Things: Quantum Mechanics and the Soul." In *The Soul Hypothesis: Investigations into the Existence of the Soul*, edited by Mark Baker and Stewart Goetz, 138–63. New York: Continuum.

Hasker, William. 2011. "Souls Beastly and Human." In *The Soul Hypothesis: Investigations into the Existence of the Soul*, edited by Mark Baker and Stewart Goetz, 202–17. New York: Continuum.

John of Damascus. 2002. *The Fount of Knowledge*. Translated by Dmitriy E. Afinogenov. Moscow: Indrik.

Kiryanov, Dmitry V. 2021. "Critical Realism in the Dialogue of Science and Religion: The Approach of Ian Barbour and John Polkinghorne." *Manuscript* 14(8): 1669–78.

Knight, Christopher. 2018. "The Human Mind in This World and the Next: Scientific and Early Theological Perspectives." *Theology and Science* 16(2): 151–65.

———. 2019. "Science, Theology, and Mind." In *Orthodox Christianity and Modern Science: Tensions, Ambiguities, Potential*, edited by Vasillios N. Makrides and Gayle E. Woloschak, 147–61. Turnhout: Brepols.

Maximus the Confessor. 2020. *Ambigua*. Translated by Dmitri A. Chernoglasov and Arkady M. Shufrin. Moscow: Eksmo.

McGrath, Alister E. 2001. *A Scientific Theology*. Vol. 1, *Nature*. Grand Rapids: Eerdmans.

———. 2002. *A Scientific Theology*. Vol. 2, *Reality*. Grand Rapids: Eerdmans.

———. 2004. *Dawkins' God: Genes, Memes, and the Meaning of Life*. Oxford: Blackwell.

Murphy, Nancey C. 2002. "Supervenience and the Downward Efficacy of the Mental: A Nonreductive Physicalist Account of Human Action." In *Neuroscience and the Person: Scientific Perspectives on Divine Action*, edited by Robert John Russell et al., 147–65. Vatican City: Vatican Observatory Foundation.

Polkinghorne, John C. 1996. *Scientists as Theologians: A Comparison of the Writings of Ian Barbour, Arthur Peacocke, and John Polkinghorne*. London: SPCK.

———. 2002. *The God of Hope and the End of the World*. London: SPCK.

———. 2011. "Mathematical Reality." In *Meaning in Mathematics*, edited by John Polkinghorne, 27–35. Oxford: Oxford University Press.

Stăniloae, Dumitru. 2000. *The Experience of God*. Vol. 2, *The World: Creation and Deification*. Brookline, MA: Holy Cross Orthodox.

Stoeger, William S. J. 2002. "The Mind-Brain Problem, the Laws of Nature, and Constitutive Relationships." In *Neuroscience and the Person: Scientific Perspectives on Divine Action*, edited by Robert John Russell et al., 129–47. Vatican City: Vatican Observatory Foundation.

Taliaferro, Charles. 2011. "The Soul of the Matter." In *The Soul Hypothesis: Investigations into the Existence of the Soul*, edited by Mark C. Baker and Stewart Goetz, 26–40. New York: Continuum.

Verschuuren, Gerard. 2017. *The Holism-Reductionism Debate: In Physics, Genetics, Biology, Neuroscience, Ecology, and Sociology*. CreateSpace.

Ward, Keith. 2012. "Bishop Berkeley's Castle: John Polkinghorne on the Soul." In *God and the Scientist: Exploring the Work of John Polkinghorne*, edited by Fraser Watts and Christopher Knight, 127–39. Farnham: Ashgate.

3

We Are More Than Our Brains
In Search of the Subjective Beginning

Alexander Kaplan

> "In fact, if any master has properly created a representation of a work, then even if such a work never existed and never will exist, nevertheless his thought is true, and the thought remains the same, whether the work exists or not."
> —Baruch Spinoza

Every day, more than two billion people on Earth connect over the now popular WhatsApp messaging application, making up a hundred million connections. Almost 80 percent of the population in developed countries have unique IP addresses that allow them to exchange confidential messages. The high accuracy of these gigantic communication systems is possible only because the connections between subscribers in this world wide web are determined by the unique telephone numbers, or IP addresses, assigned to them. Obviously, if a little noise were inserted into this network structure once and for all fixed connections, altering no more than between five and ten percent of the addresses at once, communication chaos would immediately set in.

Even a tiny fraction of communication noise is unacceptable when addressing commands in a computer processor where billions of memory cells are simultaneously at work. How, then, is the switching between 86 billion nerve cells reliably integrated in the human brain, which has a total of more than 2×10^{14} contacts and which exchanges more than 10^{15} nerve impulses every second in a kind of "ringing" between neurons (Martins et al. 2012)?

In the age of Enlightenment, the solution to this riddle was proposed by René Descartes, who understood Nature as a single cosmogonic mechanism. He inscribed the mechanics of human brain activity into this mechanism of Nature, assuming the existence in the brain of a finely tuned switching node between the sensations that arise in response to external stimuli and the response actions that are expedient for each specific case. In Descartes's own example, in response to the touch of a hot object on the finger, a person withdraws his hand due to the contraction of the muscles precisely defined for this act, presumably precisely due to the precise connection in the brain of the sensory elements of the finger with the motor elements of the hand. Proposed by Descartes, this theory began to receive a precise scientific explanation around the turn of the twentieth century with the work of a whole galaxy of great physiologists from Georg Procháska, Charles Bell, and Charles Sherrington to Ivan Sechenov and Ivan Pavlov. This apparently logical system reduced the mechanics of the brain to a large switch with almost a million billion neural contacts.

In the time of Descartes, it was not so important to ask how the address space of the brain switch turned out to be so appropriate and accurately labeled, because the answer was obvious. What was important was the very idea of Descartes about the brain as a kind of switching map of a particular person, in which all his possible actions were described. In this sense, any action of a person is determined by the map of his brain— "we are our brains." But who or what then makes this grandiose brain mechanics work? It turns out that the seemingly arbitrary subjective diversity and uniqueness of each person's behavior is actually determined by Descartes's position—a mere combination of external stimuli acting on the human senses at a particular moment.

The only question that remained open was how constant are the communication schemes in the human brain when the body is exposed to the same complex of external influences? Indeed, armchair evidence indicates that the same stimuli in different circumstances can prompt different responses: a well-fed person will hardly be distracted by the smell of food, while a hungry person will immediately react with saliva and gastric juice. Moreover, reactions to food stimuli in a hungry animal can be prompted not only by the smell of food, but, for example, by the ringing of a bell, which initially has nothing to do with food. For this, it is enough that the call and the supply of food for the dog coincide several times in time, and for a person it can even be a coincidence of events in meaning or value. In any case, reasoning after Descartes, one can come to the conclusion that the initiative of human and animal behavior belongs to external stimuli, their temporal, symbolic or semantic associations, and the expediency of this behavior is at the mercy of the initial fine-tuning of the communication circuitry of nerve cells in the brain.

A new galaxy of researchers of brain mechanisms, headed by the Nobel laureate physiologist Ivan Pavlov, explained the phenomena of "higher nervous activity" in fact within the same Cartesian scheme, adding to the unconditioned reflexes fixed from birth conditioned reflexes that are formed purely mechanically—by trial and error in response to stimuli and their complexes. This scheme of brain work, supplemented with conditioned reflexes, automatically accumulates and consolidates useful connections between neurons in the same way that we collect the necessary phone numbers in the memory of a smartphone and delete erroneous ones, without thinking at all that by doing so we are building some kind of useful communication network.

Scientists of the twentieth century preserved the same concept of the brain as a large communicator, unique to each person. It was, of course, already equipped with a memory module for frequently and rarely used connections, with refined input-output registers (receptor and motor systems), but most importantly, with an automatic mechanism for fixing inter-neuronal connections that are suited to new challenges from the environment. The result was a similar mechanics, but with an unusual feature with respect to previous concepts: this mechanics was still regulated by the stimulus environment, but under the control of the body's requests to meet current needs. Thus, a previously unknown mode was discovered in the work of the switching network of nerve cells: self-organization to achieve a specific biological result, moreover, not in the form of a plan destined "from above," but in a trivial set of control values of the parameters of the state of the internal environment of the body: the level of glucose in the blood, the oxygen content in tissues, pressure in vessels, etc. The same target settings for the formation and operation of a neural network can also be control indicators of the work of the sensory, motor and analytical apparatuses of the body, corresponding, for example, to the presence or absence of certain objects in the external environment, the positioning of body parts relative to these objects, necessary for adaptation to the habitat. Taken together, these checkpoints can be called a kind of internal target setting, deviation from which in one or another direction, activates and sets the "meaning" or "direction" of the communication mechanics of the brain.

Old theories of automatic control and new cybernetic concepts from the successful mechanic Watt, the famous mathematician Norbert Wiener to the outstanding physiologists Peter Anokhin, Nikolai Bernstein and others generalized the initiatives of the external stimulus environment with the target settings inside the body in the schemes of self-sufficient brain switching mechanics, which is reflected, for example, in the title of the book by the outstanding Dutch neurologist Dick Swaab: *We Are Our Brains* (2014).

The time came when it was possible to conduct generalized, modern tests of the mechanics of the brain experimentally. For example, technologies were developed that made it possible to simultaneously record nerve impulses from tens, hundreds, and even thousands of individual nerve cells in freely moving animals or humans. The mechanisms for the formation of new neural connections began to be identified as they comprised the unique properties of contacts between nerve cells to gradually increase or decrease the probability of conducting signals. This process depends on how much they, in the course of trial and error, turn out to be necessary to perform one or another act of animal or human activity to achieve control over individual state points in the body.

Moreover, as it turned out, clusters of nerve cells act as real memory cells in the brain for fixing impressions from objects and events that are significant for the body in the outside world, thus decomposing this world into tic-tac-toe, triangles-squares, elementary smells and sounds. The Nobel Prize-winning discovery of such detector neurons (Hubel and Wiesel 2004) has given functional completeness to the theories of brain communication mechanics. Within the framework of these theories, each object of the external environment that is significant for the body has a cluster of neurons tuned to it in the brain, the activation of which actually presents these objects in the brain and, if necessary, transfers the baton of activation to the path of a specialized response of the body. Thus, experimental confirmation was received by the idea expressed by

Sechenov that reflexes can be not only motor, but also mental, the result of which is not a motor reaction, but a brain presentation of an external object. Now it is clear that these presentations are physically carried out in the form of activation of a cluster of nerve cells specialized for each object.

The outstanding heuristic perspective of these discoveries was that it was now possible to imagine that every object or phenomenon of the external world has its agents in the brain, which in the vastness of neural fields can interact with each other and thus build a new mental world.

Furthermore, it has recently been discovered that specialized neural clusters represent in the brain not only external sensory influences, but also the results of the analysis by the brain of certain properties of the external environment. In particular, so-called "place cells" have been found in the rat brain, which are activated only when the rat is in the place where it has already been fed several times, or in contrast, where some kind of trouble has happened to it (O'Keefe and Dostrovsky 1971). For a long time, it was impossible to understand how rats found these places of activation of "food-bringing" neurons or bypassed the zones where "trouble" cells begin to signal if the coordinates of these places were unknown to the brain. A decade later, Edward and May-Brit Mosers discovered, in addition to "place cells," "lattice cells" that were activated at a very specific position of the rat in the coordinate space of the nodes of this invisible lattice (Hafting et al. 2005). This means that rats travel not only or not so much in the physical world, but in the space of the neural networks of their brains.

The discovery turned out to be so significant that it was awarded another Nobel Prize (2014) in the field of neurophysiological research into the mechanisms of brain representation of the external world. Finally, neural clusters were found in the brain that specifically activated not external objects, such as tic-tac-toe or iconic objects and faces, not on marks and coordinates of physical space, but on the very intentions for a particular motor or cognitive action. It was possible, for example, to find neural representations of intentions to move the hand in one direction or another (Georgopoulos et al. 1982).

These movement intention detectors have been especially valuable for the creation of previously fantastic, but now clinically operable, brain-computer interfaces. In these technologies, the activity of neurons-detectors of intentions to move, intercepted by electronics, is transformed into commands for executive systems, for example, for a manipulator that replaces a paralyzed arm in a person (Inoue et al. 2018).

With such a mobility of representations, recognizing how the exact communication mechanics of the brain work would greatly simplify our understanding of the self-organization of brain processes and their independence from external operators other than the external environment. Yet such a search is a dead end because it can explain neither the phenomena of intuitive knowledge, nor insights into the search for deep patterns, nor even an elementary game of chess where each move is not a calculated operation, but the result of some kind of vision of the position "in a whole."

Doubts about the existence of these exact brain mechanics creep in as soon as one considers that nerve cells are far from silicon switches, like transistors in an IBM processor, but cellular organisms with life and death problems inherent in all living things. Every day, tens of thousands of nerve cells fail in the human brain. Some of this can be attributed to the original genetic plan, some of it to various other reasons; but, in any case, such failure would cause irreparable damage to the functionality of the finely tuned communication network of neurons that make up Descartes's model.

It cannot be assumed that, along with the elimination of nerve cells, entire fragments of our life experience go into oblivion in response to the challenges of the environment, in the ability to recognize not only crosses and zeros, elements of space and images of people, but also to manage our own intentions, to travel according to brain's coordinate grid. With gross pathological processes, this is exactly what happens, but why don't healthy people notice this in themselves, although their nerve cells also die by the tens of thousands every day? Where does the clarity of memory and thought, the clarity of speech, the ability to new synthesis come from, and this is far from uncommon, in people at an age when hundreds of millions of connections have disappeared or changed in the brain over a long life?

Moreover, recently, in subtle experiments on rats, it was shown that the map of neural representations of the external world and the skills of the behavior being developed is constantly modified and drifts across neural fields, practically without fixation on any specific neural clusters, without violating either the integrity of perception, or memory, or developed skills (Driscoll et al. 2017). At the same time, morphological studies have shown that in the visual cortex of the brain, even with an unchanged composition of nerve cells, up to 1 percent of their nerve connections are rebuilt daily, and in the hippocampus and somatosensory cortex, this process already effects from 5 to 15 percent of nerve connections (Clopath et al. 2017). How is the integrity of our perception, our skills, memory, and finally, our understanding of the world at every moment of life preserved while communications between nerve cells are in a constant state of transformation?

Imagine that at least once a week the connecting wires would be mixed on the telephone switchboard in the same volume, and, meanwhile, we would somehow magically not notice anything, still successfully selecting the desired subscriber in the telephone memory by his name, despite that his current number has already changed many times. What could be the secret of such a noise-tolerant switch? Isn't it that somewhere in some other memory, not so much numbers and telephone nodes are stored, but a complete picture of the world of contacts of a given subscriber, which includes, in addition to phone numbers, a lot of details, by the combination of which you can accurately determine the desired communication channel even without knowing the specific phone number. And then, whatever the current layout of the switching lines, contacts would be established in accordance with the current expediency and according to the totality of matching signs of the necessary contact.

All this suggests that a certain process is conducted across the individual exchanges of tens of billions of neurons, which maintains the integrity of the objects and properties of the external world represented in these neurons. This suggests an analogy with a projected image that can appear on a screen, over walls, on the ceiling, without losing its integrity. But the magic of cinema here is easily explained by the fact that initially this integrity is fixed in the matrix of spatial relations of the elements of the original image, and not in relation to the elements of the screen on which this image is projected. In the case of the brain, it is hard to imagine that the 86 billion neurons are the brain's screen pixels, onto which a certain integral image is projected from some source outside the brain.

Here we permit ourselves to hypothesize that this projection exists, and can actually be simultaneously integral and mobile with respect to specific neurons, where its source is not a third-party emitter, but a built in the brain's own dynamic mental model of the external in relation to the brain's world of things and phenomena. This model is essentially a reconstruction of the external world, made on the basis of each person's experience of interacting with this world and emphasizing the elements of this world that a person needs. This model can be manifested in a person's life only in the activations of the neural clusters of his brain, but in this it does not require a rigid binding to certain neural systems, since the integrity of representations lies in the constancy of spatio-temporal, verbal-logical, semantic and spatial-figurative relations.

It is difficult to imagine the organization of brain activity without a mental model of the external world in a person illuminated by great discoveries that initially did not have an algorithmic conclusion (Fermat's Last Theorem, Poincare's hypothesis, etc.), or simply considering the next move in chess, assessing the consequences of a visit to the boss, building vacation plans, etc. Something always tells us some steps that we not only cannot explain on the basis of existing knowledge, but even with the usual logic of what is happening. This "something" is the dynamic mental model of the outside world. Like clusters of neurons-detectors, this model is not given to us from birth, but is formed as life experience accumulates. And representations of the external world, as this model develops, to a greater or lesser extent become independent and active agents of this world, the interaction between which can lead to new experience, new knowledge, and even to a new idea of the world. All these will be those clues to a scientist, chess player or agronomist, which are subjectively perceived as acts of insight or intuition, and sometimes as revelations, but in fact are based on the predictive properties of a dynamic mental model.

Any possible explanation of human perception and behavior must be based on an account of how neurons function, but one that allows for the relative mobility in respect to how they comprise the mental model. Otherwise, how could one explain the speed with which we snatch an important sound from noise, a familiar face from a crowd and images of palaces in the clouds? All this is possible because the processes of perception involve patterns developed by experience, the same neurons pick out patterns from tic-tac-toe to images of people and things. But, obviously, no templates can be found to distinguish at least specific familiar faces, dog breeds, or artistic styles, since even the same face in different lighting conditions will be recognized by formal systems as two different faces, and only in a dynamic model will this face be presented in all in all its aspects, even those which themselves are fictional or imaginary. In this sense, the dynamic mental model in everyday activity can be much richer than that of the real world. This means that such models, in accordance with their nature, can even predict things which a person has not encountered in actual experience: hypotheses that have not yet been proven by anyone, effective moves in chess, in business, or in relationships, implicit natural patterns, interpretations of events. Let us recall how the "underdrawn" Impressionist paintings with formally unrecognizable details, nevertheless, create an unusually rich impression in the conjurings of their internal world.

Only a small part of this experience includes innate and acquired representations of inputs and outputs, i.e., between sensory impressions and motor activity. Ideas about the outside world, ideas and images of this world, subjective intentions and beliefs that are formed on the basis of analytical cognitive procedures make up the bulk of this experience. In other words, the subjective experience of a person comprises our individuality up to its highest spiritual manifestations.

Setting aside the philosophical question of where the transition from the structure of connections in the nervous system to the area of mental experiences, to the world of images, thoughts is, let us consider the question of the structure and function of a computer processor: where is the transition from the connection diagram between transistors to the calculations performed in it, to learning the algorithms working in it, the formation of machine solutions regarding tasks presented from outside? Again, this system is not comparable to a computer where even a minimal error in addressing between memory cells in a computer will lead to a failure in its operation.

Finally, we note one more, perhaps the most "human" property of mental models—the "cognitive deficit." This is a kind of subjective experience of the incompleteness of the mental reconstruction of aspects of the external world. It is the cognitive deficit that sets a new vector of search behavior for a person, that forms a subjective need for an increasingly advanced mental description of the real world, which eventually goes beyond biological adaptation. Thus, a dynamic mental model born in the human brain is able to overcome the "earthly gravity" and go to the expanses of cognition of the deep laws of Nature beyond the needs of its biological essence. This desire of a person, hidden from consciousness in many respects, to feel the completeness of mental reconstructions and the ever-increasing compliance with their hidden laws of nature, perhaps gives rise to the highest spiritual needs, the sense of belonging to the universal harmony of the world. Unconscious volitional aspects, as discovered by Viktor Frankl (2014) in his search of the meaning of existential spiritual values, seem to be personal projections of the deep orientation of nervous activity towards the construction of a holistic mental model of external reality.

Turning to a metaphorical plan, one can say, in the words of Baruch Spinoza, that the subjective mental model of the world that is born and developed in the human brain is "The finite human mind, which is not able to cover the entire range of individual things due to their infinite complexity. But yet its task is to discover 'the laws according to which everything arises individually and is ordered,' and on the basis of these laws to explain the essence of things" (Spinoza 1992).

Bibliography

Clopath, Claudia, et al. 2017. "Variance and Invariance of Neuronal Long-Term Representations." *Philosophical Transactions of the Royal Society London B. Biological Sciences* 372(1715): 1–10. https://doi.org/10.1098/rstb.2016.0161.

Driscoll, Laura N., et al. 2017. "Dynamic Reorganization of Neuronal Activity Patterns in Parietal Cortex." *Cell* 170(5): 986–99.

Frankl, Viktor E. 2014. *The Will to Meaning: Foundations and Applications of Logotherapy*. New York: Plume.

Georgopoulos, Apostolos P., et al. 1982. "On the Relations between the Direction of Two-Dimensional Arm Movements and Cell Discharge in Primate Motor Cortex." *Journal of Neuroscience* 2(11): 1527–37.

Hafting, Torkel, et al. 2005. "Microstructure of a Spatial Map in the Entorhinal Cortex." *Nature* 436(7052): 801–6.

Hubel, David, and Torsten N. Wiesel. 2004. *Brain and Visual Perception: The Story of a 25-Year Collaboration*. Oxford: Oxford University Press.

Inoue, Yoh, et al. 2018. "Decoding Arm Speed during Reaching." *Nature Communication* 9(5243): 1–14.

Martins, N. R. B., et al. 2012. "Non-destructive Whole-Brain Monitoring Using Nanorobots: Neural Electrical Data Rate Requirements." *International Journal of Machine Consciousness* 4(1): 109–40.

O'Keefe, John, and Jonathan Dostrovsky. 1971. "The Hippocampus as a Spatial Map: Preliminary Evidence from Unit Activity in the Freely-Moving Rat." *Brain Research* 34(1): 171–75.

Spinoza, Baruch. 1992. *Ethics with the Treatise on the Emendation of the Intellect and Selected Letters*. Indianapolis: Hackett.

Swaab, Dick. 2014. *We Are Our Brains: From the Womb to Alzheimer's*. London: Penguin.

4

Liquid Light as a Model of Matter-Consciousness Dualism

Alexey Kavokin

Introduction

EXCITONS ARE ELEMENTARY CRYSTAL excitations that mimic properties of hydrogen atoms in different energy and length scales (Frenkel 1931). Exciton-polaritons, or, simply polaritons, are half-light-half-matter quasiparticles whose appearance may be described semiclassically as follows (Hopfield 1958): a quantum of light, photon, when entering a crystal, may be absorbed, in which case its energy is passed to the electronic system of the crystal. This energy may be expended in the creation of an exciton. In turn, the exciton can be annihilated, releasing its energy in the form of a photon. In an infinite crystal this process would go on infinitely. From the point of view of quantum mechanics, it is impossible to know where in space and time one would have an exciton and where one would have a photon until the measurement is done. Furthermore, in fact, there is no exciton and no photon while a superposition quasiparticle (exciton-polariton) exists until the measurement leads to a collapse of its wave function on the classical basis, that is either to a purely exciton state or to a purely photon state.

Excitons were studied extensively in the twentieth century (see, e.g., Wolf and Mysyrowicz 1984) and enhanced attention of the scientific community turned to exciton-polaritons in 1992 when the strong coupling regime of light and matter led to a very clear manifestation of their formation in artificial crystal structures called microcavities (Weisbuch et al. 1992). Since then there has been very active development in the field of polaritonics. The most important discoveries of the twenty-first century include the observation of Bose-Einsten condensation and superfluidity of exciton-polaritons at room temperatures (Kavokin et al. 2017). These works have demonstrated the ability of light-matter quasi-particles to form macroscopic quantum fluids that can carry information. This makes polaritons good candidates for applications in classical and quantum computing (Kavokin et al. 2022).

An interesting twist on the analogy between light-matter and consciousness-matter dualism has been introduced by the recent discussion of the role of polaritons as communication channels in the human brain (Solms 2021). Since the introduction of the idea by the founder of polaritonics J. Hopfield (1977), experimental studies of so-called life-polaritons, or polaritons formed by living cells, have been flourishing. It has been demonstrated that organic matter can be brought into the strong coupling regime with light (Dusel 2020). The resulting polariton modes do not damage living organisms, in contrast, they may help them communicate with the surrounding environment. A hypothesis related to the polariton channel for information exchange in the human brain is based on the established existence of a communicating network of cavities filled with cerebrospinal fluid that are located within the brain parenchyma (Crisan and Chawla 2016). Such cavities might be capable of sustaining a whispering gallery of modes of light that can be brought into the strong coupling regime with electronic transitions of organic molecules of the brain. A polariton-mediated information exchange would complement the communication channel provided by the neural network, enriching its learning function, a faculty still difficult to describe within contemporary brain models. It turns out that our thoughts may be conducted inside the brain by superposition states of light and matter.

Now we see that the study of exciton-polaritons may shed light on the mechanisms of interaction of human thoughts and the material world that, in turn, may reflect the way God's will is communicated to the world. What are the experimental observations in polaritonics most relevant to this problem? In the following sections, we shall review two of these: the breakdown of spontaneous symmetry showing the ability of polariton condensates "to take independent decisions" and the generation of stochastic superfluid currents mimicking spontaneous thoughts in our brain. Next, we shall discuss the concept of a polariton qubit that might shed light on a mechanism of realisation of the first two effects. In the final section we shall critically discuss these data and try to draw some conclusions.

Spontaneous Loss of Symmetry

First, let us consider the spontaneous breaking of symmetry in bosonic condensates of exciton-polaritons. This was first invoked in the experimental work of (Kasprzak et al. 2006) on the Bose-Einstein condensation of exciton-polaritons, which was then examined in detail in (Baumberg et al. 2008), and (Ohadi et al. 2012). Bose-Einstein condensates are ensembles of one hundred to one hundred thousand exciton-polaritons sharing the same quantum state, that is having the same energy and wavevector. Polariton condensates are macroscopic objects characterized by a spatial and time-dependent phase and polarization. As any second-order phase transition, the bosonic condensation of exciton-polaritons is characterized by a build-up of an order parameter. As shown in (Baumberg et al. 2008), the vector polarization of light emitted by a condensate of polaritons may be considered as an order parameter in experiments testing for polariton condensation. Below the condensation threshold, the polarization degree of light emitted by polaritons is close to zero, while above the threshold it approaches 100 percent. It is very important to note that the orientation of the polarization vector is selected by the system spontaneously and it randomly changes from one experiment to another. The statistical distribution of this vector polarization has been extracted from thousands of independent tests. It clearly shows that it is impossible to predict the polarization of a polariton condensate in each particular case, suggesting that the ensemble of polaritons "decides" which polarization to choose.

Stochastic Currents

The generation of stochastic superfluid currents of exciton-polaritons is another important manifestation of spontaneous processes in light-matter fluids. The effect has been theoretically predicted (Nalitov et al. 2017) and observed soon after in semiconductor micropillars (Lukoshkin et al. 2018). The direction of persistent superfluid currents is not imposed by any external condition but it is spontaneously chosen by the system. These observations confirm the ability of a self-organized ensemble of light-matter quasiparticles to "take decisions" either regarding their vector polarization or regarding the direction of their motion. It should be noted that we, the observers, know about the decisions taken by the studied system by looking at the photonic component of exciton-polariton condensates, measuring their optical properties. Theoretical interpretations of these experiments invoke a classical bistability (multistability) effect in a strongly-nonlinear many-body system. A similar phenomenology may also be considered in the quantum limit, where stochastic realisations of various states of a macroscopic system are considered as projections of a quantum superposition state toward a classical model. In this interpretation, before the measurement is done, the system exists simultaneously in all possible states, while the measurement collapses its wavefunction to one specific state. In this case, the "decision" is taken at the very moment of observation, and the role of an observer becomes paramount.

A Polariton Qubit

Quantum superposition states of macroscopic systems ("Schrödinger's cats") are exploited in superconducting qubits that are widely used in prototypes of quantum computers built by Google (Arute et al. 2019) and in other many-body bosonic systems (Byrnes et al. 2012). Contradictory to the intuition telling us that any quantum system containing millions of particles (such as a superconducting circuit containing millions of Cooper pairs) would not be able to keep its coherence for a time sufficient for the realization of a quantum algorithm, superconducting qubits demonstrate the ability to realize multiple quantum operations with a sufficiently high fidelity. A simple answer to the question: "How possible is it that Schrödinger's cat can be dead and alive simultaneously for such a long time?" is: "Because of the low temperature that prevents any transitions across the superconducting energy gap." Indeed, the operation temperature of superconducting quantum processors is kept well below 1K, that is close to absolute zero.

In this context, polariton condensates offer an opportunity for the realization of macroscopic many-body qubits operating at much higher temperatures, possibly at room temperature. Indeed, Bose-Einstein condensation of exciton-polaritons is observed in a variety of organic systems at room temperature (Zasedatelev et al. 2021). Topological protection of superfluid currents of exciton-polaritons gives hope that polariton qubits based on superpositions of currents with quantized orbital momenta (Xue et al. 2021) may appear extremely robust. There are multiple proposals of quantum processors based on exciton-polaritons of (Ghosh and Liew 2020). Their important advantages include not only their ability to operate at high temperatures. Being composite bosons, polaritons are subject to the bosonic stimulation effect that enables one to impose a specific quantum state onto a polariton condensate by a resonant pulse of laser light. This offers a powerful tool to manage polariton qubits that is essential for the realization of polariton logic gates. At the same time, spontaneous emission of light by polariton condensates, i.e., polariton lasing (Baumberg 2008), allows one to manipulate polariton systems while preserving information preservation and recall. It is not surprising that in parallel to the quest for quantum computing, a strong activity on neuromorphic computing with exciton-polariton condensates is currently in development, exploiting the similarity of quantum flows of "liquid light" to human neurons (Ghosh et al. 2021). This is a work yet in progress. The potentiality of strongly coupled light matter systems for non-classical information processing is yet to be explored.

Conclusion

The parallel between light-matter condensates of exciton-polaritons and a dual consciousness-matter system of the human brain may seem simplistic, but it is based on several robust experimental observations including: (1) the self-organizational ability of exciton-polaritons, (2) evidence of spontaneous "decision making" processes in polariton condensates and superfluids, (3) evidence for induced (stimulated) processes that enable one to impose a specific quantum state on a polariton condensate with use of external laser beams, (4) the ability to control matter by light and to generate light from matter that is realized in polariton superfluids. Based on these observations, one can speculate about the mechanism of interaction between spiritual and material world conducted through human thoughts, possibly spreading by means of generation and absorption of exciton-polaritons. One should clearly distinguish between spontaneous and induced (stimulated) processes in our brain. Induced processes are essentially predetermined. Human thoughts may be triggered and guided by Divine thoughts directly or through material agents. In contrast, spontaneous processes are independent of God's will. They reflect the ability of human beings to make their own choices. The combination of God's will and human will affects the material world created by God's will. Indeed, the material world is evolving in time under the influence of a great variety of internal processes. The strong coupling of material and spiritual achieved in human brains may be responsible for non-deterministic, yet not chaotic development of our world.

Bibliography

Arute, Frank, et al. 2019. "Quantum Supremacy Using a Programmable Superconducting Processor." *Nature* 574(7779): 505–10.
Baumberg, Jeremy J. 2008. "Spontaneous Polarization Buildup in a Room-Temperature Polariton Laser." *Physical Review Letters* 101 (13) 136409.
Byrnes, Tim, et al. 2012. "Macroscopic Quantum Computation Using Bose-Einstein Condensates." *Physical Review A* 85(4): 040306.
Crisan, Elena, and Jasvinder Chawla. 2016. "Ventricles of the Brain." *Medscape*. https://emedicine.medscape.com/article/1923254-overview?form=fpf.
Dusel, Marco, et al. 2020. "Room Temperature Organic Exciton-Polariton Condensate in a Lattice." *Nature Communication* 11(1): 2863.
Frenkel, Jacob. 1931. "On the Transformation of Light into Heat in Solids. II." *Physical Review* 37(10): 1276–94.
Ghosh, Sanjib, and Timothy C. H. Liew. 2020. "Quantum Computing with Exciton-Polariton Condensates." *New Physics Journal of Quantum Information* 6(16): 1–6.
Ghosh, Sanjib, et al. 2021. "Quantum Neuromorphic Computing with Reservoir Computing Networks." *Advanced Quantum Technologies* 4(9): 2100053.
Hopfield, John J. 1958. "Theory of the Contribution of Excitons to the Complex Dielectric Constant of Crystals." *Physical Review* 112(5): 1555–67.
———. 1977. "Photo-Induced Charge Transfer. A Critical Test of the Mechanism and Range of Biological Electron Transfer Processes." *Biophysical Journal* 18(3): 311–21.
Kasprzak, Jacek, et al. 2006. "Bose-Einstein Condensation of Exciton Polaritons." *Nature* 443(7110): 409–14.
Kavokin, Alexey, et al. 2017. *Microcavities*, Oxford: Oxford University Press.
Kavokin, Alexey, et al. 2022. "Polaritonics for Classical and Quantum Computing." *Nature Physics Reviews*. 4(7): 435–51.
Lukoshkin, Vladimir A., et al. 2018. "Persistent Circular Currents of Exciton-Polaritons in Cylindrical Pillar Microcavities." *Physical Review B* 97(19): 195149.

Nalitov, Anton V., et al. 2017. "Spontaneous Polariton Currents in Periodic Lateral Chains." *Physical Review Letters* 119(6): 67406.

Ohadi, Hamid, et al. 2012. "Spontaneous Symmetry Breaking in a Polariton and Photon Laser." *Physical Review Letters* 109(1): 16404.

Solms, Mark. 2021. "From Depth Neuropsychology to Neuropsychoanalysis: An Historical Comment 20 Years Later." In *Clinical Studies in Neuropsychoanalysis Revisited*, edited by Charles Salas et al., 10–30. London: Routledge.

Weisbuch, Claude, et al. 1992. "Observation of the Coupled Exciton-Photon Mode Splitting in a Semiconductor Quantum Microcavity." *Physical Review Letter* 69(23): 3314–17.

Wolfe, James P., and André Mysyrowicz. 1984. "Excitonic Matter." *Scientific American* 250(3): 98–107.

Xue, Yan, et al. 2021. "Split-Ring Polariton Condensates as Macroscopic Two-Level Quantum Systems." *Physical Review Letters* 3(1): 013099-1–18.

Zasedatelev, Anton V., et al. 2021. "Single-Photon Nonlinearity at Room Temperature." *Nature* 597(7877): 493–97.

5

The "Hard Problem" of Consciousness Elucidated Cosmologically

The Saturated Phenomenality of the Universe versus Its Object-Like Constitution

ALEXEI V. NESTERUK

> Consciousness is the most conspicuous obstacle to a comprehensive naturalism that relies only on the resources of physical science. The existence of consciousness seems to imply that the physical description of the universe, in spite of its richness and explanatory power, is only part of the truth, and that the natural order is far less austere than it would be if physics and chemistry accounted for everything. If we take this problem seriously, and follow out its implications, it threatens to unravel the entire naturalistic world picture. Yet it is very difficult to imagine viable alternatives.
> —THOMAS NAGEL

> We ourselves are large-scale, complex instances of something both objectively physical from outside and subjectively mental from inside. Perhaps the basis for this identity pervades the world.
> —THOMAS NAGEL

Introduction: The "Hard Problem of Consciousness"

THE "HARD PROBLEM OF Consciousness" (Varela 1996) is defined as a problem of explaining how the first-person embodied lived experience (understood as unique phenomenal field in which, and from which, every variety of knowledge [objectifying knowledge and participative knowledge] is assessed), with all its qualitative features, may arise from the physical processes taking place in the brains and organisms of humans (Chalmers 1995). The question is not only about consciousness as such, but about hypostatic[1] consciousness related to persons (asserted theologically, as radically different types of beings capable of articulating their own existence and createdness, imitating the source of this quality as originating in that ultimate personal Being which is associated with the Creator of all). Conversely, the problem is how to phenomenologically describe the appearance (in lived experience with its singular hypostatic specificity, with its physical conditions and mental states) of that presentation of this lived experience as one particular thing against the background of all being. In other words, how it becomes possible to describe experience in first person (as existence "simultaneous" with the

---

1. The meaning of the term "hypostatic" comes from the Greek word *hypostasis*, which was used in patristic theological context in order to underline the "personal," active, and intransitive dimension of existence as different from impersonal substance (*ousia*) or nature (*physis*). *Ousia* (as related to universals, families or species) tends to be used with regard to internal characteristics and relations, or metaphysical reality (in this it almost identical with *physis*), whereas *hypostasis* emphasizes the externally concrete character of the substance, its empirical objectivity, and the existential aspect of being, expressed through the realization of freedom, movement and will. The hypostatic aspect of individual existence is not immanent to what is included in the substance. Nature or substance can be divided and shared while the *hypostasis* of a particular being is indivisible. The reality of substance becomes evident and real only in *hypostases*, that is, in that which is indivisible. In a theological context *hypostasis* is similar to *person* in modern parlance. This implies that the nature of things becomes evident if it is *personified*. The *hypostasis*, then, is seen as the foundation of being for it is that in which its nature exists. In its application to human beings, all human beings share the same nature, they have similar biology so that flesh can be communicated from one human being to another. However, different human beings are different *persons*, that is, they have their own distinct existences, which can not be communicated to, and imitated by, different persons. All human beings are gifted with life: it is in them that life comes to itself in everyone of the community of persons, but comes as a self-hood, that is, as a *hypostasis*. As a hypostatic being man has a capacity of *enhypostasizing* reality, for example, through knowledge. The *enhypostatic* can be described as "existing in an hypostasis (or person)," "subsistent in, inherent." The *enhypostatic* points towards something which has its being in the other hypostasis.

variety of affections originating in the surrounding world) as that one particular modus of an individual among plural existences of the others.

From the perspective of perennial philosophy, either naturalistic or theistic, it seems that no "solution" to this "hard problem" can be given. In other words, no causation/transformation/transfiguration/mutation between the material world and the intelligible realm incarnate in every particular physical person can be found (this is the perennial mind-body predicament intimately related to the Hard Problem of Consciousness). In fact, it seems that the "Hard Problem" is itself generated through the search for a transition between the material and intelligible, assuming that the latter does take place, thus making it a "false" mystery constitutive of the human condition. Seen from this angle, the very task of addressing the "Hard Problem" becomes not an attempt to provide its ultimate "solution," but to generate an approach to the restatement and transformation of the problem into a new constitutive principle of the human condition. This implies a change of the basic attitude to the problem of embodied personal consciousness removing it from the metaphysical realm (that is, as reflected from the "outside") and placing it into an existential context, that is, as reflecting the essential feature of the lived experience which must be placed at the foundation and beginning of all further reasoning. Such an approach accentuates two, usually separate, directions of research about embodied consciousness (naturalistic and theistic) without giving priority to one at the expense of the other, and treating both as equally contributing to the open-ended hermeneutics of the human condition. Yet, such an attitude implies the recognition of lived experience as the ultimate presupposition of any form of investigation. The lived experience is understood widely as forming the life-world in the context of Husserl's attempts to ground all experience, including that of the sciences (Husserl 1970). To put it differently, the lived experience corresponds to that primordial realm of *existence* which Michel Henry associated with life as proceeding from the unconditional and self-affective (Divine) Life (Henry 2003a, 2003b, 2003c). Since this lived hypostatic experience is the precondition for anything to count as explanation, the "Hard Problem" transforms into the interrogation of how one would consider this lived experience as something to be explained. This kind of "explanation," if it could be effectuated, would require a radical change in the attitude of the inquirer by shifting from his/her object-oriented thinking to one in which the hypostatic subject becomes a problem for himself/herself. But perennial philosophy, including Christian patristics, as well as modernity and all modern continental philosophy, has always been aware that no constructive response to such a problematic interrogation of humanity by itself can be produced. Man is unknowable to himself, so that the implied transformation of the attitude to the Hard Problem can be compared with *metanoia* (a change of mind in ancient patristic tradition) in which this subject attempts to establish in words (that is, to phenomenalize) its own contemplation of being contingently given to itself, that is, contingently created. Certainly, one feels here a *theistic* flavor attempting to ground the facticity of subjectivity within some transcendent foundation. This foundation, unfortunately, itself becomes a certain stopping point that is itself not considerably different from the allegedly reductionist-like postulated physical substance in the foundation of mental activities and behavior. In fact, the shift to theism postulates the existence of some mental source of which human beings are miniature versions. And it is this mental source which is, allegedly, responsible for that intelligibility of the world that is manifested through the human capacity to comprehend the world under the conditions of its own ambivalence. In other words, rather than resolving the problem, the reference to theism makes it even more incomprehensible because radical contingency is ultimately related to the contingency of the world upon God.

If one abstracts from theology and looks at the possibility of readdressing the Hard Problem from a philosophical point of view, one has to admit that one can change oneself on the basis of human capacities without any reference to the transcendent. As was expressed by Michel Bitbol, such a transformation "requires from researchers nothing less than a mutation of their state of consciousness . . . when they can *see* lived experience *as* the universally presupposed background of questioning, rather than a theme to be questioned" (Bitbol 2021). This returns to our previously formulated thought that the "Hard Problem" must transform into a constitutive principle. The postulate of self-modification is radical in the sense that it implies a de facto modification of the human condition from within (not from without) to such an extent that the conventional, already existing, human condition might receive a sort of "explanation" from its modified state. Philosophically, this move could be seen as a strange self-split in the human sense of existence that could "look at itself" as if there were an access to that which is primarily forgotten at the act of birth and that is forgotten after death. Yet, once again, one feels an intrinsic influence of theistic thinking because the sought-after modification of thought, by accepting the primacy of the lived experience in its existentially irreducible and transcending intentionality, appeals to that which is not this thought and not this life. And any attempt to construct a joint picture of the world where consciousness and its intentional objects are ontologically equivalent fails because this equivalence is itself a fact that has already been constituted within the already lived contingent experience. This latter point is scarcely ever recognized by scientists, especially those who follow particular forms of speculative materialism based on the absolutization of mathematics in the natural sciences. Here we come to another version of the Hard Problem of Consciousness that can be formulated in the following paradoxical expressions: how can consciousness (in the first person) think of its own incarnation in the physical world (that is, in the person) where the question of its existence or non-existence entails thinking of that which could exist without this thinking. In order to exist in the first person (regardless whether this person is aware of its own fragile conditions), there must be certain physical conditions on Earth which make it possible to exist in embodied conditions whose articulation takes place in the person. But then, under this supposition, the first person must admit the existence of that state of the world when the existence in the third person was impossible. This implies that one observes a certain *distension* in the subject in the person when the sense of its existence in the third person experiences a tense-split pointing to a fundamentally non-local sense of coming into existence as being endowed with the possibility to formulate this coming into existence and *distension* in human consciousness between its oblique and direct intentionality.

An example of such a physicalistic attempt to express this distension between the perception of the world in first and third persons can be found in attempts of the famous physicist John A. Wheeler to introduce existential categories into the fabric of physics by employing ideas from quantum theory. He developed an idea, as a generalization of quantum mechanics's claim that observers affect the sense of reality of that which is observed, that the whole edifice of physics depends on the logic implemented by the network of intelligent observers so that the universe in its essence is not a watch-like mechanism, but the "World of Existences" (see, e.g., Wheeler 1988) contingent upon the constituting inter-subjectivity of existents. In other words, the world as it is articulated by physicists is not something in itself; it is a mental creation through historically evolving human consciousness. In a way, Wheeler attempts to say that the physical world and, hence, human observers themselves, are constituted from within the premise that they already exist. It is one thing to exist unconsciously (to experience existence in oblique intentionality), but it is a completely different thing when the fact of existence is manifested through an active exploration of nature where the very physical picture of the world represents a certain mirror of human consciousness.

Scientists did not like these ideas because of their impalpable claims and their lack of contribution to any scientific methodology. As was pointed out in my analysis of Wheeler's attempts to produce the overall constitution of the physical world by the community of observers-participants, the problem of the original lived experience, that is, of the already existent life, from within which the representation of the physical world unfolds, remained untouched (Nesteruk 2013). The reference to the community of observers remains in its essence the same metaphysical postulate of the original intelligence and intelligibility of the universe which is not advanced by such a claim. The Hard Problem of Consciousness remains untouched because all intelligent observers as hypostatic beings enhypostasizing the physical universe imply the inherent dualism between their experience of existence in the first person (as life) and in the third person as those who, while constituting the world through their observations, de facto constitute themselves as part of the physical world. The split or *distension* in the human condition is present in all such attempts to construct a model of the systematic unity of nature, but its "genesis," or the foundation of their contingent facticity, remains the primordial and ultimate mystery.

The reason why existential moves are generally problematic for physics is because the latter leaves no room for the problem of consciousness, subjectivity, and personhood to be posed in rubrics of discourse and concepts. For physicists, the hard questions related to the facticity and the structure of the inquiring mind are usually delegated to the field of vague philosophical intuitions. In many ways, this happens because of the unconditional belief in the efficacy of mathematics whose truths, while being discovered, do not refer to any personal consciousness. Yet the problem remains even for mathematics itself: man is the subject who develops and applies mathematics to the world ultimately from within the conditions of the first person (historical personality) whereas this same mathematics does not account for man as a hypostatic existence.

Correspondingly, any serious approach to the "Hard Problem of Consciousness," in particular in conjunction with the sciences, demands that we precisely locate this problem in the appropriate philosophical field which deals with the problem of consciousness as the problem of existence as such. This means that unlike in physics, where the presence of conscious observers is presupposed, philosophy makes consciousness a problem for itself, that is, the very facticity of philosophy itself is a philosophical problem. And the difficulty of such a formulation of the problem is exactly the intrinsic split of consciousness into two modes of operation within the conditions of life when existence is experienced by the human subject within first and third persons; that is, when the facticity of experience of existence in the first person depends on the facticity of existence in the third person, and vice versa. What remains solid as a rock is the dualistic structure of consciousness which while being contingent in its facticity remains closely linked to the necessities of nature. It thus encapsulates in itself the structure of the world where this consciousness is possible. Can then one conjecture that the dialogue between science and theology represents an outward dynamics of such an interplay between first and third person perspectives in one and the same man, the dynamics which contributes to the open-ended hermeneutics of the human condition?

The Natural Attitude and the Phenomenality of Objects

If one adopts an objectifying epistemic attitude in an attempt to address the "Hard Problem," then one follows the standard object-oriented ontology of scientific research and technological activity. One deals here with monistic physicalist metaphysics which accompanies a goal-oriented, objectifying attitude in investigation. This encapsulates the essence of our "natural attitude," formulated briefly as positing that which is deemed to exist as none other than object-like targets that can be extracted and stabilized out of the flow of lived experience.[2] What happens then is that

2. According to Edmund Husserl (Husserl 1980, §1), our "natural attitude" is a prephilosophical view in which the existence of a world of objects, those objects in which we are interested for practical reasons, is taken for granted. The natural attitude is related to the activity of consciousness within which one acts in a world which is real, a world that existed before this one was born and which one thinks will continue to exist after he or she dies. This world is inhabited not only by a particular human ego, but also by other human beings with whom this particular human can communicate meaningfully. This world has features which have been systematically described through the genetic-causal categories of science. The world of daily life is lived within this natural attitude and, as long as things go along reasonably well, there arises no need to call this attitude into question. Even if one does occasionally ask whether some things are "really real," whether the world is "really" as it appears to be, these questions are still

those who follow this attitude are often brought to think that the very lived experience (out of which objects are constituted) must be an epiphenomenon of some objects in the sense that the physical and biological properties somehow lead to the internal facticity of this experience, including humanity's multi-hypostatic consubstantiality.

Indeed, the naturalistic research program purports to explain every phenomenon on the basis of the laws and objects of the natural sciences. The open-ended character of making statements about phenomena (an infinite advance of science) makes naturalism allegedly immune to any objections based on the impossibility of achieving certainty with respect to some phenomena, including consciousness. However, one immediately observes that consciousness is not a particular phenomenon; it is the very phenomenality that is presupposed by any phenomenon whatsoever. Nor is consciousness an objective feature of the world. Then, a reference to the open-endedness of the naturalistic research program (its infinite advance) is *in principle* irrelevant to the problem of consciousness (although it could be claimed that the explication of consciousness is tantamount to the ongoing advance of the sciences at whose objects this consciousness is intended). Indeed, the naturalistic program only bears on an objective domain of inquiry (it deals with the phenomenality of objects). It leaves aside, by its very essence, the experiential, pre-objective, condition of any inquiry within such a phenomenality. No scientific effort can discover what has been intended in the very *decision* to enact objectification. *Intentional* acts cannot be subjected to straightforward physical causation and hence no non-existential foundation of science is possible.[3] In this sense, scientific naturalism has shown itself to be an epistemological dead-end as an explication of the very motivations of science, that is, intentional acts launching this or that particular investigation. Scientists are actors and participants in their research and not detached observers. The choice and consequent constitution of a particular

---

posed in such a way that they are questions about the natural world in which one lives. The natural attitude has a basic *teleological* tendency which finds its fulfillment in the constituted world which contains others. This is implanted in the mind's intentionality as a teleological tendency to move toward world-building. The natural attitude does not presume that manifesting something is making that which is being manifested. It is merely saying that the world appears through our production of its appearances. In the natural attitude consciousness is directed outside itself as a center of disclosure and manifestation and becomes entangled in the world as it gives it shape.

3. Husserl argued that all scientific activity is ultimately rooted in the life-world as that unmediated context of any lived experience.

object of research is dependent on *intentionality* rather than on physical causality. This is trivially the case in the science of consciousness, since here the "object" of research is identical to its subject. But this is also the case in the most fundamental theories of modern physics, dealing with the limiting questions, namely cosmology and quantum mechanics. Indeed, the constructs of these theories are, of themselves, historically and sociologically contextual and cannot therefore be detached from transcendental conditions (conditions of the lived experience, including socially conditional applications) of their objectivistic assessment (see, e.g., Bitbol 2009).

One realizes, in the context of the "Hard Problem of Consciousness," that there are indeed situations in physics and cosmology where the phenomenality of objects in respect to their constructs cannot be sustained. Hence a doubt arises about the legitimacy of the mental inference that private consciousness (as it is within the experienced phenomenon of life) can be deduced as an epiphenomenon of physical entities posited as objects (that is, one cannot deduce the phenomenality of the world in the first person from the one in the third person). In a trivial case this is related to the fact that all objects from everyday life can receive their interpretation from the point of view of the physical particles and interactions between them that sustain the object as a whole. Yet, this kind of representation will have no existential meaning. Physics in this case describes some underlying structures and relations which are abstracted from lived experience. Consciousness is present in this description as a post-factum discursive (mathematical) form of the expression of reality; however, the overall shape of objects of everyday experience (in particular of those which are constructed artificially) contains the consciousness of the whole as a basic intellectual and purpose-imbued idea drawn on the grounds of primary lived experience. In simple words, all scientific representations of reality presuppose that life as immediate experience of existence is already there. But this life is not explained by the sciences on grounds that establish sufficient conditions for life to be possible; that is to say, the conditions of this life's contingent facticity are not covered by the necessary conditions inferred through the sciences themselves.

In more sophisticated cases, some scientific claims about the ontological status of objects of investigation are challenged by ongoing scientific advances. This can be illustrated by historical examples, when some scientific "objects" become obsolete (ether, for example). This can also be illustrated by examples from those parts of cosmology which deal with not directly observable aspects of the universe (Dark Matter [DM] and Dark Energy [DE], for example), as well as with some claims on the part of cosmology for the reality of entities from the early universe, including the Big Bang itself, which as theoretical constructs have no direct empirical references. In other words, the theoretical constitution of objects does not entail their object-like phenomenality unless one commits itself to a strong mathematical realism.[4] Yet, even in this case such a problematic phenomenality of theoretical entities (a selected domain of objectified phenomena [that includes neurobiological phenomena] [Varela 1996]) does not relieve us from the obligation to recognize that all theoretical approximations have their source in the immediate lived experience (a broader domain of the immediately lived, unfabricated phenomena),[5] that is, in the already given life. The next move then is primarily dependent on how to interpret this life in order not to abandon the issue of manifestation of reality in the first person. For, speaking of the first person, one implies a particular living being with its specific body and hence with a particular trajectory in space and time.

If, as an alternative to the naturalistic trend, one interprets life as a life of consciousness, one thus retreats into a phenomenological attitude,[6] according to which the only domain of "apodictic certainty" (of which any claim of inexistence would be performatively contradictory) is the domain of "pure conscious life" ("all positions taken towards

---

4. This kind of realism implies that whatever is mathematically possible is physically possible. Even stronger, mathematics provides one with tools to think about those realities which allegedly exist without the presence of any inquiring intellect. Mathematical thinking paves the way to a belief that one can think that which is not related to this thinking (see more details in Meillassoux 2008, 112–28).

5. Once again one implies the life-world of Husserl or what Thomas Nagel described as common sense and plainly undeniable: "After all, everything we believe, even the most far-reaching cosmological theories, has to be based ultimately on common sense, and on what is plainly undeniable" (for example the very fact of life) (Nagel 2012, 29).

6. The phenomenological attitude is the opposite of the natural attitude which, as mentioned above, has a basic teleological tendency which finds its fulfillment in the constituted world that contains others. It is contingent, constitutive (world-building), and taken up with, and entangled in, the world it is shaping. In the phenomenological attitude, the transcendental reduction (epoché) as suspension of this natural naivety of world-building becomes an opposite move, contrary to the "inhuman" tendency of finding its foundation in the world, the move which returns the ego to its self-centering as a modus of the basic self-affectivity of life. The phenomenological attitude implies a move opposite to that of world-building, where through a careful insight into the constitutive acts of this building, the center of this constitution is itself disclosed as the source of "worldification" or "enworlding."

the already-given objective world" must be "deprived of acceptance" [Husserl 1960, §8]), so that the worlds of science and everyday life are downgraded to the rank of mere phenomena that "claim being," whereas "pure conscious life" is raised to the rank of "the whole of absolute being" (Husserl 1980, §51). Such a position is unsatisfactory because it relegates consciousness to the sphere of the unconditional (that is, implicitly to the theistic realm) and does not question the underlying issue of its facticity. The implied reversal of ontological hierarchy can be qualified as a variety of idealism (probably objective, that is, theistic) which cannot account for embodiment, to say nothing of the hypostatic features of consciousness, that is, persons. If one reifies the phenomenological activity that consists of "recollecting" on one's own conscious life and identifying the lived roots of one's "natural" beliefs, into something like a soul (self, mineness, etc), this creates a range of philosophical difficulties. In all possible scenarios, such a reified idealism (whether with its objective or subjective overtones) offers the problem of the first person experience (or hypostasis) no possible explanation.

It is possible then, in order to overcome the extremes of reductive physicalism and phenomenological idealism, to invoke some dualistic possibilities. Dualism, from René Descartes to David Chalmers, arises from a kind of switching over between the phenomenological and natural attitudes, associated with a naive ontologization of each of the two intertwined phenomenological domains. A phenomenological first step asserting the presence of "I think" in Descartes, or the felt "intimacy" of experience in Chalmers (Chalmers 1995), or the non-intentional immediacy of life in Henry (Henry 2003a, 2002b), tends to transform into a new "object" or property in its own right. Indeed, one is obliged to seek after the ultimate foundation of the facticity of Descartes's *cogito*, Chalmers's intimate experience, or Henry's life. The first person "I think therefore I am" is thus converted into the third person *res cogitans*, entailing that the lived experience as a precondition of any phenomenality must be converted into an additional component of a physicalist ontology.

A possible escape out of such dualism between the lived experience in the first person and post-factum representation of this experience by referring to the *hypostatic other* can be undertaken via a route of a "God's eye viewpoint" (that is, a theistic point of view) located somewhere above both consciousness and the place of its physical embodiment. In this case, the very facticity of hypostatic consciousness is associated (in Christian tradition) with man's Divine Image as being created by God. In this case these two attitudes toward lived experience—as that one which detects it instantaneously and intuitively through the fact of being created in communion with God, as well as another one which considers existence in reflection as corporeal, extended in space and time (but synthesized intellectually)—are both seen as two complementary approaches to one and the same created reality. The implied anthropology places humanity at the center of creation, unifying its visible (empirical) side with the invisible (intelligible) through their unity effectuated by God in the world and in man. Such an interplay between the personal experience of existence and its further representation in consciousness as an "objective" phenomenon can be illustrated through an analogy of a permanent circulation between the two attitudes, reaching one by way of the other and vice versa. This dynamical process can be illustrated as an "uroboros of consciousness" (Vörös 2014), as a continuous intellectual process in which one move serves as a preparation for the other. In Husserlian terms, consciousness is correlationally dependent upon the brain within a naturalistic framework, but the brain (as an object of perception and active physical handling) is *constitutively* dependent upon consciousness's acts within a phenomenological framework. Conscious experiences correlate with brain-events, but the brain as *object* is *constituted* out of a carefully selected set of conscious experiences.

The latter thought can be illustrated graphically through a "naturalized uroboros of consciousness." The task of this illustration is not trivial because it implies joining two radically non-uniform realms, that is, consciousness and the physical world. Nevertheless, this duality is the easiest problem because in principle, that is, in the natural attitude, these two realms can be "encoded" graphically as two different entities. The difficulty which pertains to the Hard Problem of Consciousness is that one needs somehow to reflect in such a graphic representation the difference between the constituting consciousness in the first person (as radically private and thus singular) and the working of consciousness that represents the outer world as a set of intentional objects, including the embodied consciousnesses of others.

Here one faces a challenge of making a symbol for the intrinsic split between the identity of the "I," expressed through the classical Fichtean formula "I=I" (and experienced only in the first person perspective), and that of "not-I," which can be treated as the outer world through which the "I's" split in itself occurs as a result of embodiment. In other words, if one fixes attention on the facticity of one's own "I," one immediately becomes aware of the boundary of one's own sphere of consciousness. The identity "I=I" cannot be unconditional because it implies the sense of the boundary as the limits of its own specificity and concreteness. But this concreteness is de facto the "I's" contingency. However, in order to detect and fix this contingency one needs to view oneself in the third person as posing this concreteness (contingency) as an "object" of this "I's" intentional gaze. One summarizes: in order to make the transition to the third person, that is to consider the "I" in the context of the "not-I," one needs to become aware of the contingency of the "I" in the first person. Both the "I's" contingency and its positioning in the context of the "not-I" in third person go inseparably together. One can provocatively claim that the Hard Problem of Consciousness is a very specific expression of the "I's" radical ontological contingency.

Thus, any attempt to graphically represent consciousness in relation to the world must implement the internal split in the "I" which makes "I's" self-identity meaningful: its self-identity implies the presence of the Other, so that, geometrically, for example, the "I's" singularity cannot be expressed as an insular point. Indeed, at this point a particular geometrical idea comes to mind if one treats consciousness, together with the French philosopher Francis Wolff as a "transparent cage":

> Everything is inside because in order to think anything whatsoever, it is necessary to "to be able to be conscious of it," it is necessary to say it, and so we are locked up in language or in consciousness without being able to get out. In this sense, there is nothing outside them. But in another sense, they are *entirely turned* towards the outside; they are the world's window: for to be conscious is always to be conscious of something, to speak is necessarily to speak about something. . . . Consequently, consciousness and language enclose the world within themselves only insofar as, conversely, they are entirely contained by it. We are in consciousness or language as in a *transparent cage*. Everything is outside but it is impossible to get out. (Wolff 2020, 42–43)

One possible concept would be to employ a so-called *stereographic projection* (where all points on the two-dimensional plane can be presented as intersections of this plane by line segments originating at the top of the sphere touching this plane at the bottom) in two dimensions. Consciousness, as a *transparent cage*, is depicted by a circle with the *transparent circumference* in a two-dimensional plane. The interior of this circle is related to its hypostatic self-identity (in a technical language, there is a generating principle of all points in this circle) whereas its boundary (circumference) contains the images of the world as result of consciousness's intentionality directed outside, that is toward the world. It is not accidental that any imagery of consciousness implies two dimensions in order to make a distinction between this consciousness as hypostatic self-consciousness "I=I" (zero dimension, that is a point) and as intentional consciousness appearing as a result of a limitation of self-consciousness because the latter must occur under the conditions of embodiment in the world. In other words, the finitude of consciousness as related to the conditions of embodiment is depicted with the help of the finite circle (in spite of the fact that the interior of this circle can unlimitedly and inexhaustively be explored by this consciousness as inner life [geometrically, the interior of the circle as two-dimensional manifold is infinitely large in comparison with that of the generating center in terms of a geometrical measure]). The fact that this circle of consciousness must be related to the world as "not-I" is depicted through the touching point at the bottom of the circle, where the physical world is depicted as a tangent line to the bottom.

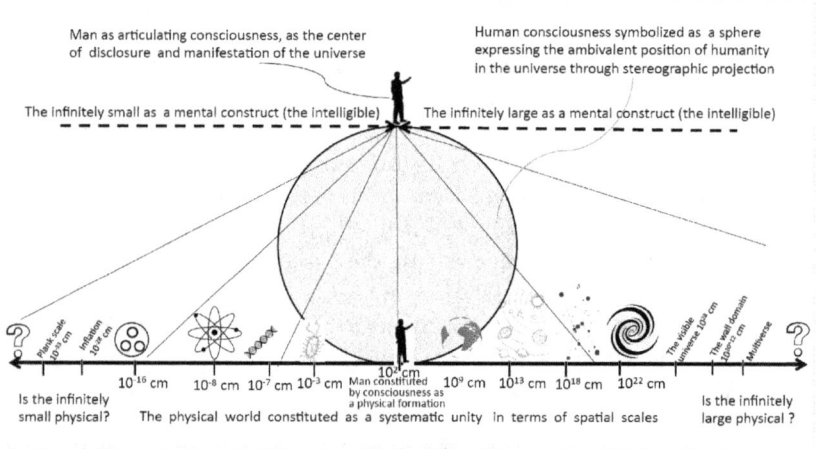

Figure 1: The relationship between human consciousness and the world presented by stereographic projection.

The top of the circle symbolizes the hypostatic core of consciousness, that is, that self-identity of the "I" which initiates all intentional acts directed (through this transcendental circle) to the world. This is depicted in the spirit of stereographic projection by straight lines originating at the top of the circle and directed towards the world depicted by the tangent straight line at the bottom of the sphere. The isomorphism between the circle and the world-line determines that any object in the world is articulated through transcendental consciousness; that is, the very structuring of the world-line in terms of scales is the result of the presence of human subjectivity depicted through the circle. World-objects appear as projections of the "I=I" through the circle of consciousness. There is only one point of "intersection" of the circle of consciousness with the world-line at the bottom of the circle and it symbolizes embodiment, that is, the fact that the circle of consciousness cannot exist without touching the world. The graph geometrically expresses that different physical objects articulated in terms of spatial scales and expressing a certain type of systematic unity of the universe are humanly constructed. This is related to human beings themselves who are constituted as physical formations from within the transcendental sphere of consciousness.

Unlike consciousness, the outer physical world is posed as *qualitatively infinite* and encapsulated in terms of spatial scales, but its *appearance* to consciousness is contingently *limited* (that is, specific and concrete and thus epistemologically limited). This contingent limitation is expressed through its projection onto the finite circle whose contingency is defined by the conditions of embodiment; i.e., the part of being that is unconcealed to man can be qualitatively infinite but epistemologically limited. This thought must be clarified further. When we talk about the world, we mean that its particular articulated presentation in forms of sensibility, categories of the understanding, and rational ideas is transcendentally specific and concrete as related not only to the cognitive faculties we have mentioned, but also to historical, social and technological circumstances. The latter amounts to the fact that the representation of the outer physical world in terms, for example, of its spatial scales, parameters of evolution in time, in terms of masses and sizes, is that of an organized structure which cannot be isolated from the structures of consciousness in a generalized sense.[7] It is in this sense that no picture of

---

7. Yet, according to those who adhere to the so called "speculative materialism" position, the recognition of the inherent contingency in the world-picture does not entail that there is no truth behind this picture because this picture is mathematical and hence predicates that which allegedly can exist without being seen or thought at all (see, for example Meillassoux [2008, ch. 5]).

the world can be non-contingent and unrelated to the human presentation unless one postulates it as a mathematical structure of a Platonic kind. This picture is formulated in human language and through human ideas. Thus the link between the circle of consciousness and the world seen through this circle on the tangent line is *constitutionally necessary, but contingent*.

One must bear in mind that the geometric representation of the circle of consciousness does not have anything to do with physical space and time. The circle simply represents the logical extension in the identity of "I=I" which manifests its contingency and radical difference with all other instances of "I" and with the world. The specificity of representation (projection) of the world through the circular boundary is determined by the specificity of embodiment. The lines proceeding from the hypostatic "center" at the top, intersecting the circle of consciousness and projected onto the line of the world represent the world's traces articulated by consciousness as its inherent desire to relate itself to that environment where it is embodied. Ultimately, one can say that the very specificity (facticity) of that which consciousness can perceive through the transparency of the circle is determined by the specificity of its embodiment which determines the extension of the "I=I" towards the world. Only that "information" can be processed by consciousness which is consistent with the conditions of the body.

At the same time, the epistemological *conditions of embodiment* are not detected and articulated in forms of consciousness because the boundaries of consciousness are not perceptible: one cannot gaze at them as "objects." The boundaries are present in all images of the world, but consciousness does not reflect upon them. It concentrates mostly on that content which penetrates consciousness through these boundaries. Here, the following analogy which is related practically to all physical observations comes to mind: physics outlines the properties of the outer world, it extends some picture of the world without necessarily describing how specific results and facts have been obtained. A clear example comes from astronomical observations: they involve telescopes, that is to say, combinations of the glass-made lenses and photographic elements, but the stated facts (as results of observations) never explicitly refer to the actual constructions of observational technologies and methods of processing observations. In other words, the boundaries of consciousness (implemented in technologies) are implicitly present in all observations of the outer physical world and its resulting picture, but they are never explicitly articulated as objective conditions of the very possibility to explore the world in the results of such exploration. All photographs are produced with the help of optical and computer technologies, but the latter are not remembered in the human evaluation of the quality, quantity and value of final results of research in spite of the fact that the transparent limiting conditions of consciousness remain tacitly in place.

The diagram at Figure 1 illustrates an interesting property of consciousness: if the latter wants to deal with the infinitely distant (either at large or deeply microscopic) "objects,"[8] the "intersecting" straight lines corresponding to consciousness's attempts to represent such "objects," become tangent to the circle at its top, that is, effectively geometrically parallel to the world-line. It seems reasonable to identify such straight lines tangent to the circle at its top with that realm of being which is perennially called the *intelligible* in contradistinction to the physical. Then it is the case that the extended finitude (not in a physical state) of the circle of consciousness as related to its embodiment expresses geometrically a finite distance between the world-line and the intelligible. Thus the two infinite parallel lines merge at infinity and, as it were, "glue together" the two realms of being into one single whole thus effectively reproducing the self-enclosed circle of transcendental consciousness. The most important thing in this representation of the whole realm of existence is that, at the intelligible level, the dramatic distinction between the infinitely small and the infinitely large disappears thus uniting them in human consciousness and thus expressing the "uroboros-like" structure of all articulated being where the human subject is present twice: as an organic physical object and as articulating consciousness (as the center of disclosure and manifestation of the universe). In order to assign to the diagram at Figure 1 a more precise "uroboros-like" character, reflecting the dualistic presence of man in the world, we make such a transformation of this diagram when the split in the embodied subjectivity will disappear and the infinitely distant (large and small) coincide (within their representations in human subjectivity) thus demonstrating a smooth transition from the physical realm to the intelligible. The result of this transformation is presented at Figure 2.

8. The reader must not be confused at this point because of the existing physical limits on the sense of space associated with the Planck length (10^{-33} cm) in depth and, let's say, ninety-two billion light years in breadth. Since modern mathematized physics allows constructs in principle with any possible sizes related either to the ideas of the infinitesimally small or infinitely large, all these constructs, being mental creations, depart from the physical and occupy a place of computable (fractals) or abstract infinities.

62 CONSCIOUSNESS AND MATTER

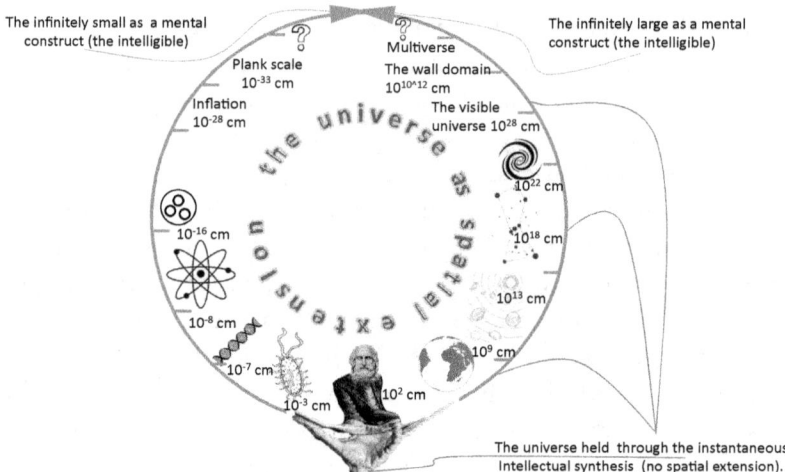

Figure 2: The "uroboros-like" representation of the radical inseparability of consciousness and the universe explicating the paradox of subjectivity: man is a physical formation in the universe as well as its articulating consciousness

The physical sense of this diagram consists of a two-fold assertion. On one hand, it unifies all known levels of physical reality starting from microscales (elementary particles, fundamental interactions, Planck scales and the possible beyond) and finishing by mega-sizes of clusters of galaxies, the visible universe, multiverse and the possible beyond.[9] This diagram positions man as a physical organism at the center thus symbolically uniting all levels of the consubstantial universe in himself, being microcosm and mediator in the perennial sense. From a physical point of view, all levels of reality are constitutive for the corporeal humanity; from a philosophical point of view, the constitution of the physical position of humanity in the universe requires an intellectual insight into those realms which in many ways have only an intelligible status. To put it differently, in order to characterize humanity's position in the universe one needs an insight not only into those entities which are observed or constituted by man through theories, but also on the real presence of human consciousness in them when their external appearances tell one how humanity functions in its attempt to disclose the sense of its own facticity.

---

9. The sense of uroboros as a snake biting its own tail, if our diagram would restrict itself only to the physical realm, is related to the fact that fundamental physics experiences a striking merge at micro- and mega-scales (see, for example, Carr 2017, 42).

Certainly, such an interpretation of the unity of physics and the centrality of man is possible in the *natural attitude* where the universe and man appear both in the phenomenality of objects, that is, both are constituted by some consciousness which oversees the universe. In other words, the physically middle position of humanity in this diagram is epistemologically misleading, because it is itself, as a fact, constituted from within the already existing life whose facticity is illustrated only in terms of *necessity*, that is, the physical and biological conditions of man's existence. The diagram as such cannot offer any descriptive explanation of the *sufficient* conditions for the existence of the consciousness which constructs the diagram. As has been stated, such a diagram represents a particular constitution of the idea of systematic unity of the universe manifesting the human capacity of producing an "instant" synthesis of it. This implies that consciousness is logically pre-existent with respect to this diagram and that it can be introduced here as that articulating gaze at the universe which the diagram reflects (not literally, of course) as if the universe were "held" in the hand of man as a hypostasis of this universe, in analogy with a theologically asserted "He had in His right hand seven stars" (Rev 1:16).

In such an uroboros-like presentation of the universe there is no inside or outside of the universe with consciousness inside of it ("consciousness and language enclose the world within themselves only insofar as, conversely, they are entirely contained by it" [Wolff 2020, 43]). One can say metaphorically that the outer universe is projected on the inside of man's consciousness, whereas its inside is immersed within its outside because consciousness is intended to be a consciousness *of* something. The spatio-temporal expanse, and the objects within the "uroboros-like" diagram, are constituted by the subject's consciousness, whereas the subject as a living body is immersed in space-time. What is encoded here is the well-known paradox of the human subjectivity of being a part of the universe while at the same time being a consciousness that articulates it.[10]

---

10. Here are two concise formulations of the paradox: "We can describe the relations between subject and world as purely intentional relations as opposed to (objective) spatial, temporal, and causal relations. We can appeal to the distinction between belonging to the world of objects and being a condition of the possibility of the world of objects (as meaning). Perhaps the broadest terms for these relations would be the *transcendental* relations and the *part-whole* relation" (Carr 1999, 116), or "It is necessary to combine the recognition of our contingency, our finitude, and our containment in the world with an ambition of transcendence, however limited may be our success in achieving it" (Nagel 1986, 9).

Yet, the possible formulations of this paradox cannot together enlighten its radical aspect that remains hidden behind its formulation; that is to say the fact that the articulating consciousness is not an anonymous and collective field in some transcendent intelligible realm, but essentially embodied and hypostatic, for whom the experience of existence in the universe is radically private and personal.

The latter point emphatically expresses the fact that there is no "symmetry" between consciousness and its objects. In other words, the phenomenality of consciousness for itself and the phenomenality of the world for this consciousness are radically different. The abovementioned symmetry is false because it itself is an intellectual construct, in which the *constituted* bodily objects and the *constituting* embodied consciousness are formally put on the same level. But whenever one becomes aware that all intellectual constructions are embedded in and originate from the lived experience, the symmetry becomes lost.

It is typical to assume that both terms of the dialogue (relationship) between science and theology enter it symmetrically. In this case theology is treated as a kind of intellectual activity that can be compared with that of science on some abstract philosophical level. However, if one treats theology existentially as expressing outwardly the lived experience (that is, experience of created existence in communion) which forms the foundation of all other phenomenalizations of the world and life, one realizes that the symmetry with the sciences is lost because scientific experience is dependent on this lived experience. One then anticipates that the only coherent strategy of balancing two kinds of phenomenalities is to dwell continuously within the lived process of constitution of the world by a concrete hypostatic consciousness, instead of *simulating* constitutive dependence of the manifest objects on an abstractly conceived (anonymous and collective) consciousness. The symmetry between the terms of this dialogue cannot be sustained because the very subject enters the dialogue asymmetrically: as the lived experience in theology and as a constituted agent of knowledge in science.

The paradoxical interplay between human consciousness and outer reality (which is constituted by this consciousness), becomes phenomenologically amplified and multiplied because humanity is multihypostatic. To put it differently, every "uroboros-like" symbol of the unity of the universe has a hidden sign of its author, a particular human person. The world is seen in the image of a concrete person. The world contains the image of this person twice. Man is present as articulating the consciousness of the universe (the universe is enhypostasized by him), but he is also present physically as a particular human being with its face (identity) and position in time and space reflected as if the world appeared to be the mirror of the human soul.[11]

Such a dualistic position of man points, in reflection, to a certain specificity of the human condition, namely to a *time-delay* between the immediate perception of the unity with the universe by the fact of existence in communion (in the first person), and the discursive representation of this existence in terms of outer space and time (in the third person). The essence of the paradox of subjectivity can then be described as the tense-split in the sense of existence when the awareness of existence (as a mental operation) must be conjugated with the perception of the same existence through the body. This requires a time-delay in consciousness itself, that is, its internal temporal extension. Here corporeality enters the discussion not only on the abstract level as a physical dimension, but as a specific and concrete body subjected to biological temporal flux and position in space. The personhood of the articulating consciousness thus demands that subjects appearing in Figure 2 be extended in space, so that this extension becomes an essential feature of that consciousness which is present behind the "uroboros-like" circle.

The split in tense-structures of experience de facto defines the difference in phenomenalities. In order for personal consciousness to make a transition from first person perspective to third person, one needs a change of phenomenality (and hence of hermeneutics) from that which is devoid of temporal flux and extended spatiality to that which represents bodies among other objects in the universe in extended space and time. One can reinterpret this as the switching over between the inner perception of existence in the Cartesian style of *ego cogito* to the perception of the physical body as enabled by the thinking subject.

By generalizing the intuition formulated above, the principle of personhood as experience of existence in the first person implies that personal consciousness has a propensity to be consciousness of space and time (compare with space and time as forms of sensibility in Kant). In this

11. One can conjecture that this biological concreteness of every hypostatic human being makes it fundamentally different in comparison with a hypothetical form of artificial intelligence which could somehow acquire hypostatic features in some disembodied state. It is because of this disembodiment that such an artificial intelligence would not be multi-personal. The way of communication with the Other would not require physical space and time and thus would be "all in all" at once leading ultimately to the disappearance of the Hard Problem of Consciousness.

sense, such a consciousness is possible only if it is incarnate in physical space and time. The latter bodily characteristics of consciousness enter the definition of multihypostatic humanity as a principle of distinction and, at the same time, communication among hypostases. Then one can say that space and time turn out to be those *modi* of consciousness which reflect consciousness's incarnation in flesh making possible in principle the distinction and relationship among persons.

If experience of the outer world either in first or third persons is related to the fact that the world affects the subject through its body, that is, physically, the experience of existence as such, that is, the sense of oneself in the first person, is prompted by the fact of being *alive*. The lived experience is that which can be associated (as was advocated by Michel Henry) with *life's self-affectivity* (Henry 2003a, 2003b). As such, this reference to a new term "self-affectivity" does not advance our discussion, referring once again to something primarily concealed and uncaused in worldly terms. Theologically, one could refer to humanity's creation in communion with God and thus relegate the problem of personal consciousness to the archetype of a personal God. Yet, this theological reference does not elucidate the major problem of how to reconcile the first person experience of the world with the third person. This problem remains a posited fact in the belief that man is made in the Divine Image. Seen in this perspective, the paradox of subjectivity becomes a constitutive part of the Divine Image with no further explanation of the ultimate origin of this paradox, as well as of the Divine Image. However, the treatment of the paradox as constitutive for the human condition in general, does not stop this condition's open-ended hermeneutics, that is, the infinite advance in attempts to explicate this condition.

The "Hard Problem of Consciousness" and the Ambivalence of Flesh

One can approach the Hard Problem of Consciousness from a different direction by considering the conditions of its embodiment (incarnation) and their dualistic phenomenality.

Indeed, the awareness *of* one's flesh, involves a dualistic approach to *this* flesh: on the one hand, flesh can be that which *is experienced*, on the other hand, the same flesh can be outwardly posed as that through which the world is experienced, that is, as *experiencing flesh*. The flesh is taken here as the locus and origin of the process of objectification, more precisely, one considers that consciousness is embodied. Consciousness is the center of disclosure and manifestation, but in the conditions of embodiment, that is, of flesh. Thus understood, flesh is split in itself onto that which is deeply transcendental as seeing, hearing and feeling, and, at the same time, as that which is "transcendent," that is heard and felt. In a way, this split serves as a different expression of the previously invoked discrimination of phenomenalities as conscious acts. At the same time, such a split in the meaning of flesh may correspond to the alleged dualism between the lived experience in the first person (flesh as experienced) and that one in the third person (flesh as that which experiences the flesh of the other). Yet, if one attempts to build a metaphysical account of the relation between conscious experience in the living body (as a particular hypostatic variation of flesh) and that of the same body in the world, one needs to start from the lived experience and then, through abstractions and objectivations, link it with to the worldly position in space. The pattern of this link is "uroboros-like" (as we have already argued through the diagrams which explicitly refer to the material flesh), yet unfolding from within lived experience.

Such an accentuation of embodiment has serious implications for how knowledge in general is conceived. In the framework of a standard ontology, one aspires to acquire knowledge about what is given out there, and this knowledge can be encoded by using thought and language. But in the framework of an ontology based on embodiment, knowledge affects two sides of the human condition that arise from the self-splitting of what is out there. Knowledge of something arises concomitantly with a transformation of ourselves as knowers: on the one hand man receives knowledge of the world through perceptions and their contextual interpretation; on the other hand, being involved in the same material fabric through embodiment, the one who is embodied becomes a knower by the virtue of being affected by the world. The transformation of oneself *as* a knower manifests itself as a mutation of one's experience that cannot be encoded intellectually, since the very processes and conclusions of the intellect depend on it. The pattern of knowledge, where one has to reflect upon the transformation of oneself from a passive observer into a knower as an active participant in the constitution of reality, is universal. In the classical natural sciences, where the objectification of a limited set of appearances is complete to such an extent that everything happens as if the objects of knowledge were separate from the act of knowing, such a pattern may seem excessive. In these cases, it is said phenomenologically, the intuitive content of that which is known is nil, because the objects are constituted and hence predicted by means of mathematics. However, the participatory pattern of knowledge becomes decisive in other situations where the phenomenality of objects becomes unattainable in principle, because the intuitive content of that at which knowledge is intended exceeds the possibility of its discursive representation.

Thus considered, the mind-body problem (that is, a transition from experience from first to third person) cannot be "solved" through a purely intellectual operation (through a change in our outward understanding *about* man in the third person) because this problem cannot be considered at the level of "objects." One cannot isolate this problem from lived experience because it is an inherent part of this experience, a part which constitutes indirectly the very phenomenality of this experience. In such a case the "Hard Problem" of the origin of phenomenal consciousness has even less of a chance of being solved. The problem is that no separability between subject and object is possible because phenomenality in first and third person originates from one and the same living being. To approach this problem one then needs a radical change in the appropriation of experience, where the above-mentioned splits in consciousness (reflecting its embodiment) will not be considered as confusing or distorting dualisms of existence, but as constitutive elements of existence. Since experience is not a term in an intellectual scheme among others, but is the lived origin and by-product of any process, including that of knowing, this experience forms the lived background of the intellectual inference (transcendence) intuiting that there is something "beyond" experience. But since the problem of experience itself cannot be confined to a part of this experience, then, to address it properly, there is no other option than to subject the problem to such a "transfiguration," where its dramatic overtones will disappear and experience will be considered as the beginning and the end of any possible justification of knowledge.

In other words, the lived experience is destined to become the existential *alpha* and *omega* of any further articulation and intellectual constitution of this experience. Repeating our thought, the problem of the split in the lived experience between first and third persons, as well as between mind (soul) and body (flesh), indicates that this experience, as very existence, as life, appears to man as that phenomenon which intuitively exceeds any capacity of being represented discursively. It falls under that class of phenomena which are called *saturated*.[12] Yet, any lived

---

12. Saturated phenomena are phenomena that cannot be represented in the

experience breaks down into two focal poles of attention, namely the sensing of the world in the first person (through the primordial perception of belonging to the world [the primordial sense of consubstantiality and epistemological commensurability, for example]) and perception of the world in the third person, mediated by the understanding and reason that guide intellectual processes whose convergence within the variety of objectified living bodies and brains yields parts of the lived experience in reflection. Here one makes a distinction between the *presence* of the lived experience (phenomenality of presence in the person) and its mental or perceptual *structure* (when this very presence is identified in perception as presence in the third person). Objects then are formed as focal points of attention, picked out and stabilized around stable poles of identity (objects) within experience as sheer presence. What can be derived from the intellectual reflection and articulating processes involving human bodies and their brains is by no means this experience as sheer presence (phenomenality of events), but an account of the *structure* of what is experienced as objects (phenomenality of objects) in space and time.

Intuitively, it is clear that in order to outline the stratified hierarchy of experience as a split of phenomenalities in one and the same subject, one needs to look at the whole picture in its intrinsic dynamics. In other words, one must dynamically describe the link between object-centered phenomenality (in the third person) and the subject-centered phenomenality (in the first person) as events, as a mutual and ever branching whole unfolded within the conditions of embodiment in time. If one concentrates on a body as a physical entity, it is positioned and moved in space in the course of time. Correspondingly, an objectivized picture of reality is itself related to such space-time representation of the body. This reality is linked to what is perceived through the body. In the case of

---

phenomenality of objects, that is in rubrics of: quantity, quality, relation and modality. The issue of saturated phenomena concerns the possibility that certain phenomena do not manifest themselves in the mode of objects and yet still do manifest themselves. These phenomena undergo saturation by the excess of intuition over the concept or signification in them; saturated phenomena cannot be constituted because they are saturated. Here such a definition of experience is implied that it cannot be determined by a transcendental subject. On the contrary, it is to the extent that *ego* cannot comprehend as a phenomenon that constitutes this *ego*. And it is flesh that reaches nonobjective phenomena, those where an excess of intuition saturates the limits of the concept already known and always foreseen. For example, this flesh attains itself as that split in the "I=I" as self-eroticizing consciousness. Before my own flesh I cannot say *I*, I cannot constitute it, foresee it and hold it at a distance in front of me. It is the phenomenon saturated with intuition, which makes me. The flesh surpasses my objectifying rationality (Marion 2000).

the phenomenality of events related to personal existence, the situation is radically different because the sense of this existence as extended is purely subjective. It is within this time-consciousness that the intentional structure of consciousness appears as a movement extended in physical time. Here the internal temporal structure projects itself onto physical space that is "materialized" through the body. The body reveals itself as sheer presence through its intrinsic dynamics in space and time. The split between first and third persons can be described alternatively as the subject-object's self-splitting. The same can be expressed as transcendence towards objects generated within the immanence of the lived experience and revealing a dynamics of inner temporality.[13] Some of these objects, like our own bodies, have an exceptional status. Their object-centered space-time dynamics is correlated with the subject-centered dynamics of reminding, willing and desiring. The living bodies are accordingly endowed with certain forms of circularity: "speaking-listening, seeing-being seen, perceiving-being perceived" (Merleau-Ponty 1968, 265), etc. The observed correlations do not prove that the object-centered dynamics of our body *cause* the subject-centered dynamics of our lived experience (such a conclusion could arise in the framework of a physicalist ontology that conflates immanent projections of transcendence with real entities and causal factors).[14] In a phenomenological account, the correlation is understood as a "mirror-like" correspondence between the structure of experience as a whole, and the structure of some of its objectified elements. Yet, the objectified items are *constituted*, by linking through laws, the experience of the present with those experiences which have been memorized. Thus, the correlation itself remains entirely internal to experience. Since no "Hard Problem" of causation between heterogenous entities (such as material brains and immaterial consciousness) is generated by this phenomenological account, it remains purely descriptive, but not explanatory.

Maurice Merleau-Ponty attempted to tackle this problem by introducing an element of temporality in perception when the split of phenomenalities (in first and third persons) happens because of a certain *distension*. Merleau-Ponty pointed out that, from a phenomenological perspective, brain processes are nothing more than perceptual or

---

13. How this can be achieved is not a subject matter of our discussion. The phenomenology of temporality can provide an insight into this mystery.

14. In the framework of phenomenology, the abovementioned correlation remains an uninterpreted basic feature of the continuum of appearances.

conceptual "logical meanings" within the lived experience of their observers. By this act of projecting "meanings," by the intentional *distension* it undergoes, the lived experience moves away from itself towards what is meant, and thus it self-splits (Merleau-Ponty 1968, 234). Merleau-Ponty nevertheless insists that there remains a permanent relation between experience and its signified items in the sense that a pattern that is given to me *now* as my lived experience, will be given to myself *a little later* as a logical meaning of my future experience.

The situation with the temporal split of phenomenalities signifying the distinction between representations of the world in first and third persons becomes acutely seen in the paradox of subjectivity understood, for example, in the following way. On the one hand, there is the *man of the world*, who is only concerned with the world and can only be so against the background of his previously conceived essence as being-in-the-world. On the other hand, there is the *man who is not of the world* because he finds himself originally determined in himself by some a-cosmic factors.[15] *The opposition between these two men relates to the phenomenological structures to which they refer.* By using the language established above, human beings deal in this situation with two types of the *given* with different phenomenalities. This situation can be described in terms of the tense-related structures employed for describing the human condition. The immediate experience of existence, when humans position themselves at the center of the reflected existence but not separated from it in their inner time-consciousness, places humanity in a nominative case as that who states this existence in the form "I am" (*ego sum*). In this case co-existence of the universe in which this "I" exists is just implied as a premise and a component of this existence as contingent. In other words, to say "I am" is the same as to say "the universe is," because to say "I=I" is de facto to say, that the self-identity of "I" implies "not-I."

---

15. Kant calls this a-cosmic factor *noumen*: "The necessity of nature, which cannot co-exist with the freedom of the subject, appertains only to the attributes of the thing that is subject to time-conditions, consequently only to those of the acting subject as a *phenomenon*.... But the very same subject being on the other side conscious of himself as a thing in himself . . . regards himself as only determinable by laws which he gives himself through reason. . . . [T]he whole series of his existence as a sensible being is in the consciousness of his supersensible existence nothing but the result . . . of his causality as a *noumenon*" (Kant 1959, 191). The famous Russian religious philosopher Nikolas Berdyaev argued for a non-cosmic origin of human personhood: "There are in the personality natural foundation principles which are linked with the cosmic cycle. But the personal in man . . . always denotes a break with natural necessity. . . . There is nature in man, but he is not nature. Man is a microcosm and therefore he is not part of the cosmos" (Berdyaev 1939, 94–95).

However, to say that I exist in the universe as its insignificant part is to say something which is temporally delayed with respect to the nominative statement, delayed because of the reflective nature of this statement, where the reflection as a psychological process is shifted in time with respect to the immediate sense of existence. The opposite statements of the paradox form a seeming tension first of all because they use two different tense-like modi of consciousness. In fact, the paradox becomes a certain expression of the fact that human beings are capable of formulating complementary statements about their existence through making extension in time by effectively stretching life in time (*distension*) and thus introducing some asymmetry between the statements of the paradox through hierarchy (before and after, primary and secondary) of the tense states of consciousness. This asymmetry has an ontological character because the state of "man of the world" is only possible from within the state of life. Thus, the facticity of life comes first.

But the paradox as such, being preoccupied with the ego's position *in* the world, by extracting this ego out of the primarily given life, gives de facto witness to the radical forgetting of humanity about the primacy of life as that immediate givenness of existence whose facticity escapes any intentional gaze. And if, with respect to the question of why humanity represents a part of the universe, one can respond that it is because of life, the question about the facticity of life (from within which everything is disclosed) cannot be referred to anything prior to this life.[16] Certainly, one can attempt to make a naturalistic inference from the universe to life, but the very assertion of the universe implies the already given life. Thus, the genuinely paradoxical feature of the dichotomy related to humanity's position in being lies in the fundamental unknowability of that life which forms a premise for any articulation of the world. Life as sheer givenness and facticity of existence cannot be conditioned by any particular modus of its manifestation, for example, by that of thinking. Life as the origin is not thinking because it is this origin that is concealed from any posterior reflection, that is, from thinking of it. In this sense one cannot remember

---

16. Michel Henry emphatically expresses this by saying: "Life is given in its own way, in a completely unique way, even though this singular mode of givenness is universal. Life is given in such a way, that what it gives is given to itself and that what it gives to itself is never separated from it, not in the least. In this way, what life gives is itself. Life is self-givenness in a radical and rigorous sense, in the sense that it is both life that gives and life that is given. Because it is life that gives, we can only have a share of this gift in life. Because life is what is given in this gift, we can only have access to life in life" (Henry 2008, 120).

that which was "before" life, because for this particular life there was no before: its contingent novelty and uniqueness can be placed in the worldly scheme of things as if they produce this life, but as such, this life, as the life of a particular self, or of an hypostatic being, does not have any trace of its pre-worldly history because life as such, as was expressed by Michel Henry, is forgetting in a radical sense (Henry 2003a, 148).

From what we have discussed it follows that there is an intrinsic inseparability between subject and object whose triviality originates in the fact that life precedes the very distinction between object and subject. Yet, the extent of the interplay between them can be different. For example, when scientists successfully predict the outcome of their research activity, and when the rules of prediction have been formalized into autonomous laws of phenomena, it is usually said that an "explanation" of phenomena has been provided. In classical physics the phenomena to be predicted can be treated as if they were occurring spontaneously in nature. Accordingly, the connecting law between phenomena behaves as if it were autonomous. Yet, there are other cases where, although "phenomena" are correctly predicted to a certain extent, these phenomena are intermingled with the researchers' activity which determines the conditions of their appearance. This is not only related to the famous claims of quantum mechanics. In a more banal sense, it accompanies many theoretical disciplines which function under conditions where their constructs (as products of the intellect) cannot be subjected to the rules of correspondence with empirical realities. Cosmology is an obvious example with respect to its theories about the wholeness of the universe as well as about its origination. The high level of "participation" in constituting the corresponding "realities" is associated with the fact that they are introduced into theory on the grounds of intentionality but not on the grounds of physical causality. Intentionality is that which forms the basis of conscious cognition and hence involves associated ideas and philosophical intuitions not directly borrowed from sensible experience.

Apart from examples from physics and cosmology, the very science of consciousness, that is, of self-knowledge, implies an even higher level of participation. In this case "predictions" cannot be made autonomous with respect to the activity of the one who predicts: predictions are based on intentional acts and do not lead to any formal invariant residue that can be called a "law" (as based on causality). As a consequence, one cannot "explain" the neuro-experiential correlation in the standard sense of considering it as an expression of some causal law-like succession (neither of a physical nor of a psycho-physical law). Indeed, one cannot predict the neural correlate of a type of experience *a priori*, before its conditions have ever been observed. One cannot predict a correlation between the internal sense of the universe as an all-encompassing experience and that which will become its abstraction before the actual intentional activity starts. Thus, building abstract models of the universe is a creative process based in the human propensity of looking for some systematic unity of nature; yet there is no evidence for any objective reference to these models apart from the human intentional consciousness itself. One can "explain" the neuro-experiential correlation in the sense of new possibilities of intuition and scientific investigation *un-folding* in us that this correlation opens, thus unfolding new possibilities of self-knowledge through an intentional construction of the whole.[17]

Such an "alternative" meaning of "explanation" as an intentional construction can no longer mean encapsulating phenomena within a rule of succession that is posited once and for all, and then considering the phenomena and their law from a distance. Instead, explaining here means participating in the production, prediction and disciplining of phenomena. Saying phenomenologically, explaining, means constituting, that is, in a way, co-creating that phenomenality of things which has not been there before. The knower becomes here an informed actor in the connection between the two types of phenomenality in the representation of reality, as opposed to a spectator of one fixed (in the natural attitude) regularity. Yet, even in this phenomenologically extended approach to how consciousness participates in constituting its reality, the Hard Problem of Consciousness can find no solution. However, there is a methodological remedy to it consisting in making the "Hard Problem" not a false mystery fabricated by our naturalistic prejudice, but the constitutive characteristic of the human constitution. Even if the "Hard Problem" is a *constitutive illusion*, this illusion must have a foundation in its own facticity as an element of the overall existence of humanity as the self-affective life of self-conscious flesh. In a way, all possible philosophical efforts to disclose this problem as the problem of existence of such flesh lead one to the final frontier where one has to invoke an idea that worldly flesh is suspended in something which is not entirely comprehensible from within it. The

---

17. In different terms, the neural-experiential correlation represents such a practical synthesis of the person who is at once an *existent* (in the rubrics of the worldly) and an *end* (the goal for the worldly realm to be articulated by humanity). It is that which realizes the scale of disproportion with the universe (expressed in the paradox of subjectivity) and thus the original fragility of the human reality (see Ricoeur 2016, 197).

assumption of such a suspension is tantamount to the already mentioned theological idea of creation as linking the immanent aspect of the world to that which transcends it. Either this is the creation of *Imago Dei* as a hypostatic unity of body and flesh, or the creation of *flesh* (distinguished from the body) defined as the initial coordination of the material and intelligible in human beings. Yet, the hypostatic dimension of this flesh remains the ultimate mystery allowing one the only possible theological *analogy*, namely that one of the hypostatic Christ incarnate in the worldly flesh of Jesus from Nazareth. This analogy is historical and theological and, as such, non-descriptive. Yet, the historical reference (realized in liturgical actions) to the hypostatic union of the Divine and human reifies the intuition of creation of the human composite in the perspective of the incarnation; in other words the reference to the creation becomes more concrete through its incarnational facticity.

If one abstains from assigning any ontological sense to such a theological insight, the invoked theological "solution" of the Hard Problem seems to be no more than another contribution to its unending (and non-descriptive) hermeneutics. This observation can be radicalized and reduced to the statement that the very presence of this problem in the background of life indicates that it is constitutive to this particular life but not explicable in discursive terms. In other words, the Hard Problem is such an inevitability which saturates intuition to the extent such that no detailed fragment of this intuition is available. The lived experience as experience in the first person is that which cannot be "looked" at in the phenomenality of objects. This experience is rather an event, or *the* event, related to every concrete human being, that event which inaugurates not only all other types of phenomenality, but human life as such. Life can then be treated as an unceasing temporal distension in the embodied man when the existence in time implies the split of phenomenalities into first and third persons.

The "Hard Problem" of Consciousness as Seen through the Split between the Universe's Saturated Phenomenality and Its Object-Like Constitution

In spite of the fact that the "Hard Problem of Consciousness" seems to be irresolvable in a mundane sense of the word,[18] it can nonetheless be

18. The classical attempt of thought to grasp its own roots and close itself inside of a hermetically sealed sphere of immanence in which only apodictic truths can present

explicated through the application of human faculties to the study of the outer world when the sense of reality in the first person encounters a tension with the sense of the same reality in the third person. This is acutely illustrated in the paradox of subjectivity as a reflection upon the dualistic position of humanity in the universe: its sense of existence in the first person when the universe as a whole is enhypostasized as commensurable with the scope of consciousness, "clashes" with the articulated sense of the physical insignificance of that one who enhypostasizes it.

Human transcendental subjectivity experiences a disjunction between the phenomenon of the universe expected to appear in the manner of ordinary objects and the ego's subjective experience of the universe through the sheer belonging to it in the event of life. Consequently, the ego cannot constitute the universe as an "object" whose concept would agree with the conditions of experience of the universe through the ecstatic reference of standing in front of it. One has here the intuitive saturation through belonging to the universe which imposes itself by excess and which makes this universe present, but *invisible* (not technically) and incomprehensible. The universe engulfs the ego's intuition to such an extent that any attempt of constituting the universe is suspended. The universe is *visible* in its particular parts and moments but, as a whole, it cannot be *looked at*. Human subjectivity finds itself in the conditions of being split between its finite physical embodiment and the intellectually all-encompassing synthesis of the universe. On the one hand, the universe enters subjectivity as a variety of objects where the human body is one among them, on the other hand, it appears as an event commensurable with an event of a concrete *personal* existence whose facticity is not entirely in the causal link with the antecedent physical circumstances. What then is that in the intentional pole of consciousness which makes the initially personal sense of the universe (in the first person) converted into that which can be approached by all men in the third person? One can rephrase the latter by posing a question of how the superabundant phenomenality of the universe as it is available in the first person transforms into that practically intuition-free content of the universe which is comprised of objects. Can then a response to this question provide another explanation to the "Hard Problem" of Consciousness?

In fact, the "Hard Problem" can be interpreted as an attempt to balance two different *phenomenalities* in this very consciousness. On the one

---

themselves, necessarily fails. One can neither stand outside of the world to make it an object of our perception, nor can we stand outside of ourselves.

hand, it deals with events of communion (events of living) with the universe (where the universe cannot be constituted because of its saturating intuition). This always happens in the first person. One can say, paradoxically, that the phenomenon of the universe is revealed in the first person and hence it is this person that "initiates its phenomenality" as a saturated phenomenon in spite of the fact that this phenomenon produces itself out of itself. It is in the first person that the saturated phenomenon is perceived as immediately given and inseparable, but not constituted through a logical function. In other words, the lived experience remains the primordial condition and "milieu" for the very qualification of some phenomena as saturated. In this sense one may conjecture that what is called "lived experience" appears always in the context of the saturated phenomenon of the universe. Thus, this lived experience as such, in its initially non-split presence with the universe, forms the saturating phenomenality of life itself.

On the other hand, the universe, containing the human body that forms the necessary condition of the very possibility of reflection upon the universe, appears as a space-time manifold of extended objects. The issue is how to balance the experiential sense of the universe as a whole, as an *event-like* saturated phenomenon co-inherent with the event of life and encompassed by the first person, with that representation of the universe in the third person, which seems to be a system of constituted *objects* (as is the case in the sciences), including human bodies.

Science and philosophy deal with the universe as a system of extended objects without being able to grasp the sense of their contingent facticity. Then through understanding that this vision of the universe is ultimately produced within the lived experience, the same consciousness poses a question about the facticity of life as such. The same can be expressed differently. What is common to both phenomenalities of life is that one cannot account for the foundation of their contingent facticity. In both cases consciousness manifests its own incapacity of dealing with the oblivion of its own origins, and hence the origins of the universe. Here theology enters the discussion by referring to the very contingency of life as originating in Divine Life understood phenomenologically as non-originary origin of its own self-affectivity and of all in the world.

The importance of a theological insight in the constitution of the universe could be dismissed if cosmology would be able to provide some clues to humanity's origin and position in the physical universe. Unfortunately, this does not happen. Not being able to understand "where from" (or "how") human intelligence was brought into existence (that is, to understand the *sufficient* conditions of their creation), the fact of existence remains for man himself fundamentally indeterminate (the same is related to consciousness). The planet, the galaxy, the cluster of galaxies, and the entire universe carry with themselves the sense of this created indeterminateness, making humanity not to be able to adapt to, and to be at home in the universe.[19] An attempt of balancing between a theological sense of existence as engulfed by the universe because of being created into it, on the one hand, and a perception of the insignificant cosmographic position in the practically infinite universe, on the other, constitutes another dimension of the dialogue between theology and science. In analogy with Jean-Francois Lyotard (1991, 4), the meeting with the world as belonging to it can be described as a return to the condition of infancy, for as infants, humans are helplessly exposed to a strange and overwhelming environment while lacking the ability to articulate what affects them. The universe-as-saturated-phenomenon poses itself to the human "I" in primacy of its consubstantiality with this "I" (within its Earthly flesh) as a constitutive element of the principle of human life.

When the universe is represented in cosmology as unfolding through the cinematographic sequence of events and places, different objects and their classes, the body of humanity as its planet becomes eidetically deprived of its initial egocentric predisposition to the universe by being displaced to the periphery of space, time, physical scales, etc. The planet Earth is displaced to a mediocre position and hence not attuned to be the home-place for man. This condition of non-attunement to the universe signifies a gap between the incarnate sensibility chaining humanity to Earth and impossibility of a mental articulation and linguistic expressibility in situations when human beings encounter the universe as a saturated phenomenon. To wrestle with the universe as a saturated phenomenon is to be in despair of chasing its escaping presence that constantly reminds the "I" about the unclarified nature of its own created finitude. The "I," being unable to constitute the phenomenon of the universe as a whole, experiences itself as being constituted by this phenomenon in the first person: this is that modus of the self-affectivity of human life which "manifests" the fact that all human beings as living creatures are affected by the universe.

19. This thought relates one to the most famous Christian ideas, discussed by many early fathers, in particular St. Augustine, that this world is not that city where man is destined to abide, implying the aspired City of God as man's ultimate harbor.

By belonging to the universe, the "I" does not have (it simply cannot have) any dominant point of view over the universe as a whole. The universe engulfs subjectivity by removing its parts and spatial extension thus saturating "I's" intuition with the sense of being hypostatically coextensive with the universe. In a temporal sense, the universe is always already there, so that all events of subjective life unfold from within the donating event of the universe as a constant coming into being. There the unforeseeable nature of every consequent moment entails the unending historicity and unpredictability of existence. In a spatial sense, the concrete factuality of the event of appearance of this "I's" life, or human life in general (phenomenologically hidden from humanity's comprehension), gives the position of human life in the universe no place in an absolute metaphysical sense. Its "place" "is" its sheer facticity, so that any cosmological reduction of the human place in the universe to a particular position in the mathematically constituted space reduces the universe's phenomenality to that of an object. But in the primary experience of existence as life of Life, the universe is not "an" object, but a saturated phenomenon coextensive with the fact of living, whose phenomenality in the first person can be described in terms of the invisible according to quantity, unbearable according quality, unconditioned according to relation and irreducible to the "I" according to modality (Marion 2000, 211).

In the natural (scientific) attitude (that is, in the first person), the universe as a whole is posited as existing out there, that is, as being transcendent to the field of consciousness. Yet, the status of its objective reality is not clarified unless the universe appears as a result of an intellectual constitution. Then the very representation of the universe as transcendent to the constituting consciousness is achieved through following an inherent *teleology* of explanation (and hence constitution) that characterizes the activity of consciousness. Hence, no objective meaning can be assigned to the universe introduced as a regulative idea formed through a teleological power of judgment (in a Kantian sense).[20] The universe as a

20. On the teleology of explanation in cosmology see (Nesteruk 2015, ch. 6). The notion of reflecting judgment is important in order to understand why and how cosmological claims about the universe as a whole can be justified in terms of the human cognitive faculties. Since the Kantian analysis of the notion of the world as a whole in *Critique of Pure Reason* proves this notion to be problematic, the question arises as to where this notion comes from. In other words, what is that faculty which allows one to consider the notion of the universe as a whole as valid, although as collectively subjective? For this purpose one needs to appeal to the faculty of judgment, which is a matter of Kant's *Critique of Judgment*. Kant distinguishes between two types of judgment which he calls determining and reflecting. In determining judgment, one

whole emerges here as a regulative notion with no pretense for an accomplished theoretical (ontological) status.[21] Being a regulative notion, the universe as a whole becomes a characteristic of consciousness as such, so that its hypothetical *reduction* (phenomenological reduction) would amount to the suspension of consciousness itself, that is, to its effective cessation. Since consciousness exists in the universe so that the universe is intrinsically present in this consciousness as communion, the universe cannot be cut off from this communion in any other way than in abstraction. One cannot suspend the reality of the *universe as communion* by using this consciousness because by insisting on such a suspension, this consciousness effectively denies itself as embodied existence and hence eliminates itself.[22] The impossibility of the phenomenological reduction of the universe as a whole points to a simple fact that the representation

applies a particular concept to intuition: one starts with a given universal (which can be a rule, principle, law, or concept), and the task is to find a particular that falls under the universal. In a reflecting judgment one creates a new empirical concept to capture common features of different intuitions. The reflecting use of judgment begins with the awareness of a particular object, or objects, and the task is to find or create a universal under which to subsume the particular object or objects. For example, observational cosmology deals with stars, galaxies, their clusters, microwave background radiation, etc. Theoretical cosmology attempts to "find" or to create a universal under which to subsume all these observable objects. This universal is the universe as a whole. But this universal is not that which can be subjected to the determining judgment. If one deals with the scientific cosmology attempting to construct the notion of the universe as a whole, one needs a particular idea of the systematicity of nature which enters the structure of the constitution on the level of reflecting judgment. However, a judgment about the universe as a whole involves judging the "object" to be *formally purposeful*, that is, without the representation of an objective end or purpose in its construction. That is, in such a reflecting judgment, one judges the "object" (the universe as a whole) to be purposeful without purpose, that is, to be only formally purposeful in order to conduct cosmological research, understanding in advance that its purpose, that is, the notion of the universe as a whole will never be achieved. When one "contemplates" the universe as a whole one does not think that the universe has an objective purpose, but insofar as it is found useful in formulating the objectives of cosmological research, one can think that the universe as a whole appears in intuition as a subjective purpose. Thus, in claiming that in a judgment of the universe as a whole the "object" is represented as purposive without purpose, one means that the object is regarded as objectively without purpose, but it is regarded as subjectively purposeful.

21. The existing mathematical models of the universe do not substantially challenge our claim because they are also constructed on the basis of human abilities to have access to eidetic worlds which in no way can become theoretical concepts.

22. Merleau-Ponty wrote: "We might say that we perceive the things themselves, that we are the world that thinks itself—or that the world is at the heart of our flesh" (Merleau-Ponty 1968, 136). In our context, the universe appears as a mirror of man's existence (compare with Figure 2), and likewise, man mirrors the world (being its center of disclosure and manifestation).

of the universe as transcendent to consciousness (that is, in the third person) can acquire no ontological quality, remaining "transcendent" only as an element of the immanent teleology of consciousness. And here phenomenology leads us back to treating the universe within the rubrics of saturated phenomena: to place the universe under saturated phenomena is tantamount to asserting that the universe defines an inherent teleology of its explication which cascades down to the human attempt to achieve self-comprehensibility. The universe as living communion in the first person remains that saturated phenomenon with respect to which the teleology of explanation acts through the universe's open-ended hermeneutics in the third person.

Phenomenology rightly suggests dismissing the intellectual idols of the universe (through the suspension of their realistic interpretation) as pretending to exhaust the reality of the universe as communion: any discursive image of the universe remains never accomplished and thus is incomplete. The universe is present in the background of existence through relationship and communion in such a way that allows one to express this presence ecstatically through music, painting, poetry, and the like. However, this experience cannot be conceptualized or expressed in the definitions of physics and mathematics. In fact, one can say that the very suspension of conceptual idols of the universe is possible only because their resulting conceptual absence is balanced by the reality of its concrete presence, manifested in the very possibility of thinking about the universe. The implicit *presence* of the created universe in all acts of the incarnate human subjectivity cannot be phenomenologically reduced because, if so, the incarnate consciousness itself would be bracketed away and hence eliminated. Obviously, this would lead to a sheer existential contradiction.

Thus, we see with a new force that the tension between the worldly experience in first and third persons (lying at the foundation of the dialogue between theology and science) deals with two complementary phenomenalities of the universe which, by the fact of their origin in one and the same human being, have to be in a constant critical attitude to each other. They must determine the sphere of their legitimate application with no claims for the priority of one with respect to another, and even less with a presumptive refusal to overcome their difference. The universe as saturated phenomenon enters the proper givens of theology because of being commensurable with human life by the fact of their creation by God. Scientific cosmology, by dealing with the universe as the constituted world of physical objects, joins a hermeneutics of the human condition by inserting into the latter the hermeneutics of the universe (outlining the necessary conditions for humanity's existence as well as for the very possibility of this hermeneutics). One can say that the ongoing inquiry into the sense of the unity of matter and consciousness forms an endless intertwining hermeneutics of experience of living in the universe as communion (and a saturated phenomenon), as well as an outward constitution of the universe as extended space and time in cosmology. Such an operation of phenomenologically dualistic human subjectivity contributes to the hermeneutics of the human condition in general and points to the irreducible and primordial facticity of the flesh as a materialized consciousness and spiritualized matter.

Conclusion

The major difficulty of dealing with the "Hard Problem" of Consciousness, or the problem of mind and body, is the fundamental unknowability of man by himself. Theology makes an ontological claim of *imago Dei*, that is, that man is created in the image of God. Thus, the "Hard Problem" of Consciousness has theistic overtones relating humanity to God through the idea of the Image. Then the riddle of humanity, its ultimate mystery, is referred to the teaching on creation of the world and man out of nothing. In a way, the "Hard Problem" of Consciousness becomes a different form of expression of that which is radically unknowable: creation of man by God out of nothing. This observation entails that if *creatio ex nihilo* is invoked in the context of the "Hard Problem" of Consciousness as a reference point, this problem acquires some theological dimension and can only be interpreted non-descriptively.

Then the question remains: what kind of ontology is needed to preserve the integrity of human beings as part of the natural world, as well as the integrity of the natural world in the presence of human existence? One might suggest the following answer: one needs a creational ontology that understands the world as *flesh*, created with intrinsic structures and with the power to unfold, to produce and to bring forth, a being constantly becoming, in which the human is a particularly rich intertwined pattern—a being woven in the prison of the flesh by a productive power made and sustained by God the Creator. Such a world has its integrity precisely as creation *and* that which creates; and human beings are precisely integral parts of this creation, of which they are also cocreators. All these metaphysical statements imply that there is a creative principle of self-affective life that is in the foundation of all. And it is in the manifestations of this life that humanity detects its own hard problems related to understanding what humanity is and related to the sense of its existence. By asking why life in men acts in that way as it does, by generating that consciousness which interrogates itself about its own functioning duality in the world, man manifests in himself this life and implicitly answers the Hard Question: his consciousness is split in itself and is capable of inquiring into the facticity of this split because it is this propensity that forms the essence of his life.

Bibliography

Berdyaev, Nicolas. 1939. *Slavery and Freedom*. Translated by R. M. French. London: Centenary.

Bitbol, Michel, et al. 2009. *Constituting Objectivity: Transcendental Perspectives on Modern Physics*. Berlin: Springer.

———. 2021. "The Tangled Dialectic of Body and Consciousness: A Metaphysical Counterpart of Radical Neurophenomenology." *Constructivist Foundations* 16(2): 141–51.

Carr, Benjamin. 1998. "On the Origin, Evolution, and Purpose of the Physical Universe." In *Modern Cosmology and Philosophy*, edited by John Leslie, 152–57. New York: Prometheus.

———. 2017. "Black Holes, Cosmology, and the Passage of Time: Three Problems and the Limits of Science." In *The Philosophy of Cosmology*, edited by Kahlil Chamcham et al., 40–65. Cambridge: Cambridge University Press.

Carr, David. 1999. *The Paradox of Subjectivity*. Oxford: Oxford University Press.

Chalmers, David. 1995. "Facing up to the Problem of Consciousness." *Journal of Consciousness Studies* 2(3): 200–219.

Henry, Michel. 2003a. *I Am the Truth: Toward a Philosophy of Christianity*. Translated by Susan Emmanouel. Stanford: Stanford University Press.

———. 2003b. "Phenomenology of Life." *Angelaki* 8 (2); 100–110.

———. 2003c. "Phénoménologie non-intentionelle: Une tache de la phénoménologie a avenir." In *De la Phénoménologie*. Vol. 1, *Phénoménologie de la vie*, 105–21. Paris: Presses Universitaire de France.

———. 2008. *Material Phenomenology*. Translated by Scott Davidson. New York: Fordahm University Press.

Husserl, Edmund. 1960. *Cartesian Meditations*. Translated by Dorion Cairns. Hague: Nijhoff.

———. 1970. *The Crisis of the European Sciences and Transcendental Phenomenology*. Translated by David Carr. Evanston, IL: Northwestern University Press.

———. 1980. *Ideas Pertaining to a Pure Phenomenology and to a Phenomenological Philosophy: First Book: General Introduction to a Pure Phenomenology*. Translated by F. Kersten. Hague: Nijhoff.

Kant, Immanuel. 1959. *Critique of Practical Reason*. Translated by Thomas Kingsmill Abbot. London: Longmans.
Lyotard, Jean-Francois. 1991. *The Inhuman: Reflections on Time*. Translated by Geoffrey Bennington and Rachel Bowlby. Cambridge: Polity.
Marion, Jean-Luc. 2000. "The Saturated Phenomenon." In *Phenomenology and "The Theological Turn": The French Debate*, translated by Thomas A. Carlson, 176–216. New York: Fordham University Press.
Meillassoux, Quentin. 2008. *After Finitude: An Essay on the Necessity of Contingency*. Translated by Ray Brassier. London: Bloomsbury.
Merleau-Ponty, Maurice. 1968. *The Visible and the Invisible*. Translated by Alphonso Lingis. Evanston, IL: Northwestern University Press.
———. 1990. *La Structure du comportement*. Paris: Presses Universitaires de France.
Nagel, Thomas. 1986. *The View from Nowhere*. Oxford: Oxford University Press.
———. 2012. *Mind and Cosmos: Why the Materialist Neo-Darwinian Conception of Nature Is Almost Certainly False*. Oxford: Oxford University Press.
Nesteruk, Alexei V. 2013. "A 'Participatory Universe' of J. A. Wheeler as an Intentional Correlate of Embodied Subjects and an Example of Purposiveness in Physics." *Journal of the Siberian Federal University. Human & Social Sciences* 6(3): 415–37.
———. 2015. *The Sense of the Universe*. Minneapolis: Fortress.
Petitmengin, Claire. 2017. "Enaction as a Lived Experience: Towards a Radical Neurophenomenology." *Constructivist Foundations* 12(2): 139–47.
Ricoeur, Paul. 2016. *Philosophical Anthropology*. Translated by David Pellauer. Malden, MA: Polity.
Varela, Francisco J. 1996. "Neurophenomenology: A Methodological Remedy for the Hard Problem." *Journal of Consciousness Studies* 3(4): 330–49.
Vörös, Sebastjan. 2014. "The Uroboros of Consciousness: Between the Naturalisation of Phenomenology and the Phenomenalisation of Nature." *Constructivist Foundations* 10(1): 96–104.
Wheeler, John A. 1988. "World as a System Self-Synthesized by Quantum Networking." *IBM Journal of Research and Development* 32(1): 4–15.
Wolff, Francis. 2020. *Dire le monde*. Paris: Pluriel.

6

The Biblical Thesis of Creation of the World *ex nihilo*, the Heisenberg Cut, Quantum Blindness, and the Ψ-*chism* of the Universe—a Final Solution to the Hard Problem of Consciousness

KIRILL KOPEIKIN

Introduction

As we shall mention elsewhere in this volume,[1] modern theoretical physics emerged as a way to study the syntax of the Book of Nature as the second Book of God, a book complementary to the Bible as Holy Scripture. Therefore, in searching for a semantic understanding of the fundamental structures of the universe, it is reasonable to turn to the biblical semantic context. The interpretation of the syntax of the Second Book, the Book of Nature, described in the language of mathematics, is a hermeneutical task and, therefore, a traditionally theological one. In a holistic conception of the world, which includes not only matter subject to causal laws, but also consciousness operating with *meanings* and

---

1. Chapter 8: Reznik and Kopeikin, "Neurotechnologies, Quantum Physics, and Theology."

setting itself various *goals*, causal and teleological approaches should each be organically linked.

The first step towards such an organic combination of explanatory, causal, and conscientious teleological discourses can be made by referring to the biblical narrative of the creation of the world. The biblical *Genesis* is truly a key text because, on the one hand, it tells about the *reasons* for the coming of all things into being and, on the other hand, it reveals the ultimate *goal* of all creation.

What is the main purpose of the creation of the world and man from the point of view of the Bible? Biblical revelation (by biblical revelation we will agree here to accept what is today normatively considered as such in the Christian tradition—primarily in the Orthodox—as well as Catholic and Protestant traditions) asserts that the Creator creates the universe and man so that all existing things may eventually unite with him and reach a state of deification when, according to the apostle Paul, "*God may be all in all*" (1 Cor 15:28).

To achieve this ultimate goal, God initially creates the world with his word "out of nothing," "*of things that were not*" (ἐξ οὐκ ὄντων, *ex nihilo*) (2 Macc 7:28). What does this mean? Often the biblical thesis about the creation of the universe is understood simplistically: God, they say, simply "made" the entire universe. Meanwhile, the meaning of this biblical statement is much more profound. In the context of the theological tradition, *creation* means *non*-self-*existence*. If, for example, a craftsman makes an object, say, a wooden table. This table continues to exist independently of the master, since in its being it "relies" on the matter from which it was made; in this case the wood. The world is created by God "*out of nothing*" in the sense that in its existence it has nothing to "rest upon" except for God.

It is the nature of the world's createdness that is the key to the possibility of future *divine union*; self-existent, inert matter, defined as the opposite of Spirit, is fundamentally incapable of such unity. It can be said that the Bible from the very *beginning* gives shape to the fundamental biblical "principle of the non-absolute nature of created existence": nothing but God is *self*-existent, every created being is relative—and everything exists relative to God.

In addition, the biblical revelation proclaims that the world is being created by the *word* of the Creator and everything *said* acquires a real—albeit relative—existence. This means that the *word* represents a special kind of being, and everything created is verbal—*logos*. Logos lies at the foundation of every being created by God: "Ἐν ἀρχῇ ἦν ὁ λόγος" (John 1:1). Of course, first of all, this refers to the word of the Creator (and hence the understanding of the world as the second Book of God)—but also to the word of a human person created in *the image and likeness* of God the Creator, who creates a new reality with a human *word*: artistic reality, mathematical reality, spiritual reality (including the reality of prayer). Note that the Greek "λόγος," traditionally translated as a *word*, has a wide range of meanings, including: (1) speech, utterance; condition, contract; tale, history, essay; philosophical position; case; (2) account (number); ratio, proportion, proportionality; weight; care; (3) reason, reasonable basis, reason, meaning, concept. The term λόγος is one of the most important (and one of the most ambiguous) terms in Greek philosophy. Later, the term *logos* penetrated into the biblical theological tradition largely due to the works of Philo of Alexandria (ca. 25 BC–ca. AD 50).

The whole history of natural science since Galileo Galilei (1564–1643) shows that its development has taken two fronts. The first pursued the path of concretizing and expanding being's *principle of relativity*. This extended from Galileo's relativity (invariance with respect to inert reference systems, strictly articulated in Newtonian physics) to the special theory of relativity (which radically intensified the extent to which the frame of reference determined the parameters of the physical system) to the general theory of relativity (where equivalence is equivalent to relativity of gravity and acceleration is local) and, finally, to quantum mechanics, the essence of which, from the point of view of the Copenhagen interpretation, is the emergence of a new principle of relativity—relativity to the means of observation. The means of observation then completes the former versions of relativity as they are relative to systems of reference. The other front pursued the deepening of the comprehension of being as imbued with the *logos*: from Galileo's understanding of the world as the second Book of God, written in the *language* of mathematics, to modern attempts to construct the *theory of everything* precisely as a *mathematical* theory (and therefore one created by the *word*).

Thus, both the fundamental physical principle of relativity and the mathematical modeling of reality acquire a natural semantic interpretation precisely in the context of the biblical tradition. This means that considering the history of science through the prism of biblical revelation allows us a lateral view of its evolution and the ability to assess the prospects of its development. In addition, this approach makes it possible to advance in solving a key contemporary problem—the problem of the correlation of "matter" and "consciousness."

The World as ψυχή

The founding fathers of quantum theory—first of all, Werner Heisenberg (1901–76), as well as John von Neumann (1903–57)—noted that one of the most characteristic elements in the Copenhagen interpretation was the need to divide the world into two parts: the observer and the devices used by him, and the quantum system under observation. At the same time, the position of the border, called the *Heisenberg cut*, depends solely on the choice of the observer (Crull and Bacciagaluppi 2011). So, for example, we can consider the measuring device itself, the observer's eye and even his brain as part of the physical world described by quantum mechanics. It is only important, as von Neumann writes in his fundamental work *The Mathematical Foundations of Quantum Mechanics* (1932), that "the measurement or the related process of the subjective perception is a new entity relative to the physical environment and is not reducible to the latter. Indeed, subjective perception leads us into the intellectual inner life of the individual, which is extra-observational by its very nature (since it must be taken for granted by any conceivable observation or experiment)." He continues:

> Nevertheless, it is a fundamental requirement of the scientific viewpoint—the so-called principle of the psycho-physical parallelism—that it must be possible so to describe the extra-physical process of the subjective perception as if it were in reality in the physical world—i.e., to assign to its parts equivalent physical processes in the objective environment, in ordinary space. (Of course, in this correlating procedure there arises the frequent necessity of localizing some of these processes at points which lie within the portion of space occupied by our own bodies. But this does not alter the fact of their belonging to the "world about us," the objective environment referred to above.)
>
> In a simple example, these concepts might be applied as follows: We wish to measure a temperature. If we want, we can pursue this process numerically until we have the temperature of the environment of the mercury container of the thermometer, and then say: this temperature is measured by the thermometer. But we can carry the calculation further, and from the properties of the mercury, which can be explained in kinetic and molecular

terms, we can calculate its heating, expansion, and the resultant length of the mercury column, and then say: this length is seen by the observer.

Going still further, and taking the light source into consideration, we could find out the reflection of the light quanta on the opaque mercury column, and the path of the remaining light quanta into the eye of the observer, their refraction in the eye lens, and the formation of an image on the retina, and then we would say: this image is registered by the retina of the observer.

And were our physiological knowledge more precise than it is today, we could go still further, tracing the chemical reactions which produce the impression of this image on the retina, in the optic nerve tract and in the brain, and then in the end say: these chemical changes of brain cells are perceived by the observer. But in any case, no matter how far we calculate—the mercury vessel, the scale of the thermometer, the retina, or into the brain—at some time we must say: and this is perceived by the observer. That is, we must always divide the world into two parts, the one being the observed system, the other the observer. In the former, we can follow up all physical processes (in principle at least) arbitrarily precisely. In the latter, this is meaningless. The boundary between the two is arbitrary to a very large extent. In particular we saw in the four different possibilities in the example above, that the observer in this sense needs not to become identified with the body of the actual observer: In one instance in the above example, we included even the thermometer in it, while in another instance, even the eyes and optic nerve tract were not included. That this boundary can be pushed arbitrarily deeply into the interior of the body of the actual observer is the content of the principle of the psycho-physical parallelism—but this does not change the fact that in each method of description the boundary must be put somewhere, if the method is not to proceed vacuously, i.e., if a comparison with experiment is to be possible. Indeed experience only makes statements of this type: an observer has made a certain (subjective) observation; and never any like this: a physical quantity has a certain value. (Neumann 1932, 418–21)

Another creator of the Copenhagen interpretation, Niels Bohr (1885–1962), had a deep realization of the need to introduce an observer into quantum theory—an observer not just as a recording device, but as a subject aware of the experimental result. Bohr was deeply influenced by the Christian existentialism of Søren Kierkegaard (1813–55). Kierkegaard believed that a person cannot become an "objective observer" without destroying everything human in himself; on the contrary, he always remains a co-participant in co-existence. In other words, the creator of the system of theoretical knowledge is himself a part of being, subject to explanation.

Surprisingly, although almost a century has passed since the publication of von Neumann's *The Mathematical Foundations of Quantum Mechanics*, no one has realized what clearly follows from the thesis about the arbitrariness of the boundary between that external "objective" reality, which we call "physical," and that internal subjective reality of the observer which we call "psychic." If you think about it, the arbitrariness of drawing the boundary between the observer and the observed system, the *Heisenberg cut*, means exactly that the quantum reality we perceive as φ-physical (Gk. φύσις, *nature*) does not differ fundamentally from the reality of the ψ-psychical (Gk. ψυχή, *spirit, soul, consciousness*), they are ontologically homogeneous! Otherwise, it would be impossible to arbitrarily shift the boundary!

Indeed, two consequences are possible from the arbitrariness of the displacement of the boundary between the observer and the observed system. Either everything—including the psyche—is material, or everything is mental. The first point of view has prevailed for the past three centuries, but today, under the pressure of immutable facts discovered by fundamental physics, such a position has been called into question. Quantum mechanics stubbornly resists all attempts at a materialistic interpretation. In addition, materialistic ontology does not allow us to explain the existence of psychic reality. The fact is that, unlike objectively existing material bodies, psychic reality is subjective, we *experience* it. And there is absolutely no understanding of how subjectivity, as such, can appear in the objective world. In addition, the mental, unlike the physical, is always *directed* at something, it is *intentional*. Today it is completely unclear what might give rise to intentionality in a world of entities (which simply *exist*)? Thus, the arbitrariness of the boundary between the observer and the observed system leads us with absolute inevitability to the conclusion that all reality—including the one we call physical—is psychic!

It should be noted that it turned out to be difficult to draw a seemingly obvious conclusion about the psychic nature of the universe precisely because, at first glance, it seems to contradict the usual classical scientific picture of the world in which things appear "material." Yet such a conclusion turns out to be quite natural from the theological context (see the section below on the "World as the Creator"). Moreover, the very arbitrariness of the boundary between the observer and the observed system is also a consequence of the fundamental biblical "principle of non-absolute created being": nothing but God is *self*-existent, each created being is relative—including the arbitrary drawing of the boundary between the observed system and the observer—and everything exists in relation to God.

Let us now try to move from qualitative reasoning to rigorous proof and consider the meaning we put into the statement that physics gives us objective knowledge about the surrounding physical world. First of all, we must pose the question: does the quantum state represent reality itself or our knowledge of reality? In other words, is the state vector an ontic state (Gk. ὤν, gen. ὄντος, *that which is*—the physical, the real or actually existing), a synonymous, co-occurring relation with real objects in the world, or is it epistemic (Gk. ἐπιστήμη, *knowledge*), a characterization of our knowledge of the quantum world (Atmanspacher and Primas 2003). At present this question has sparked a great deal of interest and discussion (Pusey 2012; Barrett 2014; Hance 2022). In order to answer this question we must first understand what sense we put into the contention that physics gives us true, objective, knowledge of the surrounding world.

Indeed, knowledge is a part of our inner, psychic reality. On what basis can we be sure that our knowledge is "objective" in the sense that it corresponds to external, physical reality? Strictly speaking, we cannot go beyond the limits of our ideas, beyond the boundaries of our psyche in any way. What allows us to hope that the knowledge we acquire through natural science is an adequate "reflection" of reality?

Consider an idealized model of a researcher, free from all the mental and computational limitations of a real scientist. Let them be called a *theoretical subject*. The basis for the possibility of introducing the concept of a theoretical subject is the unprecedented breadth and accuracy inherent in theoretical physics. Indeed, modern physics describes the world in the widest range of scales—from 10^{-19} m (the minimum resolution scale at the Large Hadron Collider) to 10^{26} m (the size of the visible part of the universe). At the same time, the value of the anomalous magnetic moment of the electron theoretically predicted by quantum electrodynamics coincides with the experimentally measured one at a phenomenal rate of accuracy—an order of $\sim 10^{-10}$. The detected decrease in the orbital period of the PSR B1913+16 binary star system located at a distance of about twenty light years (approximately 10^{17} m), owing to the loss of energy due to gravitational radiation, is consistent with the prediction given by the general theory of relativity at a rate of the order of $\sim 10^{-3}$.

The theoretical representation of the selected part of external reality (*Reality*), called the (isolated) *system* in the mental space of the theoretical subject (*Theor. Subject*) will be called the *state* of the system (*System State*). Classical mechanics has concluded that the dynamic laws it discovers are deterministic, which is equivalent to the idea of preserving knowledge about an isolated system. Based on knowledge of the state of the system at a certain point in time (initial conditions), a theoretical subject can predict its behavior in the future and calculate what it was in the past (if the system was isolated throughout the observation without interference from the environment). This can be symbolically written as follows:

Reality → *Theor. Subject* [{*System State*}]

Thus in Classical mechanics the subjective account of reality determines the theoretical subject's account of the system under analysis. When a researcher observes (measures) the (isolated) system he is studying, he only *confirms* the correspondence of knowledge about the state of the system to the real situation and therefore does not affect either the system itself or its state, i.e., the representation of reality in the theoretical subject:

Reality ← *Theor. Subject* [{*System State*}]

There is a one-to-one correspondence between external reality and its representation as the (mental) image (state) of an isolated system in a theoretical subject. In such case we can say that knowledge about the system is objective. Symbolically, it can be represented as follows:

Reality ← → *Theor. Subj* [{*System State*}]

Let us emphasize once again that, according to our definition, the *state* of an (isolated) system is an element of the mental space of a theoretical subject; it is "objective" in the sense that it observes a one-to-one correspondence between external reality and its image in the (ideal) theoretical subject. But it is also "subjective" in the sense that it is part of the inner mental reality of the theoretical subject, and not external physical reality. Note also that in both the act of separating the system under study from the physical reality surrounding it and in fixing initial conditions the theoretical subject himself is implicitly present.

In classical statistical physics, two ways of representing external reality in an (ideal) theoretical subject arise: incomplete ("subjective") and complete ("objective"). One of them, called the *Macro State, is incomplete and is characterized by a sufficient description of the isolated system for the researcher* (theoretical subject) using selected averaged parameters (for example, the pressure of the gas under study, its temperature, etc.):

Reality → *Theor. Subject* [{*Macro State*}]

At the same time, it is implied that, in principle, it is possible to give a complete (objective) description of the system, to "spy" on what it "really is" (it can be granted that an ideal theoretical subject with unlimited possibilities is able to measure, for example, the velocities of all gas molecules). Therefore, it is assumed that there is another, complete, representation of external reality in the theoretical subject, called a *microstate* and characterized by the most detailed (objective) description of the (isolated) system *(Micro State)*:

Reality → *Theor. Subject* [{*MicroState*}]

These two ways of representing external reality in an (ideal) theoretical subject—incomplete and complete—are, so to speak, on different planes. It is clear that the same macro-state can correspond to many different micro-states. Therefore, a new concept is introduced, the *Statistical Ensemble*, which is a collection of a very large (at its limits infinite) number of identical "copies" of a given system in different microscopic states corresponding to a single macroscopic state (taking negligible fluctuations into account). Our ignorance of the true "state of affairs" (for example, the coordinates and velocities of all the particles composing the gas) is compensated by the knowledge of the *probabilities* of the realization of certain macrostates from microstates. These probabilities throughout the statistical ensemble of classical physics are described by a *Distribution Function* and are simply a measure of subjective ignorance (or unwillingness to know) the situation in detail. They are in themselves attributed no ontological reality. It can be said that the probability distribution is *an epistemological* and non-*ontological* phenomenon, describing the state of our knowledge about reality and not its objective properties. This can be symbolically written as follows:

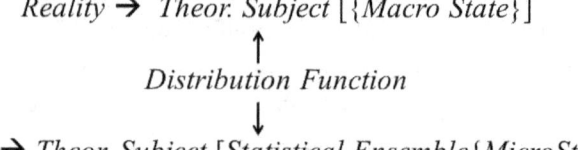

Note that, as in the case of classical physics, the micro-state and the macro-state are still elements of the mental space of the theoretical subject. The microstate is "objective" in the sense that there is (as we believe) a one-to-one correspondence between an isolated system and its image in a theoretical subject. In this sense, the microstate is *an ontological* phenomenon. But it is also "subjective" in the sense that it is part of the inner mental reality of the theoretical subject, and not external physical reality. The macrostate is "subjective" in the sense that, firstly, it is not a complete description of the system, but only sufficient for the purposes of the theoretical subject, and, secondly, it is part of the subject's inner mental reality. Thus, the macrostate is *an epistemological* phenomenon. The use of probabilistic language to describe the relationship between micro- and macro-states is associated with the incompleteness of the theoretical subject's subjective knowledge, linking the incomplete description in the language of the average values characterizing the macro-state with deterministic laws characterizing the dynamics of micro-states. This leads to the fact that the statistical laws characterizing the dynamics of macrostates are irreversible in time, entropy increases, and with it our subjective ignorance about the state of the system. Such a loss of knowledge about the system is a consequence of the initial incompleteness of our knowledge about it.

When a researcher (theoretical subject) observes (measures) the system he is studying, he receives, generally speaking, new knowledge about its macro-state, which are taken for new initial conditions. Thus, observation changes our knowledge of the system and thereby changes its macro-state; i.e., the theoretical representation of the selected part of the external reality in the theoretical subject. At the same time, observation does not change reality, since it corresponds to a microstate, into which an ideal theoretical subject can, in principle, "peep" at any moment. He does not venture to do this because, for practical purposes, it is enough for him to describe the system in the language of a macrostate. These two "planes," ontic and epistemic states, occupied by the theoretical subject do not meet. Rather, one might say that they are divided as particular "layers," as distribution functions.

In non-relativistic quantum mechanics, each of these mutually excluding positions (if we maintain the previous paradigm) co-occur simultaneously: the theoretical subject has full knowledge of the system and the observation changes our knowledge about the system and also changes its own state. Let us examine this in greater detail.

In non-relativistic quantum theory, as well as in classical statistical physics, there are also two ways of representing an external reality (an isolated system) in a theoretical subject. As already mentioned, a quantum mechanical system is mapped to a state vector in a Hilbert space over a field of complex numbers {ψ-State}. It is assumed that this gives the most complete description of a quantum system (for now we will limit ourselves to describing pure states, i.e., states that can be described in the language of state vectors). The dynamics of a quantum mechanical system is arrived at by the deterministic evolution equation, which obeys its state vector. This means, in accordance with our definition, that knowledge about the system is objective: there is an unambiguous correspondence between the external reality and its representation—the (mental) image (state) of the system in the theoretical subject:

Reality → *Theor. Subject* [{ψ-State}]

At the same time, the state vector itself, which is comparable to a quantum system, is not directly observable, and therefore we cannot experimentally compare it with reality.:

Reality ↚ *Theor. Subject* [{ψ-State}]

The coordinate, momentum, and energy are actually observable in quantum mechanics, as in the classical model; the measurement results of these observables represent probability distributions {*p-State*}. The observed (measuring instruments) correspond to linear operators operating in Hilbert space. The probability of detecting a system in a particular state with certain values of coordinate, momentum, or energy is equal to the square of the modulus of the (complex-valued) probability amplitude, which is the coefficient of the decomposition of the state vector according to the set of eigenvectors of the operator of the measured quantity (coordinate, momentum or energy). As already mentioned, the most complete result of the experiment is the probability distribution of a series of measurements (over a field of real numbers).

Reality → Theor. Subject [{p-State}]

Comparing statistics of the results of measurement (probability *a posteriori*) with theoretical (*a priori*) predictions by means of probability, the observer (theoretical subject) assures that they correctly ("objectively") describe the state vector:

Theor. Subject [{p-State}] ← Theor. Subject [{ψ-State}]

In each experiment, one of a number of potential results emerges as predicted by the initial state vector. These effected potential possibilities turn into new (subjective and thus non-exhaustive) knowledge on the part of the theoretical subject after a measurement procedure. According to this new (subjective) knowledge, the theoretical subject constructs a new state vector for the system, describing its new objective potentialities. The subsequent deterministic (and thus "objective") dynamics of the system's potentialities are defined by these new states—the theoretical subject's new knowledge. The theoretical subject can likewise construct a quantum system in a state that corresponds to its knowledge, and that quantum system's subsequent dynamics will then again be subject to the determinism of the evolution equation:

Theor. Subject [{p-State}] → Theor. Subject [{ψ-State}]

We emphasize that, as before, both ways of representing external reality in a theoretical subject are elements of its mental space. But, unlike the situation of classical statistical physics, where two ways of representing external reality in a theoretical subject existed absolutely separately, "in parallel planes," so to speak, in quantum mechanics the conjunction of both of these means of describing reality, the "adhesion" of two "planes," occurs at the moment of measurement. This "collapse" of parallel descriptions at the moment of measurement is called the "reduction of the state vector." That is to say, the theoretical subject, with full (to the extent possible) knowledge of the system described by the deterministic evolution equation, acquires, as a result of a measurement procedure, new (subjective and thus non-exhaustive) knowledge of the system. This new knowledge is juxtaposed against a new state vector likewise to the fullest possible extent (though still non-exhaustively). This state vector characterizes the system and describes its new state which will then, in the same way, evolve deterministically, and thus amount to that which is true and objective. This can be symbolically described thus:

$$Reality \rightarrow Theor.\ Subject\ [\{\psi\text{-}State\}]$$
$$\uparrow\downarrow$$
$$Reality \rightarrow Theor.\ Subject\ [\{p\text{-}State\}]$$

It is precisely this "stickiness," the union of two ways of representing external reality in a theoretical subject, that leads to numerous "quantum mechanical paradoxes."

One of the most famous of these is the *Schrödinger's cat* thought experiment. It is an especially interesting example because it does not touch on the question of the evolution of the system under consideration, but clearly highlights the main problem—the problem of the dual representation of reality in the theoretical subject observing the world and the problem of their (representations) ontological interpretation.

In 1935 Erwin Schrödinger (1887–1961) after extensive correspondence with Albert Einstein (1879–1955) published an article "The Current Situation in Quantum Mechanics" (Schrödinger 1935, 807–12, 823–28, 844–49) dedicated to the discussion of the Einstein-Podolsky-Rosen (EPR) paradox. In this article, in particular, he discusses the following thought experiment: let there be a cat and an ampule with poison in a closed box, which breaks if at least one atom of the radioactive substance located there decays. The state of the cat (whether it is alive or dead) thus depends on a specific quantum mechanical process (the decay of a radioactive atom). According to the mathematical apparatus of quantum mechanics, until the observer opens the box and sees the cat there, the system under study (the cat and the nucleus of a radioactive atom) is in a state described in the language of state vectors as the coexistence (superposition) of alternate states of a living and a dead cat, so it is "neither alive nor dead." Only as a result of the observer's awareness of the measurement result (from the point of view of the Copenhagen interpretation), can one of the alternatives be realized with a certain probability and the cat turns out to be either alive or dead. This conclusion is completely inconsistent with our intuitive idea that the cat, even if we do not open the box, must be either alive or dead.

Once again, we emphasize that the Schrödinger's cat paradox arises due to the fact that two ways of representing reality in a theoretical subject—one described by a (complex-valued) vector of state and the other representing a space (of real numbers) as the results of observations—can be given the same ontological status of "genuine reality."

Long-term attempts by physicists to simplify and clarify quantum mechanics as much as possible eventually led to the realization of the impossibility of abandoning the concept of a complex-valued state vector and reducing the description of the system only to observable (real) quantities. At the same time, as already mentioned, the dynamics of the state vector is described by the deterministic evolution equation. This argues in favor of the fact that in quantum, as in classical physics, there is a one-to-one correspondence between external reality and its representation in a theoretical subject by means of a state vector, so that the knowledge about the system described by the state vector is objective, and the reality corresponding to the state vector is "genuine reality." On the other hand, the directly observable "true reality" is the reality of the results of experiments conducted on the system. Such a dual representation of reality in a theoretical subject observing the world creates a problem and a problem of ontological interpretation of these representations: which of them is really "authentic" and "objective"?!

Note that if the dynamics of the state vector is described by the deterministic evolution equation, then this just means that it is the state vector that gives us "objective knowledge" about reality. But, as already mentioned, the state vector itself is not directly observable, which means that we cannot experimentally "touch" this "objective knowledge." Directly observable are the results of experiments conducted on a quantum system—the results of a "reduction" of the state vector, a kind of "projection" of the original "objective" state vector on a specific experimental situation. Moreover, these results do not just depend on the type of a particular experiment, they also demonstrate a certain variability described in probabilistic language. This means that *phenomena themselves cannot completely account for the whole essence of nature* (quantum reality). We can say that, so to speak, *quantum reality has some "inner dimension of being"* (Kopeikin 2014, 57–60), which it is impossible to access directly. At the same time, this "inner dimension" lives, so to speak, its own "inner life," manifested on the experimental "surface" of reality in the fact that the results of experiments cannot be predicted unambiguously, but only with some probability. There is a feeling that "inside" quantum reality there is some kind of analogue of "inner freedom," a kind of "*will*" of the universe, "on the surface" that manifests itself when projected onto external measuring instruments. The mathematical apparatus of quantum physics itself testifies in favor of the existence of an "inner dimension of being." Indeed, the "two-dimensionality" of the complex-valued probability amplitudes that we are compelled to use for a description of quantum reality (a complex number can be represented as an ordered pair of numbers) points us, so to speak, in the direction of this "inner dimension of being" and stands in contrast to the "linearity" of real numbers at the level of observation.

Let us explain what this means. Classical physics has always implied that all reality existed "outwards" and that the world had no "hidden dimension." Indeed, mass, force, distance and other classical physical quantities are all parameters revealed, so to speak, "from the outside," they can be easily measured. (This is why, by the way, the Newtonian God could be omniscient. He perceived the world through absolute space, his "sensorium," *sensorium Dei*, that inhabits the whole world). The situation in quantum mechanics partly resembles the state of affairs in psychology, where there is "something"—the psyche, "inner world," "soul" (though not every psychologist would agree that this "something" really *existed*). This entity cannot be seen or measured directly, but it manifests itself in some experiments. What is extremely strange is that the nature of the manifestation of this "something" (the psyche) depends not only on the way in which "measurements" are carried out (for example, particular psychological tests or the design of questions that are asked), but also on the sequence in which they are made. And the results of psychological "measurements" themselves demonstrate an impenetrable variability: for example, the same subject may occasionally give different answers to the same question. Traditionally, this is explained by the fact that the psyche is *subjective*, which means that it can manifest itself one way or another *in relation* to different situations and different subjects at different times. Similarly, in quantum mechanics, the results of the measurements of quantum objects not only depend on the instruments and in what sequence these measurements are made (with respect to the Copenhagen principle of *relativity to the means of observation* and the *contextuality* of quantum mechanics), but also demonstrate a well-known distribution described in probabilistic language (with respect to the fundamentality of quantum mechanical probability). Moreover, it is important to emphasize that both in quantum mechanics and in psychology, measurement (observation) as a rule radically changes the state of the system under study, and hence the healing effect of various psychotherapeutic practices (to which the sacrament of confession also applies): the act of "observation" itself, carried out by a psychologist-supervisor (confessing priest), changes the condition of the (confessing) patient. All this makes us think about the fact that quantum objects behave as if they had some internal "subjective" dimension of being—as already mentioned, the "two-dimensionality" of the complex-valued probability amplitude in contrast to the "linearity" of real numbers describing the measurement results also testifies in favor of this.

In classical physics, where the reality of the world is, so to speak, "turned outwards," "external" observations (measurements) do not affect either the system itself or its state as the representation of reality in a theoretical subject. On the contrary, in quantum mechanics, when the observer, generally speaking, does not have complete knowledge of the physical system (as already mentioned, the whole essence of nature does not exhaust itself in phenomena), the measurement performed on the system changes the observer's knowledge of reality, which means that it changes the state of the system as the representation of reality in the theoretical subject.

After the observer (theoretical subject) makes a measurement and acquires new knowledge about the (isolated) system, which is *an epistemological* phenomenon, they build a new vector of the state of the system and its further deterministic (and therefore "objective") dynamics is determined by its new state—the new knowledge of the theoretical subject. A theoretical subject can also create a quantum system in a state corresponding to the subject's knowledge, and its further dynamics will also obey the deterministic evolution equation. This means that such a state is objectively an *ontological* phenomenon. Thus, non-relativistic quantum mechanics testifies that a subject's *very knowledge about an (isolated) system (in a pure state), being subjective* (as in statistical physics), *coincides by nature with the state of the system and is thus objective,* in other words, that epistemological and ontological phenomena are essentially indistinguishable (the question of systems, being in a mixed state, requires separate consideration).

The result seems truly shocking! It turns out that *the reality we habitually consider "objective," i.e.,* φ-*physical* (Gk. φύσις, *nature*), is, in fact, ψ-*psychical* (Gk. ψυχή, *spirit, soul, consciousness*), which means that, in a sense, the "subjective" has some "inner dimension of being." This dimension cannot be penetrated "from the outside" by means of objective methods of cognition, rather it manifests itself externally in the form of a kind of *will* of quantum objects as described in probabilistic language.

This, in fact, is the position of the well-known mathematical physicist Bob Coecke. Over the past twenty years, he and his colleagues have been building a new language for describing quantum reality. The need for such a new language, from their point of view, stems from the fact that the formalism of Hilbert spaces and the operators acting on them is, to use a computer analogy, a "low-level language." That it took fifty years from the creation of quantum mechanical formalism to prove the elementary, but conceptually important, theorem on the prohibition of cloning, and sixty years to arrive at the easily deducible, but counterintuitive, phenomenon of quantum teleportation is, as Coecke has it, precisely because of the "low-level" nature of this formalism.

Erwin Schrödinger also noted that the principal character of quantum reality becomes visible only when studying non-separable states of quantum mechanical systems. Therefore, Coecke argues that searching for the adequate language to describe microreality should begin with the study of high-level principles for describing states of entanglement. His book *Picturing Quantum Processes* (Coecke and Kissinger 2017) is devoted to the systematic description of such a "high-level" diagram language. This language allows us to present quantum theory as a theory of processes. Addressing the frequently asked question: "What is new about the proposed high-level diagram language?" the authors note that the main results are not quantitative, but qualitative. This new language allows us to organically describe the specifically quantum features of the behavior of microreal elements. It allows us, in particular, to describe non-separable states that are impossible in classical physics. Some nontrivial results of quantum theory, such as the above mentioned examples, become natural in the categorical formulation. The main lesson of quantum theory, says Coecke, is that the idea of the world as a reality consisting of "things" or "bodies" (physical systems that can be isolated) is incorrect; the fabric of reality consists of *relationships* between things, and diagrams offer a natural language for describing such a relational universe (Coecke and Kissinger 2017, 398–99). In fact, he almost literally repeats our main thesis, which follows from the fundamental biblical thesis about the creation of the world out *of nothing*, which we called the "principle of non-absolute created being": nothing but God is *self*-existent, every created being is relative and everything exists relative to God.

Bob Coecke argues that one of the main lessons of quantum theory is that, strictly speaking, there is no observation in the sense that the system has some characteristics that an observer simply "spies upon." The magical feature of quantum theory is not that "observation" changes the quantum state, but that it is fundamentally impossible to "observe" a quantum system in the classical sense (Coecke and Kissinger 2017, 345). Coecke explains it this way: consider ordinary Newtonian mechanics, in which there is no idea of light. If there is no light, then there are no devices (not to mention eyes) in order to make observations. If we imagine the process of "observation" in such a model, it turns out that such a process is impossible without perturbation of the system under examination. Indeed, imagine that we are trying to "observe" some very light object, such as a balloon, in a dark room. Obviously, it is impossible to find such a ball without disturbing it. Indeed, the "detection" of an object (a ball) means that we interact with it, which means that we act upon it. If the ball is light, such an interaction inevitably leads to the ball shifting in position.

In quantum systems, says Coecke, "there is no analogue to the role that light and eyes play for mechanical objects. We can say that we suffer from *quantum blindness* and that the only way to know the quantum world involves some disturbing interaction, similar to what takes place when searching for an object in a dark room (Coecke and Kissinger 2017, 396–97). The meaning of Coecke's statement that a quantum system is in principle impossible to observe in the classical sense can be paraphrased as follows. In classical physics, observation is carried out by means of an "agent" (light), which is a kind of "intermediary" between the perceiving soul and the external bodily world (by the way, for medieval theologians, it was light that played the role of an intermediary link between spiritual, psychic and bodily, physical realities). "Quantum blindness," which Coecke speaks about, means that there is no such intermediary in quantum physics, in other words, the soul (psyche) touches the bodily (quantum) reality directly, and this, in fact, means that both of them are ontologically homogeneous! In fact, Coecke simply retells the aforementioned arbitrariness of the *Heisenberg cut* in a different way.

Note that the idea of the psychic nature of the universe immediately removes the so-called "Hard Problem of Consciousness" just as the special theory of relativity, abandoning the assumption of the existence of an ether filling all empty space, removed the problem of explaining the nature of the interaction of hypothetical ether with matter, and panrealism removes the problem of the interaction of matter and consciousness: it is not raw matter that interacts with "ephemeral" consciousness but one ψυχή interacts with another ψυχή. In addition, the idea of the world's psychic character allows us to consider resolving the ontological status of natural laws. Any physicist on a "practical" level believes in the "objective" existence of the laws they discover. After all, we say that a physicist "discovers" laws and not "creates" them. Yet as soon as he begins to submit his presuppositions to expert analysis, the question immediately arises as to "where" the laws exist, what is their ontological status, and so forth. Since the existing order is unable to answer these questions, the scientist is often forced to confine himself to the argument that laws are simply a way of ordering phenomena as they are observed. The proposed approach implies that laws exist *ontologically*, but they do not exist as things or objects, namely as mental laws, "logoi," ψυχή, at a special "me(n)ta-level" of reality. These (mental) laws exist in relation to (mental) entities and are subordinate to them, they do not just describe the way a physicist might perceive reality.

But if the reality around us is truly psychic and our subjective knowledge of the world actually affects it, then why do we not see obvious manifestations of this, why does the "physical" world around us exist as if it were "objective" and independent of our consciousness? From the modern point of view, the reason for this is *decoherence*, associated with the extreme complexity of isolating real systems. Everything said above has referred to *isolated* systems, as we stated at the very beginning. If the quantum system under study is not completely isolated from its environment, then as a result of its interaction with the surrounding (also quantum, and therefore mathematical) reality, information is exchanged. This information exchange can take place through a specially prepared detector, a person, or directly with the environment. What matters is only the transmission of information about the quantum system. "Who" will receive this information and how it will be processed does not matter in principle, the observer is just a witness to the information exchange.

It should be emphasized here that the concept of information in classical physics is very different from that in quantum physics. In classical physics, information is something non-material that contains knowledge (*information*, the tautology here is inevitable) about the state of a material physical system. In quantum physics, information is what the physical system is made of; the system is itself a carrier of information and the question of its material "basis" disappears.

At the moment when the volume of information "transmitted" to the external (quantum, and therefore psychical) environment becomes sufficient to distinguish the components of a quantum superposition that were previously coherently connected (Lat. *cohaerentio*—coupling, connection), the classical system "arises" from quantum reality. It arises in the sense that we can no longer distinguish the signs of the "quantum" (coherence) of the system. Rather, we see only its "classicity" (de-coherence of its constituent sub-systems): the superposition of quantum states passes into their mixture. Moreover, it is important to note that such an "occurrence" does not occur instantly, but gradually, and this can be experimentally observed. We can say that the environment—at its limits the entire quantum physical universe—plays the role of an "observer" for each of its subsystems, and the classical properties of subsystems arise as a result of averaging over all interactions.

An excellent illustration of the gradual decoherence process is an experiment conducted by Anton Zeilinger, winner of the 2022 Nobel Prize. Zeilinger and his collaborators conducted a classic double-slit experiment with fullerene C_{70} molecules (Hackermüller et al. 2004, 711–14) (fullerene is one of the allotropic forms of carbon, a fullerene cluster is a convex closed polyhedron made up of sixty or seventy carbon atoms). Fullerene is particularly interesting because its clusters are actually located on the border between the classical and quantum worlds. Fullerene molecules were heated and passed through a diffraction grating. At low temperatures, interference was observed, which weakened with increasing temperature until it disappeared completely at a certain temperature and fullerene clusters began to behave like ordinary classical particles. This behavior is due to the fact that when the temperature of the clusters increases, the radiation emitted by them is at such a shortwave frequency that it allows you to determine which slit the molecule passed through. Decoherence occurs due to the fact that the role of an "observer" is actually played by the environment. For the transition of a superposition into a mixture, it is not essential to have a measurement from instrument or human observer, but merely to preserve the information as to which gap the fullerene cluster passed through.

The famous American physicist John Wheeler (1911–2008) once complained: "We know how to summarize every other great idea of physics in a few simple words, but not the idea of a quantum." Reading quantum mechanics in its broad semantic context, implying the presence of a theological discourse, allows us to symbolically summarize its essence as follows:

$$\varphi \cong \psi$$

Where φ represents φ-physical reality, ψ represents ψ-psychical reality, and the sign $\cong$ refers to their identity. This identity is, however, not obvious because external "psychicity" is subjectively perceived as physical reality, owing to the spontaneous occurrence of decoherence in non-isolated quantum systems.

Despite the shocking strangeness of the foregoing, some modern researchers have put forth similar ideas. So, the famous American cognitive psychologist Donald Hoffman, professor at the University of California, Irvine, believes that what we see is not reality itself, but the "interface of reality," the minimum necessary for us to survive. From his point of view, the inability of modern science to solve the fundamental problem of consciousness stems from the fact that researchers believe reality is exactly as we see it, that is it consists of "bodies." Meanwhile, physics testifies to a completely different, non-corporeal nature of the universe. Hoffman argues that neuroscientists and philosophers needlessly ignore progress in the field of fundamental physics and believe that quantum mechanics has nothing to do with the work of the brain—the brain as a classical object. He puts forward an extremely daring thesis: "The brain—as a classical object—does not exist!" Hoffman argues that we need to get rid of the (classical) physicalism in which modern civilization has educated us. From his point of view, the most basic ontological entities, as their own kind of "elementary particles," are the most basic conscious experiences. These then comprise what we perceive as the fabric of reality (Hoffman 2019). To this should be added the views of Robert Lanza, Head of Astellas Global Regenerative Medicine, and Chief Scientific Officer of the Astellas Institute for Regenerative Medicine. Unlike most modern researchers who assume that life and consciousness can randomly arise in a lifeless universe, Lanza is convinced that the universe cannot exist without life or consciousness. Together with his co-authors, he has published several books on the concept he calls "Biocentrism," in which life and consciousness are fundamental properties of the universe inherent in it *ab initio* (Lanza and Berman 2009; 2016; Lanza and Pavšič 2020).

The World as the Creator's ψυχή

How can the above result of the analysis of the quantum mechanical measurement process be understood? If the world is really psychical, you can raise the question: *Whose psyche is it*? Since, as already mentioned, modern science arose in the context of the idea that the world is the second Book of God, complementary to the first—the Bible—then it is natural to look for an answer to this question by referring specifically to the context of biblical theology. So, if the world is a *book of the Creator*, then what is the *ontological reality* of the text he created? What conclusion can we draw when trying to comprehend the data of modern science in the meaningful context in which it originated—in the context of biblical revelation?

As has been mentioned, the fact that the Bible is revelation means that the true Author, who stands "behind" the persons of the authors of the biblical books, reveals to us his view of the universe—a view *from the other side*, "from within" being. The Bible testifies to the creation of the world by God out *of nothing* with his word. If a person wants to understand this text, he must try to take the position of the Creator *in* whose *image* he was created. Is there anything in human experience comparable to the experience of creation *from nothing*, creation in a *word*, and creation experienced by the creator himself "from within?" The only known experience of creating "out of nothing" is mathematics. Of course, mathematics initially arose from some practice, in a certain sense, through "experimentation." In the process of such an "experimental" construction of mathematics, ideal mental objects were created that began to live their own lives and increasingly aspired to "pure" ideal knowledge. The "pure" creation of mathematics, to which the "ideal" mathematician aspires, means the rejection of the use of any concepts that arise as a result of interaction with external reality. In fact, this is what the founder of set theory Georg Cantor (1845–1918) aspired to. Subsequently, a number of mathematicians, in particular, an extremely influential group of mathematicians united under the pseudonym "Nicolas Bourbaki," began to view set theory as the foundation of the entire structure of mathematics. In fact, the "pure creation" of mathematics is synonymous with the creation "out of nothing." A mathematician begins his creation of "pure" mathematics by detaching himself from any external reality and turning his consciousness inside himself, where there is still nothing. The very formulation of the problem, the awareness of this "nothing" gives rise to the concept of "nothing," which is no longer "nothing," but a kind of understanding, which means "something" is an *empty set* of Ø (Fraenkel and Bar-Hillel 1958). Creating an *empty set* of objects out *of nothing* is the first act of creation. The French philosopher Alain Badiou gave the axiom of the existence of an empty set (in Zermelo-Fraenkel's set theory) the poetic name "The First Existential Seal," emphasizing its exceptional importance for ontology. Unlike other axioms, it clearly postulates *existence* as the existence of *nothing* (Badiou 1988).

The following acts of constructing a mathematical universe are no longer a creation out *of nothing*, but a creation out of previously created mathematical constructs. It is noteworthy that it is the *word* that turns out to be a "tool" for constructing a mathematical universe. The construction of a mathematical theory, for example, Euclidean geometry or, in this case, set theory, begins with the formulation of initial axioms. Essentially, the creator mathematician reproduces God's creative act when he says: "Let there be . . ." and then postulates a system of axioms. It is the *word* that is the main "tool" of the mathematician. It is the *word* that sets the very law of the existence of mathematical objects, creates the "space" in which these objects exist. And perhaps the most surprising thing is that the theories created in such a *verbal* and seemingly quite arbitrary way turn out to be unusually "elastic."

It may seem to a person far from mathematics that axioms can be chosen as you like. This is, of course, not the case: all one needs to do is allow for an excessive level of arbitrariness and the whole harmonious mathematical construction begins to "disintegrate": theorems are not proved and, at some point, contradictory statements begin to appear. This is why many professional mathematicians have a feeling that mathematical constructs are not "created" by mathematicians, but rather "discovered" by them, that they initially exist in some special ideal reality. However, as already mentioned, this view has a number of significant flaws. The only possible evidence suggests that mathematical objects are *created* by mathematicians after all, and the result of such creation turns out to be universal due to the fact that those fundamental principles that "work" in the process of mathematical creativity are universal for all people (as the genetic code is universal for all with all the widest variability of the phenotype). It seems that these fundamental "mathematical principles of creation," so to speak, are deeply "sewn" into the psyche of a person created in *the image* of the Creator of the universe. But it is precisely because of this "depth" that they are extremely difficult to detect (as it was not easy to detect the structure of the genome); therefore it is difficult to formulate the fundamental initial axioms of mathematics (to this day mathematicians argue about what can be considered as the true foundations of mathematics; set theory is only one possible option). And yet it seems that, due to this universality of the "genetic code" of the part of the soul that is "responsible" for mathematics, "subjective" mathematics turns out to be the only one for all people. (This is the case for ordinary, "working" mathematics, and we should not be led away from an understanding of what exactly "mathematics" is by various mathematical "sects" such as formalism, intuitionism or constructivism.) Furthermore, it is also the case that mathematical constructs, which have often arisen outside of any practical purpose, simply for reasons of mathematical beauty, turn out to be perfectly suitable for describing the real world created by the One *in whose image* man was created.

The original thesis of the postulate of the two Books of God stated that the study of the Book of Nature provides the key to a deeper understanding of Scripture. The main result obtained from the study of the Book of the World is that it is written in the language of mathematics. Mathematics is created by the word "out of nothing"—from an empty set of ideas—in the mind of a mathematician-creator. It is created in *the image* of the Creator of the universe. The strikingly precise correspondence between the internal ("psychic") mathematical model of reality and the external physical ("material") world in the widest range of scales naturally leads to the hypothesis that this correspondence is not limited only to structural similarity, but can be extended to the sphere of ontology. This is supported by the above-mentioned coincidence between the subjective knowledge about the system and its objective state. Thus, giving sense to what we have now learned from the Book of Nature, we conclude that knowledge about a system, being subjective, coincides by nature with the system's state and is thus objective. Furthermore, remembering the theological context in which the formation of modern science took place—the context of the two Books of the Creator—we are forced to arrive at the unambiguous (and, at the same time, crazy enough to be true) conclusion: the *world is the ψυχή of the Creator*. His ψυχή in the sense that, firstly, the world is not dead "matter," but a living, primary fabric of being, and, secondly, God does not need an "organ" to touch the world. He has *direct* access to it just as we have direct access to our own psyche. Actually, the only reality available to us is the reality of our psyche, we know everything else only indirectly and by means of it (Kopeikin 2014, 90–93).

In order to correctly perceive the thesis that the *world is the psyche of the Creator*, one should recall the words of Ian Thomas Ramsey (1915–72), Bishop of Durham, professor of philosophy of religion at Oxford University. He was deeply interested in the problem of the relationship between science and theology (the Ian Ramsey Centre for Science and

Religion in Oxford[2] has been founded in his name) and emphasized that theological language is based on "permanent mystery" (Ramsey 1964, 61). Theological statements about God, according to Ramsey, should not be perceived as "super-science" explaining phenomena. Statements about God are only an attempt to touch the divine mystery (Gill 1976, 132, 147).

It is noteworthy that when *Science* magazine celebrated its 125th anniversary in 2005, twenty-five questions were formulated that seemed to be the most relevant at the beginning of the new millennium. It is characteristic that the first of them was the question of what the universe consisted of, and the second was what was the biological basis of consciousness (Seife 2005, 78; Miller 2005, 79). The famous American physicist Andrei Linde, one of the creators of inflationary cosmology, believes that these two issues are closely related: perhaps consciousness is as fundamental as space, time and matter. Moreover, the problem of consciousness may be closely related to the problem of the birth, life and death of the universe. Can it not be that consciousness, just like spacetime, has its own levels of freedom without an account of which the description of the Universe would be fundamentally incomplete? Is it not the case that the further development of science is in the study of the Universe and the study of consciousness inexorably knit together and that conclusive progress in one field is not complete without progress in the other? After creating a unified geometric description of the weak and strong electromagnetic and gravitational interactions, is this not the next level of a single approach to our entire world, including Man's internal world? The problem of consciousness, just as the related problem of human life and death, is not only unresolved, but is, at a fundamental level, not even being examined. It would be very tempting to show some sort of connection and analogy, even at a superficial and shallow level at first, in the examination of one other great question: the problem of the birth, life and death of the Universe. "Possibly, the future will make clear that these two problems are not so far from each other as they might seem" (Linde, n.d., 13).

Linde believes that a consistent development of quantum cosmology requires a deeper understanding of quantum mechanics than what is current today. This involves, first of all, an understanding of the problem of observation, the problem of consciousness. He believes that something

---

2. https://www.ianramseycentre.ox.ac.uk/.

similar to what happened in the theory of relativity should happen to the concept of consciousness. Space, time and matter, which initially seemed to be three fundamentally different entities, eventually merged. At first, the special theory of relativity combined space and time into a single whole. But space-time was still something like a "container" of matter. The general theory of relativity combined matter with space-time. It turned out that they were all interdependent. Now, Linde believes, it is consciousness's turn. He draws attention to the fact that the very possibility of knowing the world is conditioned by the fundamental fact of the existence of consciousness. As it turns out, our conscious perceptions obey certain laws that can be interpreted based on the assumption of the existence of an external material reality. This model turns out to be so successful that we forget about consciousness as a starting point and come to the conclusion that matter is the only reality, and conscious perceptions only "reflect" it. This assumption is just as natural (and just as false) as the assumption that space and time are only a "container" of matter. It is logical to assume, Linde continues, that, just as the unification of space, time and matter took place, in the future there should be a unification of these three components of the universe with consciousness. Only then can consciousness be organically incorporated into the scientific conception of the world (Linde 1990; Linde, n.d.).

But how can this be understood and described in the context of the scientific conception of the world? Although we are merely a *part* of this world, it is possible for us to discover the "laws of nature" as a whole because we are created in *the image* of God (Gen 1:27), and the world is *embedded in the heart* of man (Eccl 3:11). That is why, even being "inside" the universe, we dare to take a point of view that allows us to raise the question of the Legislator's *plan*. In culture, there is a technique called *mise en abyme* or "story within a story," mixing the subjective with the objective, the world of the book being read and the world of the reader himself. The term *mise en abyme* itself came from heraldry and meant placing a heraldic element in the center of the coat of arms, for example, placing a reduced coat of arms of the heiress spouse from a family without a male heir in the central area of the husband's heraldic shield, the so-called "claim shield," which meant that the husband, owner of the coat of arms, becomes a contender for the role of the head of the line on his wife's side. At the beginning of the twentieth century, André Gide (1869–1951) used this term to denote the artistic technique of reproducing a plot within a plot. Images of this kind are widely represented in the visual arts.

For example, Giotto di Bondone (1266/1267–1337) used it in his painting of the Stefaneschi Altarpiece (c. 1330) for the main altar of the old Basilica of St. Peter in Rome. The reverse side of the Stefaneschi Triptych depicts Cardinal Giacomo Stefaneschi himself (c. 1270–1343) presenting the altar he ordered to the enthroned Apostle Peter. In the short story "The Hidden Magic in Don Quixote," Jorge Luis Borges (1899–1986), listing numerous examples of *mise en abyme*, asks why it makes such a strong impression on us, and answers as follows: "These inversions suggest that if the characters of a fictional work can be readers or spectators, we, its readers or spectators, can be fictitious, too" (Borges 2011, 172).

In 1959, the famous British intellectual Charles Percy Snow (1905–80) gave a lecture entitled "The Two Cultures and the Scientific Revolution" at Cambridge University. In it he expressed regret concerning the deep gap of misunderstanding that lies between the traditional humanitarian culture and the civilization of scientific and technological progress. Snow was well acquainted with this problem from the inside: he himself had received a doctorate in physics at Cambridge, devoted some time to science, then held a number of significant government positions, devoting his free time to literary creativity. This lecture was then published as a separate brochure and it brought the author international fame with a wide public response. In 2008, *The Times Literary Supplement* included *The Two Cultures and the Scientific Revolution* in the list of one hundred books that had the greatest impact on the public discourse of the West after World War II. Snow, in particular, offered hope for the clash of the traditional humanitarian culture that grew out of the seed of theology and the civilization of scientific and technological progress also indirectly rooted in theology: "the clashing point of two subjects, two disciplines, two cultures . . . of two galaxies, so far as that goes—ought to produce creative chances" (Snow 1998, 16).

The clash of quantum physics and theology produces such creative chances—a fundamentally new understanding of the nature of reality—new for both natural science and theology. Reading quantum mechanics in the biblical theological context of two supplementary Books of God, the Bible and the Book of Nature, allows us to put forward the following dazzling thesis: there is no matter, *there is nothing but thought—the thought of the Creator Who creates us* ("We are His workmanship [ποίημα]" [Eph 2:10] *in a word* [Gen 1:3–31; Ps 33:6; John 1:3] *in our own mind* ["Known unto God are all his works from the beginning of the world" (Acts 15:18)] *in Our own image* [Gen 1:27] *so that when we know the world* [naming the names of creatures (Gen 2:19)] *we think inside His thought* ["in Him [ἐν αὐτῷ] we live, and we move, and have our being" [Acts 17:28])—*mise en abyme—and thereby we participate in His thinking* ["For of Him, and through Him, and to Him, are all things" [(Rom 11:36)]).

It is noteworthy that when *the world* is taken as the ψυχή of the Creator, the idea of decoherence gets a natural explanation. The whole universe as the ψυχή of the Creator plays the role of an "observer" for each of its subsystems, and the classical properties of subsystems arise as a result of averaging over all interactions. "In nature" quantum processes occur without any "observer" because, aside from consciousness, there is nothing else. Thus we may say that the particles themselves "know" each other. And at the same time they themselves are known by the universe as a distributed global psychic property of the Creator. Of course, the way quantum microobjects "cognize" each other is very different from human cognition, but the basic principle is the same: an exchange of information that alters the state of interacting particles.

Of course, the question arises: if the *world is the psyche of the Creator*, does this not mean that God constantly controls the entire universe, just as we seem to control the flow of our psychic life? Does it not follow from this that man has no freedom, and everything is determined only by the will of the Almighty? But then must it be that evil and sin also exist "within" Him?

Trying to answer these questions, we find ourselves forced to resort to traditional biblical anthropomorphism. Just as it is possible to distinguish two mutually complementary spheres in the human psyche, *consciousness* and the *unconscious*, then, since man is created in *the image* of his Creator, it is also legitimate to raise the question of *the "unconscious" of God*. After all, we are talking about the "right hand of God" and his "finger," about his "anger" and "repentance," about the "jealousy" and "love" of the Almighty. In the context of the biblical tradition, *heaven* and *earth* represent the two "poles" of the universe between which everything is enclosed, the fullness of being, the whole *uni*-versum. At the same time, *heaven* is the "throne of God" (Isa 66:1; Matt 5:34), the "seat" of his presence (although "the heaven and heaven of heavens cannot contain" Him [1 Kgs 8:27]), and the earth is the inheritance of human existence: "The heaven, even the heavens, are the Lord's: but the earth hath he given to the children of men" (Ps 115:16). Heaven is separated from earth, which is "his footstool" (Isa 66:1; Matt 5:35),[3] by means of the firmament,

---

3. See also Isa 66:1; Dan 7:49; Matt 23:22. "Heaven is heaven to the Lord, and He has

on which the Creator places the lights to "divide the day from the night; and let them be for signs, and for seasons, and for days, and years . . . to rule the day . . . to rule the night . . . and to rule over the day and over the night, and to divide the light from the darkness" (Gen 1:14–18). In fact, the firmament is the "place" of the existence of laws governing what is on earth. Thus, the earth—the sphere of the created world—is subordinated to the will of the Almighty not directly, but indirectly through the laws which he has established. Therefore, we can say that evil and sin are "in Him," but not "His." The words of the prayer "Our Father," bestowed by Jesus himself to his disciples, "Thy will be done in earth, as it is in heaven" (Matt 6:10; Luke 11:2), suggest that there is no direct will of God on earth right now. And in this sense this sphere can really be likened to the sphere of the un- or demon-consciousness.

Note that St. Augustine of Hippo (Aurelius Augustinus Hipponensis 354–430) in the ninth and tenth books of his treatise *De Trinitate*, proceeding from the thesis that all created nature is the image of the Creator, comes to the conclusion that man as the supreme creation bears in his soul the brightest imprint of the Deity. Therefore, he explains the dogma of the Trinity by referring to the consideration of the "inner man" (*homo interior*) and seeing threefold analogies in various aspects of the existence of the human psyche—the mind (*mens*) or the rational spirit, knowledge (*notitia*), which he knows himself, and love (*amor*), which he loves himself and his knowledge, and also memory (*memoria*), understanding (*intelligentia*) and will (*voluntas*). Thus, the assimilation of the inner world of man to the "inner" reality of God is quite natural and lies in line with the Christian tradition.

The perspective according to which the world comes to reside *in* God is called *panentheism* (from Gk. πᾶν ἐν Θεῷ, *all in God*, as distinguished from *pantheism* where God is identified with the world)). Although the term itself was introduced only in the nineteenth century by the German philosopher Karl Christian Friedrich Krause (1781–1832), a similar vision can be seen in the aforementioned St. Augustine of Hippo: "If, for example, all was sea, and an endless and immeasurable sea extended out in all directions, and there was a sponge therein of any size, but finite, so that this sponge would be soaked through on all sides, filling up with this immeasurable sea. So, thought I, of Your final creation filled with Thee, the Infinite," so wrote the St. Augustine (*Confessions* 7.5.7). The well-known modern Orthodox theologian Metropolitan Kallistos

---

given the earth to the sons of men" (Ps 113:24).

of Dioklea (Timothy Richard Ware, 1934–2022) argued that Orthodox theology can be defined as "Palamist panentheism" since St. Gregory Palamas (Γρηγόριος Παλαμᾶς; ca. 1296–1359), whose theology is revered as the highest achievement of the Orthodox tradition, speaks about the presence of God in the world and peace in God (Ware 2004, 165). The panentheistic concept is based on the Holy Scriptures, in particular, on the words of the Book of Wisdom of Jesus, the son of Sirach (or Ecclesiasticus): "We may speak much, and yet come short: wherefore in sum, he is all" (Sir 43:27).

Isaac Newton (1642–1727) stated something similar: "In Him [in God] are all things contained and moved; yet neither affects the other: God suffers nothing from the motion of bodies; bodies find no resistance from the omnipresence of God." This he wrote in his *Scholium generale*, which ends with "The Beginning" (Newton 1846, 505).

In the twentieth century, panentheism again attracted the attention of theologians and philosophers. Such a view, for example, was held by the renowned Russian religious philosopher Semen Franck (1877–1950). For him, "God not only transcends his creation, but at the same time is immanently present in it as its eternal foundation and vivifying origin" (Frank 1949, 15). Charles Hartshorne (1897–2000), one of the greatest religious philosophers of the twentieth century, had similar views (Hartshorne 1967). This view was shared by the prominent British theologian and biochemist Arthur Peacocke (1924–2006). He believed that all of both nature and man in a certain sense were located in God; but God was greater than both nature and Man and he possessed more than nature and man. In his own existence, God surpasses Man and nature, transcending their limits. Either God is in all of the creations of the world from the beginning to the end, in all places and times, or he is nowhere. All that we see around us is the creation of God and a reflection of the origins of his creativity (Peacocke 2004).

Philosophical problems held a deep interest throughout the life of one of the founders of quantum mechanics, Nobel laureate Erwin Schrödinger. This is evidenced in the very titles of his books: *Über Indeterminismus in der Physik. Zwei Vorträge zur Kritik der naturwissenschaftlichen Erkenntnis* (Leipzig, 1932), *What Is Life?* (Cambridge, 1944), *Science and Humanism* (Cambridge, 1952), *Nature and the Greeks* (Cambridge, 1954), *Mind and Matter* (Cambridge, 1958), *Meine Weltansicht* (Vienna, 1961). Being a very versatile person, Schrödinger also paid great attention to issues of ethics and religion. He believed that "this is precisely the point where our present way of thinking does need to be amended, perhaps by a bit of blood-transfusion from Eastern thought." Indubitably, he adds, during this "blood transfusion" one must take precautions against "clotting" (there is some risk in losing the validity European scientific thought has already achieved, "which is unparalleled anywhere at any epoch") (Schrödinger 1992, 130).

In the epilogue of his book *What Is Life?*, entitled "On Determinism and Free Will," Schrodinger writes from two equally valid premises:

1. My body functions as a pure mechanism according to the Laws of Nature, and

2. I know, by incontrovertible evidence, that I am directing its motions, of which I foresee the effects, which may be fatal and all-important, in which case I feel and take full responsibility for them.

> The only possible inference from these two facts is, I think, that I—I in the widest meaning of the word, that is to say, every conscious mind that has ever said or felt "I"—am the person, if any, who controls the "motion of the atoms" according to the Laws of Nature.
>
> Within a cultural milieu (*Kulturkreis*) where certain conceptions (which once had or still have a wider meaning amongst other peoples) have been limited and specialized, it is daring to give to this conclusion the simple wording that it requires. In Christian terminology to say: "Hence I am God Almighty" sounds both blasphemous and lunatic. But please disregard these connotations for the moment and consider whether the above inference is not the closest a biologist can get to proving God and immortality at one stroke.
>
> In itself, the insight is not new. The earliest records to my knowledge date back some 2,500 years or more. From the early great Upanishads the recognition A[T]MAN = BRAHMAN (the personal self equals the omnipresent, all-comprehending eternal self) was in Indian thought considered, far from being blasphemous, to represent the quintessence of deepest insight into the happenings of the world. The striving of all the scholars of Vedanta was, after having learnt to pronounce with their lips, really to assimilate in their minds this grandest of all thoughts. (Schrödinger 1946, 88–89)

Where did the notion of the multiplicity of consciousnesses come from? According to Schrödinger, such is an illusion prompted by the multiplicity of bodies in which Unified Consciousness is manifested. This illusion leads to a false sense of the multiplicity of individual consciousnesses. Schrödinger insists: "The only possible alternative is simply to keep to the immediate experience that consciousness is a singular of which the plural is unknown; that there is only one thing and that what seems to be a plurality is merely a series of different aspects of this one thing, produced by a deception (the Indian MA[Y]A); the same illusion is produced in a gallery of mirrors" (Schrödinger 1946, 90).

Yet for biblical consciousness the assertion "I am God" is not so insane or blasphemous. "Is it not written in your Law, 'I said, Ye are gods?'" (John 10:34), is what Jesus says to his disciples with reference to the words of the psalm: "I have said, Ye are gods; and all of you are children of the most High" (Ps 82:6). Man is indeed a god, though god of his own world, the world of his soul: "So God created man in his own image, in the image of God created he him" (Gen 1:27). Furthermore, as the renowned Orthodox theologian, professor of the Moscow Theological Academy, martyr Ivan V. Popov (1867–1938) wrote: "The idea of theosis (θεοποίησις, θέωσις), which has been completely forgotten in modern theology, forms the very kernel of the religious life of the Christian East" (Popov 1909, 3). That is, *salvation* in the sense of *theosis*.

At about the same time as I. V. Popov, the great religious philosopher Prince Sergei Nikolaevich Trubetskoy (1862–1905), professor and rector of the Imperial Moscow University, insisted on the need to build *religious physics*, the object of which would be the universe as the future Body of the Church, when the Church ceases to be *part* of the cosmos, but the *whole* cosmos will become the Church. Trubetskoy noted:

> We have few educated people for whom the Church is truly the Body of Christ, . . . and even fewer who would agree to consider the church life of believers as an organic process. And this demonstrates only that their faith in the Church is not sufficiently deep or alive, that it is too distracted, or that their mind has become too distracted from the objects of faith and does not sufficiently reflect on them. Moreover, the hidden iconoclasm that prevails in all of us has completely undermined the concept of a "spiritual organism," has turned it . . . into an empty metaphor devoid of vital meaning. It has come to the point that the first one who now attempts to portray the sacrament of the church as an organic process, who tries to build the philosophy of the Church as a speculative physiology of the divine Body (the *physics of the matter of God*), likely risks being considered

a heretic in the eyes of the fictive zealots of Orthodoxy.... Of course, such a philosophical task is both dangerous and difficult. Yet such a task is legitimate and even necessary in both modern and future Orthodox philosophy, because only such a higher religious physiology can give us the key to understanding the mystery of the life of all beings and together create Christian science, a Christian natural science. Such religious physics *alone is able to defeat the material and godless physics of our age* [emphasis added], and not only externally, but through the inner revelation of truth, of its overabundance. Empirical physics will not be destroyed, it will only pass into and be taken in by higher physics, which will introduce it into the Church, baptize it in itself... Moreover, one such physics is religious, philosophical, and at the same time positivist. This is a physics, which possesses not a subjective, but a universal ideal of life as the subject of its speculation, which can give in itself a true foundation for experimental natural science, which will no longer be guided by arbitrary and fictitious hypotheses, but *by positive metaphysical foundations discovered in ecclesiastical wisdom and clarified by positive speculation* [emphasis added]." (Trubetskoy 1995, 140)

In fact, Trubetskoy proposes to restore a sacred hierarchy of values. First of these is revelation, properly interpreted, of course. The Book of God, the Book of Nature, according to Francis Bacon, is then given to us so that we do not stop only at a superficial understanding of the sacred text, but penetrate into its innermost depths. It is the true source of all knowledge, including the knowledge of natural science. Such a fundamental metaphysical foundation, discovered in ecclesiastical wisdom and clarified by positive speculation, is the revelation of the creation of all things out *of nothing* by the *word* of the Creator and the creation of man *in the image* of his Creator, a man capable of creating images of things in his inner world *by the word*.

Bibliography

Atmanspacher, Harald, and Hans Primas. 2003. "Epistemic and Ontic Quantum Realities." In *Time, Quantum, and Information*, edited by Lutz Castell and Otfried Ischebeck, 301–21. Berlin: Springer.
Augustine. 1945. *Confessions*. London: Dent & Sons.
Badiou, Alain. 1988. *L'Être et l'Événement*. Paris: Seuil.
Barrett, Jonathan, et al. 2014. "No ψ-Epistemic Model Can Fully Explain the Indistinguishability of Quantum States." *Physical Review Letters* 112(25): 1–10.

Borges, Jorge Luis. 2011. "Partial Magic in the Quixote." In *Labyrinths*, translated by James E. Irby, 171–74. Sidney: Penguin Australia.

Coecke, Bob, and Aleks Kissinger. 2017. *Picturing Quantum Processes: A First Course in Quantum Theory and Diagrammatic Reasoning*. Cambridge: Cambridge University Press.

Crull, Elise, and Guido Bacciagaluppi. 2011. "Translation of: W. Heisenberg, 'Ist eine deterministische Ergänzung der Quantenmechanik möglich?'" http://philsci-archive.pitt.edu/8590/.

Fraenkel, Abraham, and Yehoshua Bar-Hillel. 1958. *Foundations of Set Theory*. Amsterdam: North-Holland.

Frank, Semyon. 1949. *Light in the Darkness: Experience in Christian Ethics and Social Philosophy*. Paris: YMCA.

Gill, Jerry H. 1976. *Ian Ramsey: To Speak Responsibly of God*. London: Allen & Unwin.

Hackermüller, Lucia, et al. 2004. "Decoherence of Matter Waves by Thermal Emission of Radiation." *Nature* 427(6976): 711–14.

Hance, Jonte, et al. 2022. "Could Wavefunctions Simultaneously Represent Knowledge and Reality?" *Quantum Studies: Mathematics and Foundations* 9(3): 333–41.

Hartshorne, Charles. 1967. *A Natural Theology for Our Time*. La Salle, IL: Open Court.

Hoffman, Donald. 2019. *The Case against Reality: Why Evolution Hid the Truth from Our Eyes*. New York: Norton.

Kopeikin, Kirill. 2014. *What Is Reality? Reflecting on the Work of Erwin Schrödinger*. St. Petersburg: St. Petersburg State University Press.

Kuratovskij, Kazimierz, and Andrzej Mostovskij. 1976. *Set Theory*. Amsterdam: North-Holland.

Lanza, Robert, and Bob Berman. 2009. *Biocentrism: How Life and Consciousness Are the Keys to Understanding the True Nature of the Universe*. Dallas: BenBella.

———. 2016. *Beyond Biocentrism: Rethinking Time, Space, Consciousness, and the Illusion of Death*. Dallas: BenBella.

Lanza, Robert, and Matej Pavšič. 2020. *The Grand Biocentric Design: How Life Creates Reality*. Dallas: BenBella.

Linde, Andrei. 1990. *Particle Physics and Inflationary Cosmology*. London: CRC.

———. n.d. "Universe, Life, Consciousness." https://static1.squarespace.com/static/54d103efe4b0f90e6ca101cd/t/54f9cb08e4b0a50e0977f4d8/1425656584247/universe-life-consciousness.pdf.

Miller, Greg. 2005. "What Is the Biological Basis of Consciousness." *Science* 309(5731): 79.

Neumann, John von. 1932. *Mathematical Foundations of Quantum Mechanics*. Translated by Robert T. Beyer. Princeton: Princeton University Press.

Newton, Isaac. 1846. *The Mathematical Principles of Natural Philosophy*. Translated by Andrew Motte. New York: Adee.

Peacocke, Arthur. 2004. *Evolution: The Disguised Friend of Faith? Selected Essays*. West Conshohocken, PA: Templeton.

Popov, Ivan. 1909. *The Idea of Theosis in the Early Eastern Church*. Moscow: Kushnerev and Co.

Pusey, Matthew, et al. 2012. "On the Reality of the Quantum State." *Nature Physics* 8(6): 476–79.

Ramsey, Ian T. 1964. *Models and Mystery*. Oxford: Oxford University Press.

Schrödinger, Erwin. 1935. "Die gegenwärtige Situation in der Quantenmechanik." *Naturwissenschaften* 23 (48, 49, 50): 807–12, 823–28, 844–49.
———. 1946. *What Is Life?* New York: MacMillan.
———. 1992. *What Is Life? Mind and Matter: Autobiographical Sketches.* Cambridge: Cambridge University Press.
Seife, Charles. 2005. "What Is the Universe Made Of?" *Science* 309(5731): 78.
Snow, Charles P. 1998. *The Two Cultures and the Scientific Revolution.* Cambridge: Cambridge University Press.
Trubetskoy, Sergey. 1995. "About Hagia Sophia, the Wisdom of God." *Voprosy filosofii* 9: 120–68.
Ware, Kallistos. 2004. "God Immanent yet Transcendent: The Divine Energies according to Saint Gregory Palamas." In *In Whom We Live and Move and Have Our Being: Panentheistic Reflections on God's Presence in a Scientific World*, edited by Philip Clayton and Arthur Peacocke, 157–69. Grand Rapids: Eerdmans.

7

Theology and Thermodynamics of Life and Mind

The Legacy of Nikolai Kobozev (1903–74)

SERGEY KRIVOVICHEV

Introduction

AT SEVERAL POINTS, THE history of twentieth-century science witnessed an interesting phenomenon: prominent scientists who had devoted their lives to studying "non-living" matter, turned their attention to the problems of life and the mind during the later stages of their careers. The names Vladimir Vernadsky, Erwin Schrödinger, Eugene Wigner, and Walter Elsasser immediately come to mind. Among lesser known luminaries, those who spent most of their lives in the Soviet Union and were unable to contradict its dominant materialistic dogma, one may recall Sergey Vavilov, Karl Trincher, and Nikolai Kobozev. In his book *Origin and Eternity of Life* (published in Petrograd, 1922), Vladimir Vernadsky pointed out that "there are no problems more important than the problem of the mystery of life, the eternal problem that humankind has been facing for thousands of years and which it tries to resolve by all the striving of its personal and collective effort" (Vernadsky 2013, 373). Later he pointed out that "the concept of living was not created by science.... It was introduced into science by a common conception from pre-scientific common knowledge.... Defining the distinction between the living and nonliving, as well as the existence of life itself, are real issues in the field of the exact sciences just as are the definitions of space, time, matter, force, among others" (Vernadsky 2013, 145–46). According to Sergey Vavilov, a prominent Russian physicist and president of the USSR Academy of Sciences between 1945 and 1956, the recognition of life and mind as primary realities along with such basic indefinable entities as matter and space would lead to "a new science and new worldview" (Vavilov 2012, 334).[1] The shadows of this "new science" have always been and still are on the horizon of the modern scientific enterprise, especially since the dawn of the "new physics" at the beginning of the twentieth century. However, the purpose of the present work is not to explore all the possibilities and consequences of the inclusion of life and mind into scientific worldview as indefinable entities, but to concentrate on the analysis of these entities and the process of thinking in the works of the prominent Russian-Soviet chemist Nikolai Kobozev (1903–74), professor at Moscow State University. We start with a brief biographical sketch and an overview of his work, followed by sections outlining basic points of his analysis of life and mind. Kobozev's work was based on thermodynamics and includes theoretical models expressed in mathematical formulas and calculations. We shall try to avoid the use of advanced mathematics in order to get the principal message that Kobozev derived from science to the point reachable by minds inclined toward theology. There is little doubt that he himself was such a mind, as he has always been remembered as and expressed himself as an Orthodox Christian.

N. I. Kobozev: A Biographical Sketch

The name of Nikolai Ivanovich Kobozev is well-known to the readers of Alexander Solzhenitsyn. In his book *Invisible Allies* (*Nevidimki*), a supplement to *The Oak and the Calf* (*Bodalsya Telenok s Dubom*), there is a chapter devoted to Nikolai Kobozev, who was the doctoral supervisor of Solzhenitsyn's first wife, Natalia Reshetovskaya, at Moscow State University. "Nikolai Ivanovich Kobozev was one of the most brilliant men I

---

1. Sergei Ivanovich Vavilov (1891–1951) never discussed the problem of mind in his scientific works. However, from his recently published diaries, it is more than evident that this problem was central to his worldview in his later years. It should be noted that Sergei Vavilov was one of the teachers of Nikolai Kobozev during his student days at Moscow State University.

have ever met. He was a renowned specialist in physical chemistry, but he went beyond this field, and in the best tradition of pre-revolutionary Russian science combined his main line of research with reflections on comparable phenomena and problems in parallel branches of knowledge, as well as in philosophy, Russian history and Orthodox theology" (Solzhenitsyn 1995, 26–27).

Nikolai Kobozev was born on May 12, 1903, to the family of Ivan Iosifovich (Ioasafovich) Kobozev (1874–1943) and Sofia Adolfovna Faist (†1952). His father was a lawyer. In 1920, Kobozev entered the Natural Sciences section of Moscow State University, which he finished in 1924 and enrolled in doctoral studies (*aspirantura*) under the supervision of Russian physico-chemist Prof. Eugene I. Shpitalsky (1879–1931). During his student years, Kobozev was already thinking about the relations between science and theology. To his friend and collaborator, Sergei Vasiliev, he mentioned that "he . . . was pondering the question on the origins of scientific knowledge and came to the conclusion that theoretical science cannot be justified without the belief in God as a source of any truth. . . . Newton believed that God gave the first impetus to the world He created. But this understanding of the act of creation is mechanistic since it considers motion as a directed movement of some body or some particle in space only. The more general viewpoint is that God created the universe by means of an adiabatic compression" (Vasiliev 1999, 169–235). Once, in a dispute with a fellow student, Kobozev mentioned that he could prove the existence of God from scientific principles. However, his religious practice was not only theoretical. According to Solzhenytsyn, "Kobozev was acutely aware of the Russian spiritual collapse in the twentieth century, but in religious terms he was a simple Orthodox free of intellectual pretensions" (Solzhenitsyn 1995, 30).

Kobozev's scientific life was associated with the Faculty of Chemistry, Moscow State University, where he was a Professor from 1935 and the Head of the Laboratory of Inorganic Catalysis, later transformed into the present Laboratory of Catalysis and Gaseous Electrochemistry (Lunin 2007). He made great contributions to the theory of catalysis and chemical technology, including explosives and oxidating conversion of methane, new methods of ozone and hydrogen peroxide production, a theory of active ensembles (clusters) in catalysis, among other contributions. After the Second World War, his laboratory was actively involved in exploratory studies on the possibility of using ozone in rocket fuels (with negative results).

The scientific achievements of N. I. Kobozev were recognized by many fellow scientists, in particular, by such renowned chemists as Academicians N. D. Zelinsky (1861–1953) and N. S. Kurnakov (1860–1941), who repeatedly nominated him to the Academy of Sciences of the USSR. However, the opposition was also strong,[2] and their nominations were unsuccessful, despite the nominee's high scientific reputation.

According to Solzhenytsyn, the peculiarities of Kobozev's life "were linked to his chronic ill health. . . . Kobozev suffered from an endless number of physical ailments; I would not be able to enumerate them all. One arm was chronically dislocated at the elbow and lacked all strength; with the other arm he could barely manage his spoon and fork, so that his wife had to cut his food into tiny pieces as if he were a child—this was also necessary in order to control his stomach ulcer. He suffered from a discharge of cerebral fluid into his nasal cavity; his legs became so feeble that he had to be pushed around in a wheelchair. . . . Afflictions had rained down upon him as though he were God's chosen, perhaps in even greater abundance than those that had fallen upon the biblical Job. But Kobozev never raged against his lot, smiling as he submitted to God's will" (Solzhenitsyn 1995, 27–28).

Nikolai Kobozev died on February 27, 1974, in Moscow. According to his bibliography, he was an author of 333 scientific books and papers. Some of them were republished in two volumes of his *Selected Works* in 1978 (Kobozev 1978), including his book on the thermodynamics of thinking, which is most relevant to our present study.

N. I. Kobozev: Scientific Works Related to Theology

The problems of life and mind central to this paper were of interest for Kobozev from his student years. However, he started to work on them more closely during the 1940s, which culminated in his first paper on the subject published in *Bulletin of Moscow Society of Naturalists* (Kobozev 1948a).[3] In this paper, Kobozev developed basic principles of cybernetics, working independently from Norbert Wiener and Ross Ashby. It is

---

2. The reasons behind such an opposition were, in part, due to the N. I. Kobozev's criticism of the group of influential chemists headed by Acad. A. N. Frumkin and A. N. Bakh. See Vernadsky 2013, 23:60–62.

3. The list of Kobozev's works relevant to theological issues is given in Appendix A to this article. In the following, we will refer to them by indicating the year of publication and their respective pages.

very likely that his interests in the subject were significantly enhanced by the appearance of Erwin Schrödinger's book, the translation of which was published in Soviet Russia in 1947 (Schrödinger 1947). Kobozev criticized Schrödinger's concept of negative entropy, pointing out that it is essentially equivalent to the concept of free energy and emphasized the importance of thermodynamics for the understanding of life and mind. In Kobozev's words: "The thermodynamic criterion that established itself well in the study of molecular processes and microstructures in physics and chemistry seems to be applicable, but is not sensitive enough, or, to be precise, it is insensitive to the application to a living substance. Thermodynamics may well distinguish liquid from vapor, solution from suspension, mechanical mixture from chemical compound; it is much less sensitive to the optical stereoisomerism of molecules, whereas nuclear isotopy is at the limit of thermodynamic sensitivity. The state of living matter is below even this threshold. Here we need *a new system of thermodynamics and statistics* [emphasis added], the creation of which is a possible and extremely timely aim" (Kobozev 1948b, 32–33). Following this research programme first outlined in 1948, Kobozev published between 1961 and 1970 a series of papers in the Soviet *Journal of Physical Chemistry*, which was the most prominent Soviet physical chemistry journal at the time.[4] The most important was the series of six papers under the general title, "On the Physico-chemical Modeling of Processes of Information and Thinking," which later constituted the core of the Kobozev's book *Investigations in the Field of the Thermodynamics of Information and Thinking* published in 1971 by Moscow State University. In 1974, Alexander Solzhenytsyn pointed out that this book escaped "political vigilance" of Soviet authorities, since "herein, the existence of an antientropic center in the Universe has been proved, which, leaving aside physical terminology, presumes the existence of God" (Solzhenitsyn 1997, 495–96).

The collection of Kobozev's works on life and mind is a systematic, deep and profound scientific research program, which has important theological resonance for those who had "ears to hear" (Matt 11:15). It is hard not to connect it to the promises of the young Nikolai Kobozev to use thermodynamics to prove the existence of God. Below we provide a brief introduction to Kobozev's scientific ideas on the problems of the essence of life and mind which bear strong theological implications.

---

4. See Appendix A.

Energy, Entropy, and Thinking

In the paper on the "Elements of the general theory of vector-Brownian processes and the laws of biological kinematics" (Kobozev 1948a), and a subsequent series of papers on "the problem of ordered and disordered energy in chemical thermodynamics" (Kobozev 1961a, 1961b, 1962), Kobozev proposed a vectorial representation of thermodynamic functions and defined two types of energy. The first type of energy is "ordered" and vectorized (free energy), whereas the second one is "disordered" and corresponds, for instance, to Brownian motion. The difference between two types of energy can be illustrated by the Brownian motion of inorganic or "non-living" particles and microorganisms. The movements of the latter consist of two components: chaotic and vectorized, i.e., purpose-oriented. The obvious conclusion is that any natural process has both chaotic and ordered contributions with the totally ordered process possible at absolute zero temperature and therefore prohibited by the Nernst-Planck theorem, sometimes called a "third law of thermodynamics." All natural processes happening above absolute zero invariably contain chaos, expressed as a non-zero entropy of the system.

On the basis of thermodynamic considerations, Kobozev points out that "thinking is the only natural phenomenon that contains an actual transition to the limiting case, i.e., to the completely zero-entropy state. This is the true mystery of mental activity" (Kobozev 1971, 100). The main problem in the thermodynamics of thinking lies in "the incompatibility between the entropy law for molecular structures, including molecular machinery of the mind and the law of identity for thinking" (Kobozev 1971, 7). Kobozev distinguishes between physical space (μ-space) and the Ψ-space of thought and analyzes the relations between them. As an example, let us consider the two rows of symbols given below (Kobozev 1971, 155).

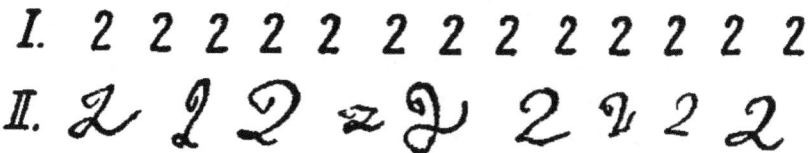

Figure 3: Two rows of symbols (Kobozev 1971, 155).

Obviously, the first row compared to the second one possesses the lower code entropy and can be compressed to a single symbol. The volume of the symbol in the μ-space (paper sheet or computer screen) is relatively small, in contrast to the second row. However, in the Ψ-space of mind the two rows are identical, though the mind should apply more work in order to compress the row II. The latter operation is possible only due to the supply of negative entropy (or antientropy) to the Ψ-space that compensates for the entropy of symbols in the μ-space. This is why abstract thinking is possible for humankind, since the same symbols in the Ψ-space have the same meaning for any mind.

According to Kobozev, "thermodynamic analysis shows that the process of ordered thinking is related to the violation of the balance of generalized entropy: entropic physico-chemical operations of brain . . . are able to produce a zero-entropy production of thought." This is the essence of the "thermodynamic paradox of thinking" (Kobozev 1968a, 5). The possession of the antientropy is the major aspect that distinguishes a mind (or generally, living system [see below] from an automaton.

The Definition of Life

The definition of life is one of the currently unresolved issues in biology (Trifonov 2011, 259–66; Krivovichev 2022, 335–37). As it was pointed out in the introduction, Vernadsky believed that life does not need a special definition, being one of the primary indefinable concepts, along with matter, space, time, etc. When considering the criteria of "living" entities and their difference from "non-living" in terms of Brownian and vectorized processes, N. I. Kobozev (Kobozev 1948a, 26–29; Kobozev 1971, 170–72) proposed to use the dependence of diffusion coefficient of an object from its mass. According to the kinetic theory, the diffusion coefficient of a (non-living) particle, D_{nl}, decreases with its mass, m_{nl}, increasing:

$$D_{nl} = D_{nl}^{\circ} \times m_{nl}^{-1/2}$$

where $D_{nl} = D_{nl}^{\circ}$ for some particle with unitary mass $m_{nl} = 1$.

In contrast, for a living object, the diffusion coefficient D_l increases with the increasing mass m_l:

$$D_l = D_l^{\circ} \times m_l^{2/3}$$

Kobozev points out to the difference between the "dead" Newtonian mass of non-living objects (m_{nl}) and the "living" mass of biological objects (m_l), highlighting the difference between living and non-living matter, well in the spirit of Vernadsky's works. The increasing diffusion coefficient with the increasing mass is a criterion of discrimination between living *versus* non-living objects. According to Kobozev, the increasing diffusion for the increasing biological mass "indicates that this mass is in thermodynamic inequlibrium with its environment, and the degree of the inequlibrium increases with the increasing mass" (Kobozev 1971, 172).

It is rather remarkable that Kobozev's criterion of living objects is based purely on their motion, without taking into account any other aspects of their existence and activity such as metabolism, information-based genetics, reproduction, etc. However, it is obvious that stationary or immobile objects can be alive as well, thus violating Kobozev's criterion if the latter is defined for a physical space.

Antientropy and the Origin of Life

Physical entropy is a measure of disorder of physical systems: more ordered systems possess lower entropy compared to disordered systems. For instance, liquid (e.g., water) and crystal (e.g., ice) with the same composition have high and low entropies, respectively. In statistical physics, the entropy S of a given macrostate is calculated by means of the Boltzmann-Planck equation:

$$S = \ln W$$

where W is the number of microstates that realizes the given macrostate. For instance, the macrostate of a liquid water can be realized by the higher number of microstates than the macrostate of a solid ice, since, in the latter, molecules are more or less "frozen" in certain positions, whereas, in the former, they move more freely. The W parameter is also called a thermodynamic probability.

Since each macrostate has at least one corresponding microstate, $W \geq 1$, then entropy cannot be negative: $S \geq 0$. The condition $W = 1$ and $S = 0$ corresponds to the absolute zero temperature, which is prohibited according to the third law of thermodynamics.

The keypoint in Kobozev's analysis of the entropy of living organisms (Kobozev 1968b, 1046; Kobozev 1971, 160–62) is in the extension and reconsideration of the concept of thermodynamic probability W in an algorithmic sense. First, he points out that "the existence of the complete procedure for the reconstruction of a given macrostate is the mandatory limiting assumption of molecular statistics." Then Kobozev suggests that W be understood as a number of any procedures that realizes the macrostate. If there are no procedures that realize the macrostate, then $W < 1$ and $S < 0$, i.e., the entropy of the macrostate is negative or becomes antientropy. This step is crucial for the understanding of Kobozev's argument, since then he introduces a distinction between algorithmic states (for which there are algorithms that realize them) and non-algorithmic states (for which there are no algorithms in principle). The former states have positive entropy, whereas the latter states necessarily possess negative entropy or antientropy.

According to Kobozev, it is antientropy that lies at the core of living organisms, since there are no procedures that results in their origin from non-living matter. Francesco Redi's principle "*omne vivum ex vivo*" ("life always comes from life") and Rudolf Virchow's principle "cells come from the existing cells" agree well with the non-algorithmic property of life and even provide support for it from the empirical observations of nature.

Of course, organisms possess positive entropy as well, due to their molecular-based nature (see below), so "in living substances, molecular material adopts both entropy levels: positive molecular entropy and negative (potential) entropy. One can imagine that elements of a living system oscillate between these levels of entropy.... As a result of such an oscillation (or superposition of the two levels), the living system occupies some intermediate biological entropy level, which is reduced relative to the entropy level of its molecular material.... Therefore, the partially antientropic state of living creatures leads to the conclusion that their construction from entropic molecular material requires a supply of negative entropy; i.e., the reconstruction of all the statistics of the organism" (Kobozev 1971, 168).

The concept of negative entropy or antientropy is fundamental to Kobozev's thought on life and the mind (see below). From a terminological point of view, it may well be inspired by Schrödinger's book, but the essence of the Kobozev's concept is principally different.[5] As mentioned above, Kobozev associated Schrödinger's negative entropy with free energy, emphasizing that "life and death are isoenergetic and isoentropic

---

5. It is worthy to note that the initial rejection (or at least harsh criticism) of Schrödinger's concept by Kobozev (Kobozev 1948b) later was reconsidered in the direction of its re-interpretation (Kobozev 1971, 68).

states and Schrödinger is incorrect when he suggests the existence of thermodynamic entropic barrier between them" (Kobozev 1948b, 32).

In some sense, the concept of a non-algorithmic state of living organisms (in particular, of a cell) recalls the concept of an irreducibly complex system advocated by Michael Behe (Behe 1996) and William Dembski (Dembski 2002). At the same time, Kobozev did not reject the principle of biological evolution, leaving aside the problem of the initial origin of a living cell.

Ψ-Particles and the "Physics of Thinking"

With respect to the activity of a human mind, Kobozev distinguishes two levels, pre-logical, associated with the information handling and production, and logical—thinking *sensu stricto*. The latter is impossible without antientropy, which is not an emergent property, that is, it "did not emerge in the form of *Deus ex Machina*," but is necessary for organized thinking. "Without this new factor, the usual atomic-molecular matter of the brain is unable to provide the process of thinking and even the simplest information process if it is associated with the most elementary symbolic entry" (Kobozev 1971, 173).[6] However, the pre-logical operations, e.g., the production of information, can be modeled on the low-entropy level, reachable for quantum systems. Kobozev considers a strongly degenerate Fermi gas composed of superlight particles, which he called Ψ-particles or psychons.[7] These unknown Ψ-particles are one hundred thousand times lighter than electrons and are relatively large ($\sim 10^{-6}$ cm^3). The hypothetic Ψ-neuronal net formed by the Ψ-particles is potentially able "to produce low-entropy operations that are specific to the psychics as a whole and to the transmission of information (disturbance) over the net" (Kobozev 1971, 182).

According to Kobozev, "the participation of elementary particles greatly expands the possibilities of mental activity of the brain, not only by reducing its entropy, but in other important ways." The atomic-molecular matter bound by the law of conservation of mass is "only suitable for

---

6. Thus the antientropic property of life and mind is given and does not emerge at higher levels of material organization, as it was stated by "dialectical materialists."

7. The term "psychon" was first used by McCulloch and Pitts (1943) for the identification of an "ultimate psychic unit," "no less than the activity of a single neuron." Later J. C. Eccles (1994) defined psychon as an "elemental or unitary mental event" linked to a particular dendron.

building soma," whereas "carriers of mental functions and antientropy necessary for life should be sought in the field of elementary particles" (Kobozev 1971, 183).[8]

It is important to emphasize that N. I. Kobozev associated the psychon gas with a pre-logical level of mental activity only, whereas logical operations are provided by antientropy, which is not achievable even in quantum systems (due to the Heisenberg's uncertainty principle).

Conclusions

Since its origin in the nineteenth century, thermodynamics as a science dealing with the order and distribution of energy had significant implications to theological issues such as origin and fate of the universe, the source and evolution of structures (Kragh 2008). The essence of the research program by Nikolai Ivanovich Kobozev was focused on the entropic characteristics of life and mental processes. His numerous works on the application of thermodynamics to the investigation of thinking and information processes led him to the concept of antientropy, which is an inherent feature of any living organism, non-derivable from any physical structure or property. Well in line with the contemporary research in the West, Kobozev hypothesized on the role of quantum structures in life and mental activities, though the essence of life and mind could not be explained by any natural processes. Through the concept of antientropy, he postulated the existence of the non-physical basis of life and mind, at least in the sense of modern science. Antientropy sustains the existence of any living being that cannot be reproduced from any molecular material.

As with many other great naturalists, the scientific interests of Nikolai Kobozev in the problems of life and mind were driven by his deep religious convictions, remarkable in the context of mid-twentieth century Soviet history. In his attempt to build a theory that proves the non-physical basis of life and mind, he belongs to a unique group of faithful scientists of the past century that invested considerable intellectual efforts to reconcile their beliefs and science into a single worldview.

---

8. The hypothesis about the role of Fermi gas of (unknown) elementary particles in life and mind was first expressed by Kobozev (1970; the work was submitted for publication in 1969). In 1968, German physicist H. Fröhlich suggested that quantum condensates such as Bose gas play an important role in biological systems (Fröhlich 1968). In contrast to Kobozev's paper, his work has been cited more than 1,400 times since its publication.

Bibliography

Behe, Michael. 1996. *Darwin's Black Box: The Biochemical Challenge to Evolution.* New York: Free.
Dembski, William N. 2002. *No Free Lunch: Why Specified Complexity Cannot Be Purchased without Intelligence.* Lanham, MD: Rowman & Littlefield.
Eccles, John C. 1994. *How the Self Controls Its Brain.* Berlin: Springer.
Fröhlich, Herbert. 1968. "Long-Range Coherence and Energy Storage in Biological Systems." *International Journal of Quantum Chemistry* 2(5): 641–49.
Kobozev, Nikolai I. 1978. *Selected Works.* Moscow: Moscow University Press.
Kragh, Helge. 2008. *Entropic Creation: Religious Contexts of Thermodynamics and Cosmology.* Hampshire: Ashgate.
Krivovichev, Sergey V. 2022. *Orthodoxy and Natural Sciences: A Textbook for the Bachelor of Theology.* Moscow: Poznanie.
Lunin, Valery V., ed. 2007. *Our Sunny House: Laboratory of Catalysis and Gaseous Electrochemistry: In Commemoration of its 60th Anniversary.* https://www.kge.msu.ru/files/kge_sun_house.pdf.
Mcculloch, Warren S., and Walter Pitts. 1943. "A Logical Calculus of the Ideas Immanent in Nervous Activity." *Bulletin of Mathematical Biology* 5: 115–33.
Schrödinger, Ervin. 1947. *What Is Life?* Moscow: Nauka.
Solzhenitsyn, Aleksandr. 1995. *Invisible Allies.* Translated by Alexis Klimoff and Michael Nicholson. Washington DC: Counterpoint.
———. 1997. "On N. I. Kobozev's Book *Investigations in the Field of Thermodynamics of Information and Thinking.*" In *Publizistika.* Vol. 3, *Articles, Letters, Interviews, Prefaces,* 194–96. Yaroslavl: Verkhnyaya Volga.
Trifonov, Edward N. 2011. "Vocabulary of Definitions of Life Suggests a Definition." *Journal of Biomolecular Structure and Dynamics* 29(2): 259–66.
Vasiliev, Sergey S. 1999. "Memories about N. I. Kobozev (1903–1974)." In *Chemical Design: Context-Chronicle as an Experience of Reflection in Natural Sciences (to the Biography of N. I. Kobozev),* 169–235. Novosibirsk: Chem. Lab NCD.
Vavilov, Sergey I. 2012. "Diary Entry, 26. XII. 1946." In *Dnevniki* [*Diaries*]. Vol. 2, *1920, 1935–1951,* 334. Moscow: Nauka.
Vernadsky, Vladimir I. 2013. *Collected Works.* Moscow: Nauka.

Appendix A: Bibliography of N. I. Kobozev's Scientific Works Related to Theology

Kobozev, Nikolai I. 1948a. "Elements of the General Theory of Vector-Brownian Processes and the Laws of Biological Kinematics." *Bulletin of the Moscow Society of Naturalists, Biology Section* 53(1): 3–29.
———. 1948b. "Several Critical Notes on the Schrödinger's Book *What Is Life* from the Viewpoint of Physicist." *Bulletin of the Moscow Society of Naturalists, Biology Section* 53(3): 3–29.
———. 1961a. "The Problem of Ordered and Non-ordered Forms of Energy in Chemical Thermodynamics. I." *Soviet Journal of Physical Chemistry* 35: 2736–44.

———. 1961b. "The Problem of Ordered and Non-ordered Forms of Energy in Chemical Thermodynamics. II. Brownian-Vectorial Energy Equilibrium in Chemical Thermodynamics." *Soviet Journal of Physical Chemistry* 35: 2745–50.

———. 1962. "The Problem of Ordered and Non-ordered Forms of Energy in Chemical Thermodynamics. III. Application of the General Principles." *Soviet Journal of Physical Chemistry* 36: 266–73.

———. 1966a. "On the Physico-Chemical Modeling of Processes of Information and Thinking. I. Thermodynamics of the Process of Information." *Soviet Journal of Physical Chemistry* 40: 281–94.

———. 1966b. "On the Physico-Chemical Modeling of Processes of Information and Thinking. II. Thermodynamics of the Process of Thinking." *Soviet Journal of Physical Chemistry* 40: 784–94.

———. 1967. "On the Physico-Chemical Modeling of Processes of Information and Thinking. III. System Processes and the Types of Their Representation." *Soviet Journal of Physical Chemistry* 41: 1723–30.

———. 1968a. "On the Physico-Chemical Modeling of Processes of Information and Thinking. IV. Thermodynamics of the Process of Thinking on the Level of Systems." *Soviet Journal of Physical Chemistry* 42: 5–12.

———. 1968b. "On the Physico-Chemical Modeling of Processes of Information and Thinking. V. On the Sense of Negative Entropy." *Soviet Journal of Physical Chemistry* 42: 1045–51.

———. 1970. "On the Physico-Chemical Modeling of Processes of Information and Thinking. VI. Modeling Low-Entropic Information-Thinking Functions on the Basis of Degenerate Fermi Gas." *Soviet Journal of Physical Chemistry*, 44: 2969–74.

———. 1971. *Investigations in the Field of Thermodynamics of Information and Thinking*. Moscow: Moscow University Press.

8

Neuroethics, Quantum Physics, and Theology

Oleg Reznik and Kirill Kopeikin

Introduction

IN 2002, THE DANA Foundation brought together experts from the field of neuroscience, bioethics, psychiatry, psychology, and law for the conference "Neuroethics: Mapping the Field." At this conference, the famous American man of letters William Safire proposed a new term, "neuroethics," giving it the following definition: "the study of what is right and what is wrong, what is good and what is bad when it comes to treatment, improvement, unwanted invasion and dangerous manipulation of the human brain" (Safire 2002, 3). The term "neuroethics" had already been coined (Illes 2003), but Safire's definition for the first time narrowed in on the ethical component of the field.

The field of neuroethics is the study of dilemmas that naturally arise as a kind of natural fruits of progress in neuroscience (Rabadán 2015). Ethical reflection here automatically requires some delicacy, if not intimacy, since it is addressed to conflicts arising from the study of the brain—the material carrier of consciousness, the organ in which our perception, sensations and thoughts exist.

The uniqueness of neuroethics, in the words of cognitive scientist and philosopher Adina Roskies, in comparison with other areas of bioethics, is determined by the very fact of the existence of "a close connection between our brain and our behavior, as well as a special relationship between our brain and ourselves" (Roskies 2002).

It turns out that neuroethics, in its short twenty years, is directly related to the study of the most authentic and profound aspects of the existence of a particular person, to the search for an answer to the question "What is it to *be* human?," or, in a less broad formulation, "What is consciousness?"

It is well known that the phenomenon of consciousness, the nature of human behavior and the importance of the brain as their source and regulator have occupied thinkers since ancient times. For example, already in Hippocrates there are records about the brain as a "messenger of consciousness" or that "the brain is the interpreter of consciousness." This is not the place for a detailed description of the concepts of consciousness that took place at different times, including the religious interpretation of its nature, the concept of the soul and the idea of Cartesian dualism. The authors take the liberty to assert that none of the answers we have today are particularly clear and that the search for these answers is the main task of modern neuroscience.

At the same time, it is also important to note the heterogeneity of views of modern thinkers on the accessibility to the study of the phenomenon of consciousness. With James Watson, Francis Crick is known as the primary discoverer of the structure of DNA. Crick devoted the last twenty-five years of his life to the study of the brain and the phenomenon of consciousness. He published many articles and two books on neuroscience and consciousness (Kaplish 2016). Crick was convinced that the brain and consciousness are things that can be studied and, at some point, will be understood. The British thinker Colin McGinn, on the other hand, called for recognizing that the "secret" of consciousness is something that cannot, in principle, be revealed (McGinn 1989). We can only know de facto that consciousness "exists" inside the brain; how exactly this happens is a priori beyond understanding. Finally, John Searle defines consciousness as a set of specific biological processes that are quite accessible to study, but because of their complexity remain at present virtually unexamined (Searle 1990).

From the "Mystery of Consciousness" to Modern Neuroscience

Consciousness is often portrayed as a deep mystery, one deep enough to call forth such radical solutions as the revision of the fundamental laws of quantum physics (Kent 2018). Despite the ongoing debate over the problem that consciousness creates for science at the conceptual level, it is already obvious that the current status of research itself serves as a source of discoveries valuable both for fundamental science and for applied research and medicine. Advances in this field entail the need to solve a number of pressing legal and ethical problems, such as, for example, assessing the status of consciousness in patients under general anesthesia or in a vegetative state (Owen et al. 2006); the status of consciousness in infants, animals and machines (Dehaene et al. 2017); measuring well-being and happiness or moral responsibility (Levy 2014).

Before proceeding to the consideration of concrete examples, let us outline the current state of affairs in the field of consciousness. We have pointed out above that McGinn (1989) put forward the thesis about the unsolvability of the "mystery of consciousness." In 1994, the Association for the Scientific Study of Consciousness was founded in Berkeley and the twenty-fourth annual Congress of this authoritative organization was held in June 2020. In 2014, the journal *Trends in Cognitive Sciences* published an article by Ken Paller and Satoru Suzuki (Paller and Suzuki 2014), who, in rather harsh terms, gave the following characterization of consciousness research:

> Why does an unrelenting stream of thoughts and experiences usually fill your mind? We have no satisfactory answer. We do not know how the normal operation of the human brain turns into subjective experience. Consciousness therefore seems some sort of miracle, and research a waste of time and money doomed to failure. Nevertheless, there are grounds for optimism that need to be shared with the public in order to justify continuation of research. (Paller and Suzuki 2014, 87)

Beyond just this fragment, the authors' text as a whole is imbued with skepticism, and even sarcasm; yet ends with an optimistic note. After describing the fragmentary nature of the scientific community's ideas about the nature of consciousness, the authors then indicate promising directions for further scientific research. In particular, they highly appreciate the importance of studying the mechanisms of neuronal interactions as the substrate of material consciousness.

The authors' sharp formulations were likely meant to be provocative because, only three months later, a response was published in the same journal, in which a team of authors led by Ned Block tried to clearly indicate noticeable progress in the study of consciousness. This, however, looked more like an enumeration of disparate facts that could not add up to some complete picture. For example, the authors pointed to the proven disconnection of attention and awareness, successes in the study of the neuronal foundations of metacognitive processes, separately highlighted significant progress in the study of consciousness levels in people during the deep sleep phase, anesthesia and in the vegetative state as being of particular importance for modern medicine (Block et al. 2014). And still today consciousness research lacks the integrity, complexity and scale required of its aims. The medicalization of scientific fields of research, on the other hand, would intuitively seem to be well-justified because medicine can give empirical studies of the phenomenon of consciousness a practical application.

The above is covered in the July 2019 issue of *Nature* (Emmons 2019) in which a special section consisting of 8 articles is devoted to brain and consciousness research. Anil Seth, professor of cognitive and computational neuroscience at the University of Sussex and an authority in the field of consciousness research, offers what would be a good epigraph for the course of these articles: "The existence of consciousness is still a fundamental mystery" (Seth 2017). In his eminently accessible TED Talk Seth describes the current state of the study of consciousness:

> More recently, life itself seemed to people to be an inexplicable, miraculous phenomenon that was perceived as something more than a manifestation of the work of a well-coordinated mechanism, but today, thanks to the fact that systems biology has explained the properties of living systems from the standpoint of physics and chemistry, even ordinary citizens can understand terms such as metabolism, homeostasis, and reproduction at least at the intuitive level. The sciences of consciousness have yet to arrive at a solution of the "hard problem of consciousness" from the same positions. (Seth 2017)

Note that at the time of writing this article, there is no space to argue about any *movement* towards the discovery of the "secret of consciousness," but only about the process of accumulating data for subsequent analysis. At the same time, the volume of this data is its own problem that has yet to find a solution. Let us demonstrate some of the scale. Paller and Suzuki's article noted the future promise of the study of neuronal interactions. A superb article by an international team of scientists entitled "Architecture of the mouse brain synaptome," published in the journal *Neuron* (Zhu et al. 2018), offers data on the amount of information received during their experiment. At one stage of the study, one hundred million images from twenty-five thousand samples of the visual cortex of laboratory animals were recorded and then reconstructed into a three-dimensional model. The volume of data was two petabytes, or two hundred million gigabytes, which is approximately equal to one trillion printed A4 sheets. The entire existing volume of satellite images of the Earth is about 1.3 petabytes. Astonishingly, this study examined one cubic millimeter of mouse brain, approximately the size of a grain of sand (Zhu et al. 2018). This gives a new meaning to Blake's words "see the world in a grain of sand."

These examples indicate that none of the theses about the fundamental possibility or impossibility of studying consciousness can at present be confirmed nor refuted. The phenomenon of consciousness remains one of the great mysteries of the twenty-first century. In this light, there is little hope for neuroethics to have any clear boundaries or definite guidelines in its own field of inquiry.

Presuming that progress in the field of neuroscience is not bringing humanity closer to answering the question of the nature of consciousness, we arrive at a branch of human activity that is almost impossible to assess as a whole from the standpoint of socio-humanitarian expertise with all the moral risks that are associated with such a state of affairs.

Brain Research Projects

Against the background of achievements in the field of neuroscience, neuroethics not only took shape as a branch of bioethics, but also acquired the specific features of an independent discipline. This has taken place primarily due to major research projects taken up in the United States and the European Union. These two projects, respectively, are BRAIN (Jorgenson et al. 2015) and The Human Brain Project (Rose 2014).

In the US government's description, the BRAIN project employed formulations that are apparently traditional for Western practice: the project was initiated in order to "catalyze" the development and implementation of technologies in order to "revolutionize existing ideas about the brain." The project's program identifies seven priority areas:

1. Study the features of the work of neural circuits in health and in illness.
2. Map information transmission paths at various levels from an individual synapse to the brain as a whole.
3. Develop methods for large-scale brain monitoring.
4. Study how brain activity changes in relation to behavior.
5. Research how the brain encodes and transmits information.
6. Organize and maintain integrated networks for the study of the human brain.
7. Based on the analysis of data obtained during the previous levels of the project, determine how dynamic patterns of neuronal activity are transformed into processes of memorization, emotions, and the particulars of perception.

The project is planned to be completed in 2025 and all relevant information is presented on the official Internet resource of the project (BRAIN Initiative n.d.). It is important to note that only a few lines are devoted to the ethical risks of a large-scale brain research project with state funding in an article devoted to this project (BRAIN Initiative n.d.). On the contrary, Nicholas Rose, head of the social and ethical department of Europe's Human Brain Project, takes a balanced position and addresses ethical issues directly (Rose 2014). First of all, he questions the very fundamental possibility of forming a "corpus of unified scientific knowledge about the brain." As early as 2014, the "Society for Neuroscience" had included more than forty thousand people from more than 90 countries. The volume of scientific output of the members of this community was such that even with the use of special search programs, algorithms for data collection and analysis, it was not possible to constructively comprehend the results of a huge number of experiments. This serves as an indirect confirmation of the fact that, since the term "neuroscience" was proposed in 1960, the field has not overcome the "pre-paradigm" stage of its development, which is characterized by an independent and fairly balanced coexistence of different scientific schools, theories, hypotheses and experimental directions.

Another problem is that such large research projects put the confidentiality of subjects who provide their data at risk. When it comes to global research initiatives aimed at the "common good without exception," compliance with the principles of individual privacy may fall by the wayside, a possibility which is ethically unacceptable.

The main task of the European project is to create a simulation of the human brain in a neuromorphic supercomputer. Such a stated effort leads directly to the problem of "simulated consciousness/mind." Can consciousness arise in a sufficiently accurate computer simulation/ simulation of the human brain? If it can, then how would we relate to this entity? Should it be considered as a separate "entity," or "essence" at all? If, for example, such a "simulated consciousness" turns out to be transferred into an autonomous humanoid robot, then how should such a construct be considered? Within the framework of a thought experiment it would be easy to permit the use of humanoid robots with certain levels of consciousness for, say, military purposes as well as for the needs of healthcare work or for general public service. In this regard, it is noteworthy that the US Defense Advanced Research Projects Agency (DARPA) is a financier of the BRAIN project.

Today there are six major brain research projects in the world (Grillner et al. 2016), there are also many individual initiatives and consortia with more specific research goals. Let us mention the "Adolescent Brain Cognitive Development Study" (ABCD n.d.) conducted by the National Institute of Mental Health, which is the largest initiative in the United States to study the features of childhood brain development and the PsychENCODE project dedicated to studying the molecular mechanisms behind psychiatric diseases.

A common feature of brain studies is that they are all at the stage of active data collection and the completion of one study only signals the launch of a new series of studies. In the ABCD Study, the survey of the first group of subjects (4,500 people) yielded more than thirty terabytes of information. According to the authors, this amounts to around three times the collection of the Library of Congress (National Institutes of Health n.d.)—more than thirty-eight million books, fourteen million photographs, 3.5 million audio recordings, among much else. In total, the library's repository contains about 160 million unique sources of information (Library of Congress n.d.).

In December 2018, a special issue of the journal *Science* published seven articles representing the results of the PsychENCODE consortium (Psychencode Consortium 2018). Three more articles have been published in the thematic journals *Science Translational Medicine* (Chen et al. 2018; Meng et al. 2018) and *Science Advances* (Rhie et al. 2018). These ten papers are remarkable for their experimental organization and the volume and complexity of results. They set out new paths toward understanding the biology of the human brain and new means of neural modeling using transcriptomic, epigenomic and genomic studies of the structures of the adult and developing brain. The content of the publications is built around the materials of three principal articles: the first treats the development of the human brain, the second transcriptomics of psychiatric diseases, and the third integration of single-cell and tissue research data with deep machine-learning algorithms.

Issues of the journal *Science* are published from one to three times a month, while only one special issue of the journal is usually published in December. Over the past few years, the PsychENCODE Consortium has brought together scientists from fifteen research institutes, and the fruits of their work are presented as one of the most significant achievements of science. Yet it must be noted that this research project is, in fact, a failed attempt to explain the phenomenon of human behavior through the study of individual molecules, genes and their regulators. Characteristically, such ambitious research involves collecting massive arrays of various types of data on neuronal regulatory networks and passing them through specially developed coordinated algorithms of deep machine learning (Wang et al. 2018). Thus we observe a paradox: researchers delegate to self-learning artificial intelligence a problem that they themselves are not able to solve and, it seems, not even able to meaningfully formulate.

From the above, it is clear that two main elements are guiding the scientific community in its effort to *fully* study the brain. The first is characterized by an increasingly accelerating accumulation of scientific data in volumes that a human being, without special training, would have a very hard time estimating. As mentioned earlier, thirty terabytes of information is approximately equal to the data volume of three Libraries of the US Congress, where millions of books are stored. According to surveys by the Pew Research Center (2016), the average American reads about twelve books a year. Thus, twenty-five-year-old man who will live up to eighty-two years old will be able to read about one thousand books in his lifetime at a reading speed above average. Recall that thirty terabytes is the volume of one database obtained within the framework of one research project in which less than ten thousand people participate.

The question evidently arises as to who and when could someone at least be able to read the data accumulated by mankind about the brain, much less analyze them. The first question is followed by the second—about the ambiguous value of information in and of itself.

It is easy to imagine a gloomy picture of the near future where members of the scientific community occupy the position in relation to deep machine learning algorithms that the average person occupies today in relation to representatives of the scientific community—passive, silent recipients of so-called "scientific knowledge." Popular plots of post-apocalyptic fiction, where humanity loses in a struggle against out-of-control artificial intelligence, begin to seem quite feasible considering the automation of processes analyzing the brain's accumulated knowledge.

The second element is the inferiority of existing approaches to the study of the structure and function of the human brain. While remaining methodologically confirmed, they demonstrate vicious cycles of inconsistency in solving fundamental problems that are multiplied each time a new case is given practical application. The impressive results of recent research in the field of neuroscience paradoxically confirm this thesis: an outside observer sees a whole spectrum of unsuccessful attempts to approach a holistic understanding of the nature of consciousness and the principles of its "messenger"—the brain—through the mere study of individual structures and processes. It seems that the study of the brain is based on a logical defect that makes induction, as it were, impossible.

Neurotechnologies as the Main Object of Neuroethics

We shall now turn to the "by-products" of large research projects—the achievements of neurotechnologies, which are easily applied in healthcare as new tools for monitoring protocols and interventions. These are neuroimaging devices (Porzio 2016), neuropharmacological drugs (Sahakian et al. 2015), cranial stimulation devices (Bell et al. 2014), neurosurgical techniques (Giordano 2015) and many other tools and techniques that allow for solving all new applied medical problems. Let us first consider the most interesting technologies from at least the perspective of neuroethics.

Neuroimaging

The main focus of neuroethics is reasonably aimed at means of functional neuroimaging, that is, techniques for measuring brain activity. This is because functional neuroimaging first made it possible to *measure* such complex phenomena as existential reflections, decision-making processes (Greene et al. 2001), moral and immoral social judgments (Moll et al. 2002) even motives such as altruism and the abstract feeling of falling in love (Bartels and Zeki 2004). The mass media have assigned to the techniques of functional neuroimaging the image of a certain "window into the brain" (Raeburn 2005). Despite the fact that this comparison is not quite correct, the term has firmly come into use.

It is important to understand that all currently existing means of functional neuroimaging allow us to study brain activity only *indirectly* through the determination of surrogate biomarkers of neuronal activity: oxygen uptake for functional MRI, glucose metabolism for positron emission tomography, electrical activity for electroencephalography or magnetic fields for magnetic encephalography (Illes and Racine 2005), (Illes et al. 2006). The apparent simplicity of "neural images" of brain activity can easily mislead an observer with its visual persuasiveness. In fact, it is impossible through such images to objectively assess the incredible complexity of processes behind the "increased" or "reduced" neural activity of neurons. The process of interpreting and generalizing the results of visualizing the work of brain structures is itself complex, requires strict adherence to protocols for fixing brain reactions to typical stimuli, includes complex statistical analysis that allows you to separate significant activation from artifacts of brain activity, and many other techniques. The totality of these practices persists as-is since no one has formulated a single paradigm in contemporary brain research, nor are there any universal standards and practices (Illes and Racine 2005; Racine et al. 2010).

Methods of functional neuroimaging are actively used in medical practice to identify features of brain functioning in conditions such as depression, schizophrenia, and attention deficit hyperreactivity disorder (Agarwal et al. 2010) in order to assess the effectiveness of treatment and to develop methods for more accurate diagnosis of brain diseases.

Of greater interest is not the pragmatic approach to solving specific problems that dominates medical practice, but these abstract and "non-medical" phenomena that functional neuroimaging can help us to examine: the organization of personality, aspects of behavior, decision-making process. There is a separate "neurosocial" trend of research, in which visualization methods are translated into such areas as education (neuroeducation; Meltzoff et al. 2009), law (neuro-jurisprudence; Garland

2004), economics (neuroeconomics and neuromarketing; Plassmann et al. 2007) and religion (neurotheology; Whitfield 2003). Methods that use nothing more than the results of research eventually transform into outright attempts to encroach on "cognitive freedom" and the fundamental right of a person to think independently. These methods then become ways of gaining access to consciousness for purposes of monitoring and observation (Sententia 2004). The only factor limiting these undesirable trends is the imperfection of existing technologies. In addition, some crude forms of "mind reading" are able to establish contact with patients with severe disorders of consciousness that have no other way to communicate. There are practical bounds of functional neuroimaging beyond which it ceases to be an effective medical tool and becomes, rather, a potential means of monitoring the consciousness of members of society.

Neurocognitive Improvement

Neurocognitive improvement is understood as the use of drugs to modify processes in the brain in order to improve memory, mood, and concentration of attention by people without a diagnosis or obvious violations of any brain functions (Hall 2004).

It is noteworthy that one must "improve" one's consciousness as if that given to us by nature somehow needed automatic updates. We have already noted that the scientific community does not yet have a sufficiently complete understanding of the mechanisms of the brain. A layman's knowledge about the structure of the brain is often limited to the school curriculum and, at best, is supported by information from popular science. It does not take much to presume that a single representative of the general public does not know anything about the work of his own brain. At the same time, the idea of neuropharmacological improvement of consciousness easily resonates with the layman. It is surprising to see the desire to improve the work of a structure whose principles we do not understand. We cannot assess our current position with respect to our knowledge and can therefore scarcely assess, let alone understand, whether neurocognitive improvement is something which is actually required.

In the scientific community, the discussion is built around medical and non-medical improvement of cognitive functioning. In medical practice, neurocognitive improvement has a clear focus and denotes a *therapeutic* effect directed to improve the cognitive functions of patients with neurodegenerative or psychiatric diseases. Outside the medicine, the term "neurocognitive improvement" loses its clear outlines, some researchers consider it synonymous with "over-the-counter use of drugs," "drug abuse," or "drug dependence" (Racine and Forlini 2010; Forlini and Racine 2009).

We are sympathetic to the position of a research team from Australia, whose members in their article predict that today's fashion for "improving" consciousness by taking, for example, modafinil or methiphenidate will be replaced by public censure, as was the case with today's banned narcotic substances (Bell et al. 2012).

The main problem of the concept of neurocognitive improvement is the prospect of hypermedicalization and the stratification of society using the achievements of medical science and technological progress against human nature. The scenario that artificially "advantaged" social groups might exploit the "disadvantaged" seems realistic, as well as the forced "advancement" of employees in order to increase productivity, or to use tools for neurocognitive improvement for military purposes.

Neurostimulation: Deep Brain Stimulation

Neurostimulation is the newest neurotechnology combining a variety of invasive and non-invasive brain stimulation techniques. These include deep brain stimulation, vagus nerve stimulation, repetitive transcranial magnetic stimulation, and direct transcranial stimulation. Let us consider the most widely discussed practice of deep brain stimulation today.

Deep brain stimulation is carried out through electrodes implanted in various parts of the brain, connected to a special device—a pulse generator implanted in the upper part of the chest (Benabid 2007). Initially, deep brain stimulation was quite successfully used for the treatment of psychiatric and neurological diseases, including depressive disorders (Holtzheimer et al. 2012) and Alzheimer's disease (Laxton et al. 2010). In 1997, the technique was approved by the Food and Drug Administration (FDA) for the treatment of essential tremor and refractory Parkinson's disease. The FDA approval was the impetus for the commercialization of these procedures.

Today, anyone in the United States can independently purchase a device for transcranial brain stimulation and use it at their discretion in order to improve cognitive functions or mood. Since the legal regulation of this area is even more imperfect than in relation to neuropharmacological drugs, this is effectively a marketing device. For example, the company Foc.us openly declares that their device is not a medical and so requires no permits and can be used unrestrictedly to improve cognitive functions. The interest of the general public in this technology is successfully fueled by the mass media, which details the positive effects of brain stimulation and reports no side effects (Dubljević et al. 2014). Neurostimulation technologies are positioned today as absolutely harmless and ready for use at home. For the average person, this seems to be a perfectly reasonable solution. The inadequate response of the law to this matter has arisen because the legal field has not kept pace with the challenges that have arisen from the transfer of knowledge from neuroscience to society. Of this, the layman is unaware. A similar situation is observed in the ethical sphere where specialists can scarcely get beyond immediate concerns.

Artificial intelligence, NBIC technologies, the Internet of Things, virtual and augmented reality, cyberspace, large databases in public or private hands, neuromarketing, are far from a complete list of technologies and technological challenges that are the basis for rethinking the field of neuroscience itself. Everything that affects our consciousness—from a smartphone in a child's hand to cloud storage of information—all these are part of digital and, hence, neurotechnologies. They change the status of consciousness, cognitive skills and functions and, as a result, the status of the human brain, changing its position in the world. The future is determined by a change of human neuroprocesses themselves, by delegating the thinking capabilities themselves not even to machines, but to the "swarm intelligence" of devices and systems where decisions will be made independently of human consciousness and by the imposed algorithmization of mental processes. Therefore, it is necessary to determine whether this path leads to the strengthening of human cognitive functions or, conversely, to their diminution. Accordingly, there are questions of the correlation of morality and intellectual potential.

The possibility of neurotechnological intervention into teaching, legal proceedings, criminology, and other fields must also be taken into account when neurotechnological algorithms will be used to identify individual citizens, and then entire groups, as socially undesirable. Neurotechnologies that enhance cognitive abilities, if they are energy-consuming and expensive, on the contrary, can lead to the creation of a "higher stratum" of human society, simply put, to a "higher race" of superhumans. In our opinion, without recourse to theology it is impossible to understand the proper role of neuroscience. The tools of philosophy are in this case insufficient.

Today, neuroscience comes at the intersection of cognitive sciences, chemistry, computer science, engineering, linguistics, medicine, physics, philosophy, and psychology. The list of neurosciences is continuously increasing: neuropsychology, neuropsychotherapy, neuropedagogy, neuromarketing, neuroeconomics, neurosociology, cognitive neuroscience, neurotheology, neuropolitics, neurobiotics, neurolinguistics, military neuroscience, etc. Attach the prefix "neuro-" to any scientific term and get a new scientific field. Methodologically speaking, the development of neuroscience is distinct from the development of neurotechnology. Neurotechnologies convey a mechanism of direct action while neuroscience poses as the comprehension and generalization of neurotechnological contributions. The fundamental inability of neuroscience to independently approach the solution of the "mysteries" of the brain and consciousness seems obvious.

Thus, success, if not guaranteed, is likely with an interdisciplinary approach that combines the efforts of scientists, philosophers, bioethicists, and theologians. The peak of the development of the organized matter of the universe is the apex of the evolution of organic matter in the form of the human brain, a thinking substance capable of reflecting the surrounding world in all its manifestations. Most intriguing is the very possibility of the transition of the "ideal" (the world of the imagination) and the "non-existent" into the material, into existence, into being, into objects of material culture. Therefore, the attempt on the part of the global scientific community to penetrate the secrets of the universe, which include the principles and mechanisms of the human central nervous system, is natural. And here it would be appropriate to consider the concept of "neurotheology."

Are There Philosophical and Physical Grounds for Such a Term as "Neurotheology"?

The term was introduced into scientific circulation in 1984 in James Ashbrook's article "Neurotheology: The Working Brain and the Work of Theology." Ashbrook allocated the research fields that would serve to unite neuroscience and theology. In the 1980s, there were attempts (primarily by Charles Laughlin and Eugene d'Aquili) to investigate the neuropsychological determinants of ritual behavior. They pointed to the connection of neurobiological substrates of brain structures with religious practice and experience and suggested the possibility of studying theology from a biological point of view (Vinnik 2015; Malevich 2012).

Researchers who resort to the term "neurotheology," regardless of the goals of scientific research, produce an epistemological and ontological narrowing of the problems of relations between these fields. Let us take the liberty to assert that the term "neurotheology" is itself speculative and useful only because it serves to introduce the concept of theology into the neuroscience vocabulary. Why is theology necessary to understand the essence of neuroscience?

For centuries, materialism has dominated science. All concepts that question the materialist approach to explaining the essence of the phenomena around us, both in the natural sciences and in the humanities, are immediately rejected by the scientific community. The broadly accepted scientific ideas that do not have satisfactory materialistic explanations are accepted on the grounds that such explanations will appear later. Karl Popper and John Eccles. Eccles called this kind of argument *hopeful materialism* (Popper and Eccles 1984; Whitfield 2003). Do all events, however, have a material cause? The answer to this question today is delegated to quantum physics.

Neuroethics, Quantum Physics, and Theology

The main difficulty encountered by neuroscience in the attempt to explain the nature of human consciousness is the problem of subjectivity and the intentionality of the psyche. Indeed, unlike objectively existing "bodies" consciousness is subjective, we *experience* it. And it is absolutely incomprehensible how subjectivity, as such, can appear in the objective world. David Chalmers, the most famous modern philosopher dealing with the problem of consciousness, formulates the main question as follows: how is it that objective processes in the brain do not "go into the dark," but are "accompanied" by subjective experience? If the brain can process incoming information and transform it into actions without any subjective experiences, then why do we need subjectivity at all? (Chalmers 1996). In addition, the mental, unlike the physical, is always *directed* at something, *intentionally*. If there *are* just physical bodies, then consciousness is always *about something*: I think about something, worry about something, get disturbed at something. But if the brain and neurons are the physical *bodies* like any other object in the material world, and obey the "objectively existing" laws of nature, then it is completely incomprehensible how they can generate the subjectivity and intentionality inherent in the human psyche? "If the brain is just atoms and emptiness," asks John Searle, one of the most influential modern American philosophers, "then how can it be *about anything*?" (Searle 1984, 16).

Gradually, the academic community is coming to the realization of the fact that an effective solution to the problem of consciousness is impossible without the involvement of theological discourse, implying the presence of a personal view of psychic reality "from within." In 2017, the *Mindscience of Reality* symposium was held in Pisa, Italy. This was the first of a series of planned events aimed at launching the term *Mindscience* as an alternative to the term *Neuroscience*. The researchers who took part in the conference expressed the belief that the holistic study of *mind* and *consciousness* should combine the "third-person" approach, typical of Western sciences, and the so-called "first-person" approach, "from within," characteristic of the religious tradition. In order to initiate such a dialogue, the symposium organizers invited the Dalai Lama to take part (Mindscience of Reality n.d.).

The reasons for the scientists' appeal to the mystical tradition of the East are clear: the impersonal Buddhist approach, it seems, is a better fit with the objectivism of European science. However, it is the impersonality of the Buddhist tradition that inevitably becomes an obstacle to understanding the personal nature of the human psyche.

In our opinion, the origins of the customary separation of natural science and theology—today taken for granted—lie in the medieval doctrine of "dual truth" that encompasses faith based on divine revelation and knowledge acquired through "natural reason." From this doctrine, the division of knowledge into the *sciences of nature* and the *sciences of the spirit* later solidified. If the sciences of nature investigate the vital *circumstances* of human existence, then the sciences of the spirit try to comprehend its *meaning* and *purpose*. At the same time, of course, it is implied that a holistic vision of reality is possible only in the harmonious conjunction of both discourses.

The dichotomy of the natural sciences and the spiritual sciences is associated with the distinction between two approaches: "explaining" (predicting) and "understanding," they are also designated as "causal" and "teleological." At the same time, if "explanation" as a rule involves bringing a specific phenomenon under a known general pattern, or involves a clarification of its causal conditionality, then "understanding" is related to the need to "decipher" an initially opaque meaning and is conditioned by the possibility of a human consciousness to "penetrate" another consciousness through external forms of expression. Gradually, the explanatory discourse that characterized the natural sciences came to the fore as all but the only standard of scientific knowledge. However, we should not forget that only a teleological, *comprehending*, view allows us to see an harmoniously arranged *order* obeying unchangeable *laws* through the apparent chaos of the universe.

Belief in the existence of such universal laws is akin to religious faith. Einstein called it "cosmic religion," or "cosmic religious feeling."

As is well known today, modern science appeared in the context of the biblical tradition as an "explanatory," "causal" way of studying the second Book of the Creator—the Book of Nature. This was a complement to the First Book, the Bible, divine revelation (note that the concept of "two Books" has become a kind of refraction of the doctrine of "dual truth"). It was taken that God gives revelation in two forms: the first is the Bible, the second is the Book of Nature. There is and cannot be a contradiction between these two Books, since they were written by one and the same Author. Understanding the world as God's second Book had important consequences. Since the world is a text similar to the Bible, the same research methods can be applied to it as to the Bible. Semiotics can approach signs syntagmatically, in their relationship with other signs, semantically, in their relation to the denoted object, or pragmatically, in relation to the message's creator or addressee. With a certain degree of conventionality, we can say that early Christian theology was primarily occupied with the study of the pragmatics of the Book of Nature. It was realized that the world is a text of the Creator addressed to man. Medieval theology, which investigated the symbolism of the universe, studied the semantics of its various "elements." The pathos of the scientific revolution of the seventeenth century was that, from the study of the semantics and pragmatics of the universe, the new science turned its gaze to the study of the syntagmatics of the Book of Nature, to the description of its "syntax," the structure of the universe (Kopeikin 2014, 16–22).

Indeed, Modern physics creates a model of the world by introducing *quantities* that make it possible to juxtapose mathematical objects that do not exist in nature, i.e., *numbers*, with elements of the real physical world. Such a juxtaposition is carried out during the implementation of the *measurement* procedure, the study of the relationship of one element of physical reality to another. In this manner science as an objectifying practice does not describe the world "in itself," but only *projections* of various elements of the universe in instruments of measurement. The resulting physical theories turn out to be *theories of relations* and this is, in fact, the "syntax" of the Book of Nature. Due to this "relativity," mathematical (structural) theories of the physical world are open to meaningful *interpretation*. The problem of interpretation, strictly speaking, goes beyond physics and implies the possibility of further deepening of physical theory into philosophy, metaphysics and hermeneutics.

In classical physics, the interpretation that seemed self-evident was the materialistic one. And, until the beginning of the twentieth century, the materialistic interpretation of physics received ample justification. But after the emergence of the theory of relativity and, especially, quantum mechanics, the situation radically changed. In classical physics, the concepts of mass, distance, time, and force seemed intuitively comprehensible. Meanwhile, in quantum mechanics, the mathematical representation of reality is a wave function, or the state vector. We have learned to predict the probabilities of possible experiments, but we have yet to understand which physical reality corresponds to the mathematical construct we use—the state vector (Carroll 2019).

It turned out that at the deep, fundamental, quantum-mechanical microlevel, physical reality behaves not at all like dead inert "matter," but rather like an informational, almost quasi-psychical reality. Even the so-called *measurement problem* supports such an assertion. Quantum mechanics demands that the behavior of quantum objects be differently described when they are subject to observation then when they are not. As it turned out, the state vector, which is a mathematical representative of a quantum mechanical system, can change in two ways: over time, the state vector of the system when unobserved changes, continuously obeying the deterministic equation of evolution, as a result of measurement. When measured, it leaps ahead according to the law of probability. There is an impression that the observer seems to "influence" the system under study by the very act of questioning—and the system seems to "understand" this and "respond" to the observer.

Furthermore, it was found that, at the fundamental quantum mechanical level, physical reality has the following amazing properties

1. *Reality is* indeterministic in the sense that we cannot unambiguously predict the results of measuring a quantum mechanical system, we can only estimate the probabilities of one outcome or another. And this is not because we do not know any "hidden parameters" inherent in reality at some fundamental level, but because reality seems to "answer" our inquiry. In the answer itself there is an element of *will*, an element of freedom. In 2004, mathematicians Simon Kochen and John Conway demonstrated a *theorem of free will* (Conway and Kochen 2006; 2009). It says that if experimental physicists really have free will, i.e., their choice of what they will measure is not determined by the previous history of the universe, then the result of the measurement performed on a quantum mechanical system will also not be determined by the previous history of the universe, i.e., it will be absolutely unpredictable. Conway argues that this result is a clear evidence in favor of the fact that there are glimpses of life and freedom in every element of the universe (Thomas 2011).

2. *Reality is contextual* in the sense that some of the parameters attributed to it do not exist "objectively," "by themselves," but acquire certain values depending on the experimental context. For instance, this may include the sequence of operations and the types of measurements made, just as in psychology. In 1967, Simon Kochen and Ernst Specker proved *the quantum contextuality theorem*, the essence of which boils down to the following: the state of a quantum system can neither be described deterministically nor independently of the experimental setup (Kochen and Specker 1967).

3. *Reality is non*-local in the sense that two systems connected by a common past remain connected further, and this connection is not transmitted by any material carrier, but is carried out "directly" at any distance (Bell 2004).

Of course, such strange properties of quantum mechanical reality contradict our intuition about how the *material* world should be arranged, but they have all been experimentally tested and confirmed on numerous occasions. Currently, quantum mechanics is the most accurate physical theory working in the entire field available for experimental verification.

So, since modern theoretical physics emerged as a way to study the syntax of the Book of Nature as the second Book of God complementary to the Bible, then searching for the semantic significance of the fundamental structures of the universe would logically demand that we turn to the biblical semantic context. The interpretation of the syntax of the Second Book, the Book of Nature, described in the language of mathematics is a hermeneutical task and, therefore, a traditionally theological one. In a holistic picture of the world, which includes not only matter subject to causal laws, but also consciousness operating with *meanings* and setting itself various *goals*, causal and teleological approaches should be organically linked to one another.

An important step towards such an organic connection of explanatory, causal, on the one hand, and, on the other, comprehending, teleological discourses was made by one of the founders of quantum mechanics, Nobel Prize winner Wolfgang Pauli together with the founder of analytical psychology Carl Gustav Jung. Pauli, one of the greatest physicists of the twentieth century, was a rationalist and intellectual of the highest order, maintaining that there was no existence of anything other than matter that obeyed causal laws. Jung, on the contrary, was a pure humanitarian. He tried to comprehend the deep purposefulness of the soul, while paying special attention to the psychological study of the Bible, as in, for example, his work *The Answer to Job* (1952). At the age of about thirty, Pauli experienced a serious existential crisis, the external reasons for which were the suicide of his mother, an unsuccessful marriage that ended in divorce less than a year after the wedding, and professional problems associated with the collapse of the former, classical scientific picture of the world. Pauli even considered whether he should continue studying physics, and took up writing a utopian novel *Gulliver's Journey to Urania*. But most importantly, Pauli began to be tormented by vivid archetypal dreams, as if trying to tell him something that his "daytime" rational consciousness refused to accept. In the end, Pauli turned to Jung for help. The experience of the unconscious, which "presented" itself to Pauli in dreams, forced him to move away from the idea formed in his childhood that everything in life can be explained with the help of reason alone (Kopeikin 2016).

Trying to understand how to approach a holistic worldview, Pauli turned to Kepler's scientific work. Kepler lived at a time when the *Weltanschauung* was not yet divided between the religious and the scientific. According to Pauli, Kepler was a key figure, his ideas mark an important intermediate stage between the former magico-symbolic and modern quantitative-mathematical description of nature. Pauli presented the results of his research in the work *The Influence of Archetypal Ideas on the Formation of Kepler's Theories of Natural Science* (Pauli 1952). When writing it, he was not only inspired by Jung's ideas, but also used the advice of his closest colleague and assistant, Dr. Maria-Louise von Franz (who helped Pauli with translations of Kepler's Latin texts). He also turned to the works of Kepler's opponent, a prominent representative of the hermetic tradition, Robert Fludd, whose philosophical views were influenced by Renaissance magic and Kabbalah. As described by the English researcher of the history of ideas, Frances Yates, Fludd belonged to the same hermetic Kabbalistic tradition that shaped the work of Marsilio Ficino and Pico della Mirandola. He knew the *Corpus Hermeticum* perfectly, which he had read in Ficino's translation, and *Asclepius*, and it would hardly be an exaggeration to say that quotations from the works of Hermes Trismegistus can be found on almost every page of his work (Yates 1964).

If Kepler believed that the task of science was to discover objective, mathematically describable *explanations* (although the choice of these *explanations* was largely predetermined by Kepler's original unconscious religious attitudes), then Fludd insisted on the need to achieve an *understanding* of symbolic correspondences between the phenomena of the external world and the processes taking place in our inner psychic reality. In the treatise *The History of the Macrocosm and the Microcosm* (1617), Fludd symbolically depicted the universe in the form of a Pythagorean "monochord of the world," the upper end of the string of which originates in the divine Trinity, the lower one is fixed on Earth, the Sun is in the middle, and the various levels correspond to spiritual hierarchies, planets and the four elements. With the help of a system of symbolic analogies between the internal micro- and external macrocosm, Fludd tried to comprehend the innermost meaning of the Book of Nature. Kepler, on the contrary, considered the proper sphere of objective science to be only the discovery of the *structures* of the Book of Nature—that which can be quantified and proved mathematically—everything else was to be attributed to the sphere of the subjective.

Pauli associated the difference in the views of Kepler and Fludd with the division of thinkers into two classes: some consider quantitative relations between *parts essential*, others, on the contrary, the qualitative indivisibility of the *whole*. As a result of his research, Pauli came to the conclusion that a complete understanding can be achieved only by combining both of these discourses. If Kepler's point of view prevailed in the seventeenth century, then today, striving to create a holistic picture of the world, we must also take into account Fludd's views, which also contain an element of truth. Kepler's objectifying "explanatory" approach must be supplemented by an "understanding" interpretation in the spirit of Fludd. It is the organic combination of two complementary types of discourse—Kepler's causal and Fludd's teleological—that, according to Pauli, is able to solve one of the central problems of European intellectual history (*Geistesgeschichte*)—the problem of the interaction of spirit (*Geist*) and matter (*Materie*) (Kopeikin 2009).

In their joint research, Pauli and Jung paid special attention to strange, inexplicable semantic coincidences of various "objective" events within the framework of the traditional causal scientific paradigm, the presence of which cannot be explained by cause-and-effect relationships; Jung called such events *synchronistic*. Almost all of us have encountered such strange synchronistic coincidences in our lives, as if connected with the inexplicable influence of the states of our inner world on the events of the external world: we think about some person and suddenly meet them on the street or they call on the telephone; we are tormented by some question and suddenly get an answer on the radio or through a television broadcast. Many people encounter similar cases, but most often do not attach importance to them, considering them accidental coincidences. A serious scientific examination of them is confronted by great difficulties. Synchronistic coincidences indicate that not only at the microscopic, but even at the macroscopic level, physical reality can behave like an informational, quasi-psychic reality. If this is true, this means that we can interact with the world not only "from the outside," exerting an "external," forceful influence on it, but also "from the inside": by changing the state of our soul, we are able to "attract" certain life situations to ourselves. Pauli, with all his hypercriticism (colleagues even called him *Die Geissel Gottes*—"The Scourge of God") believed this. Synchronistic coincidences of this kind had haunted him his entire life. Almost all physicists who knew about the so-called "Pauli effect"—a series of inexplicable accidents that surrounded the scientist—recognized its reality. But they were unable to explain the nature of what was happening and so preferred to interpret it only as a chain of odd, amusing coincidences. For his own part, Pauli was absolutely convinced that behind all the synchronistic events taking place in his life there was some deep connection that remained incomprehensible to science.

As a result of many years of searching for a holistic vision of reality, Pauli and Jung came to the conclusion that the physical and mental are not two different "substances," as is commonly believed after Descartes, but rather two mutually complementary ways of manifestation (two "aspects") of a single underlying reality of the whole world. Supporters of this point of view, called "neutral monism" or "two-dimensional ontology," were, in particular, such famous thinkers as Benedict Spinoza, William James, Bertrand Russell and, today, John Searle and David Chalmers.

Unfortunately, Pauli's early death prevented the successful implementation of the research he and Jung had begun. However, the synchronistic coincidences they study indicate that, even at the macroscopic level, physical reality can behave like an informational, quasi-psychic reality. This leads to an extremely important practical conclusion, significant for everyone: the relativity of being means that changing one's state "relative to the Creator" and (re)ordering it (first of all through prayer that has its own special "verbal power"), we can change both our own way of being and the way of being of the reality around us. In the Orthodox tradition, this has found its embodiment in the well-known saying of the St. Seraphim of Sarov: "Save yourself and a thousand around you will be saved." Yes, perhaps these changes are almost imperceptible—but they are happening; today we are only at the very beginning of the journey. The smallness of the changes we are making is due to the fact that so far only a small number of people are really working on cultivating their own souls. Each of us, as John Donne said, is part of a huge Continent—Humanity. If quantum physics is read in an organic, semantic, biblical, theological context, one can realize oneself as a part of the Whole and feel one's responsibility for mankind and the whole Earth. Such is an important ethical conclusion that we are able to reach today.

Conclusion

Thus, neuroethics, the main object of which is neurotechnology, urgently demands engagement with theological discourse. It is particularly worth emphasizing that neurotechnologies have exceptionally weak ontological foundations since they reduce any examination of consciousness to the study of the material substrate of the human brain and the processes occurring within it. The risks that arise in this case are ethical in nature, the term "neuroethics" itself has an applied element, just as does "neurotheology." The problem of studying consciousness is inextricably linked with modern theories of quantum physics and demands a paradigm shift in the course of scientific research. Without defining such a paradigm, neurotechnologies can turn into an unregulated tool for manipulating humanity. In this regard, we emphasize once again what we have already stated: the generally recognized regulatory function of secular neuroethics must involve a religious expert assessment. This would be applied to scientific initiatives that might carry potential risks to human nature, even if those who represent this scientific knowledge are themselves not believers.

Bibliography

Adolescent Brain Cognitive Development (ABCD). N.d. "About the Study." https://abcdstudy.org/about.html.
Agarwal, Niveditaet, et al. 2010. "Update on the Use of MR for Assessment and Diagnosis of Psychiatric Diseases." *Radiology* 255(1): 23–41.
ASSC. 2021. "The 24th Meeting of the Association for the Scientific Study of Consciousness." https://theassc.org/wp-content/uploads/2021/08/PROGRAM.pdf.
Bartels, Andreas, and Semir Zeki. 2004. "The Neural Correlates of Maternal and Romantic Love." *Neuroimage* 21(3): 1155–66.
Bell, Emily, et al. 2014. "Beyond Consent in Research: Revisiting Vulnerability in Deep Brain Stimulation for Psychiatric Disorders." *Cambridge Quarterly Healthcare Ethics* 23(3): 361–68.
Bell, John. 2004. *Speakable and Unspeakable in Quantum Mechanics*. Cambridge: Cambridge University Press.
Bell, Stephanie, et al. 2012. "Lessons for Enhancement from the History of Cocaine and Amphetamine Use." *AJOB Neuroscience* 3(2): 24–29.
Benabid, Alim Louis. 2007. "What the Future Holds for Deep Brain Stimulation." *Expert Revue of Medical Devices* 4(6): 895–903.
Block, Ned, et al. 2014. "Consciousness Science: Real Progress and Lingering Misconceptions." *Trends in Cognitive Sciences* 18(11): 556–57.
BRAIN Initiative. N.d. "Neuroethics Working Group." https://braininitiative.nih.gov/about/neuroethics-working-group.
Carroll, Sean. 2019. "Even Physicists Don't Understand Quantum Mechanics: Worse, They Don't Seem to Want to Understand It." *New York Times*, September 7.
Chalmers, David. 1996. *The Conscious Mind: In Search of a Fundamental Theory*. Oxford: Oxford University Press.
Chen, Chao, et al. 2018. "The Transcription Factor POU3F2 Regulates a Gene Coexpression Network in Brain Tissue from Patients with Psychiatric Disorders." *Science Translational Medicine* 10(472): eaat8178. DOI:10.1126/Scitranslmed.Aat8178.
Conway, John H., and Simon Kochen. 2006. "The Free Will Theorem." *Foundations of Physics* 36(10): 1441–73. https://arxiv.org/pdf/quant-ph/0604079.pdf.
Conway, John H., and Simon Kochen. 2009. "The Strong Free Will Theorem." *Notices of the American Mathematical Society* 56(2): 226–32.
DARPA. N.d. "DARPA and the Brain Initiative." https://www.darpa.mil/Program/Our-Research/Darpa-And-The-Brain-Initiative.

Dehaene, Stanislas, et al. 2017. "What Is Consciousness, and Could Machines Have It?" *Science* 358(6362): 486–92.
Dubljević, Veljko, et al. 2014. "The Rising Tide of Transcranial Direct Current Stimulation (Tdcs) in the Media and Academic Literature." *Neuron* 82: 731–36.
Emmons, Scott. 2019. "Editorial." *Nature* 571 (7763): S2–S19. https://www.nature.com/nature/volumes/571/issues/7763.
Fludd, Robert. 1617. *Utriusque Cosmi Maioris Scilicet Et Minoris Metaphysica, Physica Atque Technica Historia: In Duo Volumina Secundum Cosmi Differentiam Divisa.* Vol. 1. Openhemii: Aere Iohan-Theodori De Bry, Typis Hieronymi Galleri. https://archive.org/details/utriusquecosmimao1flud.
———. 1617. *Utriusque Cosmi Maioris Scilicet Et Minoris Metaphysica, Physica Atque Technica Historia: In Duo Volumina Secundum Cosmi Differentiam Divisa.* Vol. 2. Openhemii: Aere Iohan-Theodori De Bry, Typis Hieronymi Galleri. https://archive.org/details/utriusquecosmimao2flud.
Forlini, Cynthia, and Eric Racine. 2009. "Disagreements with Implications: Diverging Discourses on the Ethics of Non-medical Use of Methylphenidate for Performance Enhancement." *BMC Medical Ethics* 10(9): DOI: 10.1186/1472-6939-10-9.
Garland, Brent. 2004. *Neuroscience and the Law: Brain, Mind, and the Scales of Justice.* Washington, DC: American Association for the Advancement of Science.
Ghosh, Sudip. 2008. "Functional MRI: A Radiological Window into the Mind: Part 1." *Brain Blogger*, March 19. https://brainblogger.com/2008/03/19/functional-mri-a-radiological-window-into-the-mind-part-1/.
Giordano, James. 2015. "A Preparatory Neuroethical Approach to Assessing Developments in Neurotechnology." *Virtual Mentor* 17(1): 56–61.
Greene, Joshua D., et al. 2001. "An Fmri Investigation of Emotional Engagement in Moral Judgment." *Science* 293(5537): 2105–8.
Grillner, Sten, et al. 2016. "Worldwide Initiatives to Advance Brain Research." *Nature Neuroscience* 19(9): 1118–22.
Hall, Wayne D. 2004. "Feeling Better Than Well." *EMBO Reports* 5(12): 1105–9.
Holtzheimer, Paul E., et al. 2012. "Subcallosal Cingulate Deep Brain Stimulation for Treatment-Resistant Unipolar and Bipolar Depression." *Archives of General Psychiatry* 69(2): 150–58.
Illes, Judy. 2003. "Neuroethics in a New Era of Neuroimaging." *American Journal of Neuroradiology* 24(9): 1739–41.
Illes, Judy, and Eric Racine. 2005. "Imaging or Imagining? A Neuroethics Challenge Informed by Genetics." *American Journal of Bioethics* 5(2): 5–18.
Illes, Judy, et al. 2006. "A Picture Is Worth a Thousand Words, but Which One Thousand?" In *Neuroethics: Defining the Issues in Research, Practice, and Policy,* edited By Judy Illes, 149–68. Oxford: Oxford University Press.
Jorgenson, Lyric A., et al. 2015. "The BRAIN Initiative: Developing Technology to Catalyze Neuroscience Discovery." *Philosophical Transactions of the Royal Society B: Biological Sciences* 370(1668): DOI: 10.1098/Rstb.2014.0164.
Kaplish, Lalita. 2016. "Crick on Consciousness." *Welcome Library*, September 14. https://wayback.archive-it.org/16107/20210312182608/http://blog.wellcomelibrary.org/2016/09/crick-on-consciousness/.
Kent, Adrian. 2018. "Quanta and Qualia." *Foundations of Physics* 48(9): 1021–37.
Kochen, Simon, and Ernst Specker. 1967. "The Problem of Hidden Variables in Quantum Mechanics." *Journal of Mathematics and Mechanics* 17(1): 59–87.

Kopeikin, Kirill V. 2009. "The Abyss of the Soul and the Abyss of Creation." *Voprosy Filosofii* 7: 107–14.

———. 2014. *What Is Reality: Reflection on the Work of Erwin Schroedinger.* St. Petersburg: St. Petersburg State University Press.

———. 2016. "In the Footsteps of Jung and Pauli in the Search for the Contact between the Physical and Psychical Worlds" In *Known and Unknown Discoveries of the 20th Century*, edited By Tatiana S. Iur'evaya, 85–97. St. Petersburg: St. Petersburg State University Press.

Laxton, Adrian W., et al. 2010. "A Phase I Trial of Deep Brain Stimulation of Memory Circuits in Alzheimer's Disease." *Annals of Neurology* 68(4): 521–34.

Levy, Neil. 2014. *Consciousness and Moral Responsibility.* Oxford: Oxford University Press.

Library of Congress. N.d. "Fascintating Facts." https://www.loc.gov/about/fascinating-facts/.

Malevich, Tatiana V. 2012. "Neurotheology: The Theory of Religion and Brain Science." *Religious Studies* 1–2: 62–83.

Marcus S. J., ed. 2002. *Neuroethics: Mapping the Field.* New York: Dana.

Mcginn, Colin. 1989. "Can We Solve the Mind-Body Problem?" *Mind* 98(391): 349–66.

Meltzoff, Andrew N., et al. 2009. "Foundations for a New Science of Learning." *Science* 325(5938): 284–88.

Meng, Qingtuan, et al. 2018. "The DGCR5 Long Noncoding RNA May Regulate Expression of Several Schizophrenia-Related Genes." *Science Translational Medicine* 10(472): eaat6912. DOI:10.1126/Scitranslmed.Aat6912.

Mindscience of Reality. N.d. "1st Symposium / The Mindscience of Reality." http://mindscience.webhost1.unipi.it/en/homepage/.

Moll, Jorge, et al. 2002. "The Neural Correlates of Moral Sensitivity: A Functional Magnetic Resonance Imaging Investigation of Basic and Moral Emotions." *Journal of Neuroscience* 22(7): 2730–36.

National Institutes of Health. N.d. "NIH Releases First Dataset from Unprecedented Study of Adolescent Brain Development." https://www.nih.gov/News-Events/News-Releases/Nih-Releases-First-Dataset-Unprecedented-Study-Adolescent-Brain-Development.

Owen, Adrian M., et al. 2006. "Detecting Awareness in the Vegetative State." *Science* 313(5792): 1402.

Paller, Ken A., and Satoru Suzuki. 2014. "The Source of Consciousness." *Trends in Cognitive Sciences* 18(8): 387–89.

Pauli, Wolfgang. 1952. "Der Einfluss Archetypischer Vorstellungen Auf Die Bildung Naturwissenschaftlicher Theorien Bei Kepler." In *Natureklärung und Psyche*, 109–94. Studien Aus Dem C. G. Jung-Institut. 4. Kascher: Zurich.

Pew Research Center. 2016. "Appendix A: Additional Demographic Tables and Charts." *Pew Research Center*, September 1. https://www.pewresearch.org/Internet/2016/09/01/Book-Reading-2016-Appendix-A/.

Plassmann, Hilke, et al. 2007. "Orbitofrontal Cortex Encodes Willingness to Pay in Everyday Economic Transactions." *Journal of Neuroscience* 27(37): 9984–88.

Popper, Karl R., and John C. Eccles. 1984. *The Self and Its Brain.* Oxford: Routledge.

Porzio, Umberto di. 2016. "The Brain from Within." *Frontiers in Human Neuroscience* 10: 265. DOI: 10.3389/Fnhum.2016.00265.

Psychencode Consortium. 2018. "Revealing the Brain's Molecular Architecture." *Science* 362(6420): 1262–63. https://www.science.org/doi/10.1126/science.362.6420.1262.

Rabadán, Alejandra T. 2015. "Neuroethics Scope at a Glance." *Surgical Neurology International* 6(1): 183.

Racine, Eric, and Cynthia Forlini. 2010. "Cognitive Enhancement, Lifestyle Choice, or Misuse of Prescription Drugs? Ethics Blind Spots in Current Debates." *Neuroethics* 3(1): 1–4.

Racine, Eric, et al. 2010. "Can We Read Minds?" In *Scientific and Philosophical Perspectives in Neuroethics*, edited by James J. Giordano and Bert Gordijn, 244–70. Cambridge: Cambridge University Press.

Radin, Dean. 1997. *The Conscious Universe: The Scientific Truth of Psychic Phenomena*. San Francisco: Harper.

Raeburn, Paul. 2005. "MRI: A Window on the Brain." *MIT Technology Review*, December 1. https://www.technologyreview.com/2005/12/01/229970/mri-a-window-on-the-brain/.

Rhie, Suhn K., et al. 2018. "Using 3D Epigenomic Maps of Primary Olfactory Neuronal Cells from Living Individuals to Understand Gene Regulation." *Science Advances* 4(12): eaav8550. DOI: 10.1126/Sciadv.Aav8550.

Rose, Nikolas. 2014. "The Human Brain Project: Social and Ethical Challenges." *Neuron* 82(6): 1212–15.

Roskies, Adina L. 2002. "Neuroethics For the New Millenium." *Neuron* 35 (1) 21–23.

Safire, William. 2002. "Introduction: Visions for a New Field of 'Neuroethics.'" In *Neuroethics: Mapping the Field*, edited by Steven J. Marcus, 3–9. New York: Dana.

Sahakian, Barbara J., et al. 2015. "The Impact of Neuroscience on Society: Cognitive Enhancement in Neuropsychiatric Disorders and in Healthy People." *Philosophical Transactions of the Royal Society B: Biological Sciences* 370(1677): 20140214. DOI: 10.1098/Rstb.2014.0214.

Searle, John R. 1984. *Mind, Brains, and Science*. Cambridge: Harvard University Press.

———. 1990. *The Mystery of Consciousness*. London: Granta.

Sententia, Wrye. 2004. "Neuroethical Considerations: Cognitive Liberty and Converging Technologies for Improving Human Cognition." *Annals of New York Academy of Science* 1013: 221–28.

Seth, Anil. 2017. "Your Brain Hallucinates Your Conscious Reality." *TED*. https://www.ted.com/talks/anil_seth_your_brain_hallucinates_your_conscious_reality?autoplay=true&muted=true.

Thomas, Rachel. 2011. "John Conway—Discovering Free Will (Part III)." *Plus Magazine*, December 27. https://plus.maths.org/content/john-conway-discovering-free-will-part-iii.

Vinnik, Dmitriy. 2015. "Religious Experience as an Object of Psycho-Physical Investigation." *Philosophy of Science* 1: 58–77.

Wang, Daifeng, et al. 2018. "Comprehensive Functional Genomic Resource and Integrative Model for the Human Brain." *Science* 362(6420): eaat8464. DOI: 10.1126/Science.Aat8464.

Whitfield, William. 2003. "Towards a Neurotheology?" *International Journal of Psychiatric Nursing Research* 8(3): 941.

Yates, Francis. 1964. *Giordano Bruno and the Hermetic Tradition*. Chicago: University of Chicago Press.

Zhu, Fei, et al. 2018. "Architecture of the Mouse Brain Synaptome." *Neuron* 99(4): 781–99.

9

Seed and Law
Neuroscience and Virtue Ethics in Christian Anthropology

WALKER TRIMBLE

General Introduction

WHEN THE PSALMIST EXCLAIMS to God the wonders of the heavens, he turns and asks "What is man that you are mindful of him, the Son of Man that You care for Him?" (Ps 8:4). In the vastness of the created universe, why have You turned, and why should You turn Your heart to us? The parallelism in the verse would lead us to expand upon this exclamation, or propose it as an answer. We may read the Father's mindfulness in the incarnation of the Son, the God-man whose care is the salvation of the world.

The question "what is man" is conceived these days quite differently. The human is a bundle of cells, a set of chemical reactions. When we turn to the mind, we are told "you are your brain," "the mind is what the brain does." The human is a competing set of chiefdoms—the interest of the digestive system against that of the immune system, the circulatory system matched against the nervous system, the "selfish gene." The "eloquent" parts of the brain may sometimes succeed in overreaching the baser instinctual parts and sometimes may fail.

Historically the relationship between different parts of the mind and soul, and the different types of knowledge which populate them, has been a major source of speculation and difficulty. At the risk of giving too general an account of a complex history, we shall say that the opposition between the "rational" and "irrational" is often paired with an opposition between the "practical" and "theoretical," the body and the soul. The Aristotelian vegetative and animal souls are contrasted with the rational. "Ethos" is contrasted with "ethics." As Gilbert Ryle formulated an observation already present in Plato's *Theaetaetus* "knowing how" is contrasted with "knowing what" (Ryle 2009, ch. 2). Against this have been set streams of thought which emphasize the unity of action on the part of a moral being. The first divides forms of knowledge and behavior on the basis of observation, the second examines how they must all be gathered together to thrust toward coherent action. The second position is always challenged by arguments that show how inconsistencies in action give the lie to the integrity of that "gathered together." The first is always confronted by the difficulties of determining the boundaries between these parts and in showing how they do come together when they do.

The subject of Orthodox theology as a therapeutic discipline has been covered in a number of places to good theoretical and practical value (Weber 2003; Trader 2012; Hierotheos 2000), especially when it includes the profound psychology of our ascetic tradition. However the science that has emerged over the last twenty years—the so-called age of the brain—has a different practical and theological significance because it claims to have defined what it means for humans to do and to think at the most fundamental levels. We know the physical mechanisms behind what we do better now than we ever have. The picture that has emerged is one of a vast population of behaviors spreading in a universe of directions. But rather than conceiving of this complexity as a concert of activities all leading to a spiritual and biological goal, we conceive of it as a cacophony of competing functions. Science no longer has the methods or conceptual foundations that would allow it to arrive at an understanding of a coherent self.[1] As cultural critique of the Modern has argued, the picture of reality we have created no longer has a place for us.

While it is common to portray this as the result of advancements in technology and the accumulation of knowledge, in fact we will show that medicine and anatomy up to the sixteenth century had a clear

---

1. This is also the argument of Knight 2018.

understanding of a relationship between brain function and behavior without necessarily adopting the position that there must be no place for the self. Our fragmented conception of the person comes as much from our ideology: utilitarian notions of the "function" we have in society, Darwinian notions of our "function" with respect to the species. These rob us of our primary function: to realize ourselves as the children of God and the primary mediators of his creation.

Some of the most important discoveries in brain science have to do with the fundamentals behind reason. Whereas it has been typical to associate the "animal" part of the brain with desire and contrast this with the "rational" part, it has famously been shown that those suffering from depression also suffer from impairments to their reasoning abilities. As Antonio Damasio has argued, we have been led to believe that reason is a cool calculator lodged in the upper recesses of the brain, but neuroscience has shown us that desire and motivation are inexorable parts of reasoned activity. For Damasio this means that Plato and Aristotle were wrong (Damasio 2008),[2] yet reason in the ancient world was no mere calculation, but that which was enabled through (and solely through) virtuous desire. Pace Damasio, reason is not the problem, nor desire, nor the forces which combine them, but how we have come to understand the contents of these categories and their relations.

Brain science and the study of consciousness have become among the most important objects of scientific investigation. Hundreds of thousands of publications engage theories of consciousness, biology, information, complexity, theoretical and applied mathematics, and even fundamental physics. Thus, to some extent, this topic must confront the theology of creation and natural theology in general. Orthodox theology has mostly taken a hostile view of this "rationalism" to the extent that it sets man-made laws above divine ones, deduction above revelation, as Paul Gavrilyuk has written (in Swinburne and Bradshaw 2021, x). Yet the science of the brain lies at the juncture between reason and experience. Our ascetic tradition, anthropology, and theories of creation have much to offer when viewed from these sources. But this requires a fundamentally different approach.

This paper will examine the extent to which brain science as now conceived operates on foundations that prevent a reasonable conception

---

2. Lorraine Daston discusses the historical movement from human reason to algorithmic rationality (Erickson et al. 2013). The importance of reason and the senses in patristic sources has been richly examined (Gavrilyuk and Coakley 2011).

of the human person as a living, flourishing agent in its own affairs and in the ways of the world. It will then propose new foundations for this science with the resources of the patristic tradition. To do this we will not make lists of who is naughty and nice with respect to Orthodox anthropology, nor will we show happy and unhappy juxtapositions. In the terms of natural theology, this is not an effort at "correlationism."[3] It is not "neurotheology" that subjects theology to neuroscience, or that uses neuroscience to analyze religious experiences (Whitfield 2003), but the reverse: we will see what the fruits of the science of the brain have to offer theology. Our method is as follows. After a historical survey of the problem, we will identify two false categories which are widely presupposed by both neuroscience and most contemporary Christian anthropology (Section 2). The first false category is the means by which mental content is "encoded" in the brain. This is falsely understood as a semiotic system that flows according to a discrete, but undefined, mechanism between a semiotically ordered world and a semiotically organized brain. The second false category is the source of the motivations that supposedly fill the content of this machinery. Desires are taken to be utilitarian instincts that are determined by Darwinian evolution. With a set of rules for operation and a set of motivations to set the rules in motion, nineteenth- and twentieth-century man would seem to be complete. Recognizing the vacuity of these categories, we will replace them with more empirically defensible and theologically cogent ones.

Indeed, our project is not merely negative. We have alternatives. We will show that one can determine a relationship between mental contents and their referents in the world not as they are encoded, but as they are *encoding* (Section 3). The active, intentioned means by which persons engage with the world is the best way by which to determine the causal relationship between the two. Thus it is not the passive following of rules but the active forming of patterns of behavior which determine complex

---

3. In natural theology, "correlationism" is the notion that scientific and theological facts are modally the same. Natural theology is then a matter of finding the right fit between facts. Some established physics is theologically good, other physics is bad and so we do not write about it. Under the scope of the modern, this position always sets theology under the aegis of scientific validity. If theology is to mean anything, it must maintain that all facts only have truth value so long as they are nourished by an ontology. And the basis of ontology is theology. See a summary of the problem in Smith 2005, 38. This does not mean that the results of correlationist theology are *ab initio* false but that they lack the proper method to isolate their validity.

mental activity. This is possibly the only way in which the biological embodies conscious content.

In the relationship between activity and desire, we will show the extent to which moral instincts are the result of long-established sets of patterns of activity. This is not because rules have been inserted from the world, or from the Ten Commandments, into the brain. This is because there is a demonstrable relation between what we think to do now and what we have been doing for a long period of time. Rules of behavior act primarily through a set of dispositions. This shows that neuroscience would advocate for a model of moral activity that starts with virtues rather than a semantically based system of encoded rules (Section 4).

Finally, we will show that the best explanation for why we have such an extraordinary organ as the brain aids in explaining the basis for our existence as ethical beings. Furthermore, our ethical nature can become the foundation of a metaphysical justification for our discrete existence as individual beings and as members of a species—just the problems which are plaguing the foundations of biological theory (Section 5). Since the application of Orthodox theology to neuroscience is as yet very uncharted ground, we will lightly touch upon such important themes as to how Eastern theology may approach the question of natural kinds and free will. These will require much further investigation set upon the foundations we hope to establish. I maintain that a "neurotheology" that does not seek to reestablish the theological foundations of science and the anthropological foundations of neuroscience will fail to make relevant contributions either to theology or to neuroscience.

From the perspective of cognitive science, the orientation of our work comes primarily from what is called Multi-E theories of cognition: enactive, ecological, environmental, ethological, etc., (Shapiro 2014) an increasingly important position (Linson et al. 2018). This view tends to take the perspective that the brain is an organ which is meant, first and foremost, to interact with and manipulate the world around it. At first blush this is the last theory one would expect to be amenable to theology. It grounds its perspective in evolution and presumes no inherent Logos to creation. Yet our point here is that the *logoi* cognitive science presumes are false ones that put the human-generated semiotic cart before the living, creaturely horse. We should not expect the brain to do anything else for the self but to help that self live and thrive, like any other organ. Multi-E theories of cognition return the brain to its organic nature as an instrument (ὄργανον) for the living organism. God did not create the body as a biological entity on the basis of some lack of forethought, like Plato's gods who "did as well as they could." Our biological life *means* something. Furthermore, science is never going to understand consciousness without arriving at theories that are compatible with the principles of biology, something that, as we shall see, it is loath to do.

Some might see this view as morally or pastorally problematic. Exaltation of the living body can lead to libertinism. To this we would employ the patristic tradition to show that morality is intimately connected with the body. Asceticism is constantly attentive to the body and its motions. Fasting and chastity do not reject the importance of the body but that necessitate it. Theology is not there to ignore the body, but to understand its place and lead it to higher things.

Yet more important to academic investigation, and to the pastoral care of those under the technocratic ideology that so dominates our public discourse, we argue that the current image of the body, mind, and brain is fundamentally damaging to *theological anthropology*. Our conception of how the brain and self come together relies on a historically-determined set of presuppositions. It then employs the authority of anatomy to make these presuppositions an inexorable part of our nature. For example, in a compelling and sensitive interview, Fr. (now Bishop) Alexis (Trader), a great authority on the relationship between the ascetic life and psychology, remarked on the effect of asking for God's help in dealing with our impulses:

> It's no longer me and my impulses, but it is my impulse and God with me. That automatically changes you. We all know that impulses come from the survival part of the brain, the center part of the brain. That's not where we connect with God. Once we connect with God, once we ask for His help, once we touch His garment, a change takes place, and we can dare to really believe. (Rossi 2019)

We could put his Grace's sense in different words: we must consciously call upon God for help with those parts of the self we sense we cannot control. This is inestimably good advice. However the use of anatomy suggests there is a part of us that has been, as it were, left to the dogs. This descends from a particular understanding of brain anatomy which puts reason only in the frontal cortex and emotion in the so-called "limbic system" (the "center part of the brain"). This view, like the so-called "Hard Problem of Consciousness" (Chalmers 2002), conceives of reason from an Enlightenment perspective. Calculating reason is the only type of reason which makes us conscious. We will argue here that patristic theology requires a view of reason more broad than conscious calculation, more broad than even subjectivity, and thus requires a view of neuroscience that allows *all* of the brain to connect with God. For what other reason would he have made it?

The penetration of the rational into the whole range of our behavior and experience has been considered with philosophical rigor since the development of phenomenology. When two people shake hands they are operating in a habitus that is culturally determined. One does not generally calculate before extending one's hand, or in saying "please" and "excuse me" when about one's daily business. Does that mean that the automaticity of such activity is irrational? Are the moral contents of these automatized activities thus null and void? It is certainly more reasonable to presume that rules and habits are in a constant give-and-take where a conscious decision to initiate or alter a course of behaviors eventually arises as a new set of habits which change the condition in which the reasoning mind can act. We may argue that neuroscience can teach us that ethics is founded upon ethos, but that ethos is the result of long established patterns of individual decisions. A concept of the brain that opposes a cortical watcher over and against a chemical beast is not going to accommodate a sense of give and take, or a notion of the interactions of neurochemicals, hormones, diet, immunity, and genetics—all the things we now know to be crucial to the brain's functioning.

This distinction is, in the end, of a species to that which St. Paul refers to in his subtle dialectics of law and spirit in the Epistle to the Romans, an endlessly rich text for those over the course of the last century who have pursued his line of thought (Macken 1990). It is also that of the seed which grows or withers in response to the word in Christ's parable of the sower, and the kernel of wheat in John 12. It is in the stuff of modern humanity to see purpose in words and laws and to look with impatience at that which must meditate, sprout, and grow.[4] We maintain that a cognitive science that empirically sets the aim of the body (brain included) as life and flourishing will naturally move toward a more comprehensive understanding of the act of the organism as reason through ethics and morals and, in consequence, an understanding of right dispositions and

---

4. This is Iain McGilchrist's argument: the Modern has favored the left-brain's need to make decisions now rather than the right brain's need to prepare for them (McGilchrist 2021).

attitudes. This is a fundamentally empirical approach to relations between mind and matter.

For some four decades, bioethics was richly nourished by Tristram Engelhardt who, in his later years, took up incarnational theology and the ascetic tradition in his work (Engelhardt 2000). But Engelhardt's conclusions, if not his approaches, were always centered around a legal subject that was inevitably Kantian and deontologically ordered within a society that had to make health care choices in relation to that subject. Neuroscience has redefined what the subject is in ways that the great Orthodox bioethicist justly chose not to recognize in his practical, legal questions addressed to the liberal, commercially-defined health care system of the United States. Rather than looking at the legal subject, or the psychological subject, we shall look at the biological subject in this essay.

While it is debatable whether Bp. Alexis's understanding of the brain would have much of a negative effect on pastoral concerns (his teachings on asceticism are much more likely to have a very positive effect), the manner in which contemporary science understands ethics is intensely destructive to any notion of moral personhood. What theology can provide are the principles upon which a normative decision can be made. Any system which would consider itself an ethics must address questions such as: "What is a choice?," "What is an agent?," "What does it mean to act?," "What is the will?" That neuroethics has not yet arrived at any pertinent answers to these questions stems not just from its positivist methods but from the fact that its philosophical foundations do not permit them to arise.

Beyond, and through ethics, the claims of neuroscience put upon us further, and unexpected, metaphysical claims. While we do not have the space here to examine all of them in detail, I am persuaded that the rejection of Cartesian categories of thought requires that we reassess the foundations of realism. Christian theology must at some level be realist, but that does not require the presupposition that a set of categories for the real, on the lines of an *analogia entis*, be at some point locally available to logical inquiry. We may consider that God sets out the principles of creation to be discovered through science as a maieutic that advances toward the real but is only presently accessible through revelation. Just as physics has often in the twentieth century had to turn toward the nature of consciousness to advance its understanding of realism, so cognitive science must rearticulate its very different access to the real.

Essential to that access is the direction toward which revelation guides creation. The Darwinist perspective has always had at its center a conflict between the hierarchical notion of man at the pinnacle of all species and the idea that all processes are random and undetermined. If evolution means change over time, that change needs to be going somewhere. The silent butler of this change has been utilitarianism and the "Whig" ideology of progress which regards the advance of reason over superstition as the only acceptable direction of history (Abadía 2008).

A revived theology of creation could reorder the hierarchy of being within a historical teleology centered on divine rather than human measures. This would serve to locate not only time, change, and development, but also the metaphysics of essences, and natural kinds.

How an entity chooses depends on what it is and, most fundamentally, what gives it the force and capacity to make the kinds of choices it does. The fault of contemporary neuroethics, like experimental ethics, is that it proffers itself as a mere description that can inform how we make choices and not what they should be or how we might be shaped in a way to make them. It lacks a metaphysics of agency and openly professes its lack of a system of values. A chi-square analysis of a set of decisions, or the types of brain activity a certain population engages in when it makes decisions, cannot truly be a complete ethics because this amounts to an analysis of choices that have been made. Ethics needs to prepare us for the study of choices that have not been made. While neuroethics might be able to come up with a statistically likely set of decisions for a reliable cohort of the population, it can never give us that moment where within the self that fateful step is taken. For that it needs to operate with a presupposition of autonomy. St. John of Damascus took nature, will, activity (ἐνεργεία), autonomy and self-determination (αὐτεξουσία), and wisdom as equal elements of divine and human nature (*De Fide Orth.* I [PG 94:1033A)])—each informing the other as part of the hypostasis of the divine and human person. In contemporary biology where effective causes have replaced agency with activity (Oliver 2019), the notion of conscious agency becomes, essentially, unrecognizable.[5] Proper ethics requires qualitative, subjective, and normative analyses.

St. Gregory of Nyssa composed his *On the Soul and the Resurrection* as a Christian philosophical dialogue between himself and his sister, St. Macrina, as the latter lies on her deathbed. She, "the Teacher," explains

---

5. This is not the case, however, with theoretical and mathematical biology, see Nowak 2006; Friston et al. 2020, 516.

the *nous* as "a created being, a living being, conscious, impressing upon an instrumental and sentient body the power of living and of grasping sensual objects." Here there is no Aristotelian division between animal and rational soul, though Gregory is well aware of that distinction. The mind has life that is conveyed to the body because the body is an instrument made to receive it. Furthermore, the body receives sense impressions directly but only so much as the soul gives it the capacity to do so. St. Macrina then pointed to the physician at her side:

> There is a demonstration of what I say right here. How, I ask, does this man, by setting his fingers to the pulse, hear through his sense of touch the manner by which nature disclaims to him and dictates its particular pain? (PG 46:29C)

She tells us of the soul of the physician reading through his enlivened touch, her soul, that speaks to him so that he may convey in his knowledge her diagnosis. A living soul living through an enlivened body, giving testimony of itself through that sentient body and soul to another is the model of the human to which we need to return.

Historical Introduction

Western philosophers were in general agreement in dividing functional cognition into practical knowledge and the vital or "living spirit" (ψυχή) from general knowledge and the faculty of mind (νοῦς). This did not mean that faculties were mechanisms that stood over and beyond the agent as a whole. The Christian and pagan moral traditions demanded a cultivation of both the practical and contemplative. For St. Gregory of Nyssa, as mentioned above, the *nous* is both a faculty and an essence as the primary agent of a rational being. For this reason translators often find it more comprehensible to render "*nous*" in the Greek Fathers as "soul" rather than "mind." This tells us something about what *nous* is and also about the substantial instability of "mind" in English. With respect to moral sensibility, doing good was an indication that the *nous* was healthy and in charge. As we shall see, the virtuous actions of the *nous* are where we most resemble the image of our Creator and where we most realize our future image in salvation. The exaltation of the *nous* as mind and soul in pre-modern Christianity is set against the background of its immaterial, sensible, and all-pervading nature, its role as the purveyor of life, and a doctrine of universal resurrection and bodily salvation. In his *On the Making of Man*, St. Gregory of Nyssa rejected the views of those who would locate the soul in the head, heart, and liver (Plato), or the heart alone (Aristotle, among others): "For he who makes mention of the heart speaks also of the reins, when he says, God 'tries the hearts and reins' (lit. kidneys; Jer 17:10); so that they must either confine knowing to the two combined or to neither" (*De opificio hominis* 12.8 [PG 44:160]). Since a unified self cannot have two seats for the soul, the faculty of reason has the *whole body* to reside in. For this reason, while the Eastern fathers broadly recognized the Aristotelian division between *psychē* and *nous*, their body-soul dualism as anthropology is one of instrument and vivifying agent and not the competing fiefdoms we tend to see in Platonic and Western medieval anthropology. The conflict between reason and the passions was not a battle between organs, and thus divided selves, but a question of the proper faculties to make moral and spiritual choices. This preserves a soul-body dualism, but opposes essence-agent (the soul) and matter-instrument (the body). Though many of St. Gregory's fourth-century observations are completely, and sometimes ludicrously, at odds with our current knowledge, they represent a clear understanding of what physiological and biological mechanisms mean. After all, Cappadocia was famous for its physicians. Rather than there being worse parts of the soul matched to worse parts of the body, the question centered around the harmony, the soundness, of spiritual and physical health and the unsoundness of disease.

The "mind-body" problem had a different articulation in the ancient and medieval Mediterranean world than it does in our modern, Cartesian one. Hippocrates (c. 460–c. 370 BC) regarded mental illness as resulting from lesions of the brain[6] and Galen (AD 129–216), the ancient world's most influential physician, held that different mental functions were stored in its ventricles (Rocca 2003). The fourth-century bishop and "physiologist" Nemesius (d. 420) expanded this theory in his theological anthropology (Eijk 2008) which had a great effect on later thinking, including that of St. Maximus the Confessor (e.g., *Ambigua* 10 [PG 1109B–D]). Like St. Gregory, Nemesius held that brain disease can have a direct effect on the *nous* (Nemesius 2008, 122). Nemesius also seemed to have been very influential in shaping the anatomy of Arab physicians, who are the likely sources of Thomas Aquinas's subtle understanding of

---

6. If we can regard his "On the Sacred Disease" as authentic.

the role of the brain lesions in mental illness (Kemp and Fletcher 1993).[7] The doctrine of the inner senses that dominated the Western medieval understanding of the brain seems to have come from Ibn Sīnā (Avicenna [980–1037]) who relied upon Greek sources (Aristotle's *De Anima* and Galen are evident) as well as the best contemporary understanding of anatomy. He accounted for three ventricles which governed six mental faculties. The first dealt with practical processing and imagination, the second with cogitation and estimation, and the third with memory. Sensory perception entered the first ventricle where it was (1) ordered and rendered into an image, then it was (2) actively processed and compared with other cogitations which might result in some judgment or behavior, finally it was (3) stored in memory. In dreams this process was reversed.

Notably, much of what we attribute to higher functioning—imagining unreal objects or events—"pictures in the brain"—was considered to be part of the sensible faculty just as the ascetical tradition regards *logismoi* as distinct from the activity of the *nous*. The spirits that filled the ventricles worked according to a very mechanical form of operation, but that seemed to have bothered no one. The tremendous advances in sixteenth- and seventeenth-century anatomy led to more salient theories of nerve function and a better understanding of the differences between the nervous and circulatory systems (Mehta et al. 2020), and that there was much more to this jelly-like organ than three vesicles and some "wormlike" objects. Cardinal figures such as Andreas Vesalius (1514–64) eventually (and correctly) concluded that gross anatomy could not explain imagination and memory (Kemp and Fletcher 1993, 565–66). Thus the foundations for Cartesian dualism do not come from a lack of causal explanations as to brain function, but from the presumption on the part of moderns that all physical processes can have only mechanical explanations and, if they do not, they are supernatural. The limitation of all activity to only material and effective cause has done more to displace the faculty of abstract reasoning from biology than any particular scientific progress. Thus it is not that Descartes is the *auteur* of Cartesian dualism, but that his brand of empiricism, and causality, attributed to the faculties of the soul what could not be explained mechanically in the body.[8] Furthermore, the fact that the soul does what we cannot explain

---

7. See Aquinas, *Summa Theologiae*, I q. 84, a. 7.

8. Jean-Luc Marion (Marion 2018) has argued that this caricature of body/soul Cartesian dualism is indeed not Cartesian. In part this is because Descartes retained some of the scholastic concepts of his contemporaries, including an Aristotelian understanding

mechanically is directly analogous to the position that what we cannot explain about the world is attributed to God and his will. The soul of the gaps comes from the God of the Gaps (Collins 2003). Just as in many enlightenment thinkers, including Newton, Descartes used his theology as constant informant for his natural philosophy. Just as with Newton, questionable theology became fixed in hard science (Oliver 2001). The views of earlier thinkers certainly relied on empirical observation and a realistic estimation of the brain and its powers, but they regarded the moral and rational life as that which pertains to the *whole person* and the soul as the essence of that life. To them this was as self-evident as the fact that, when you agree to sign a contract, its terms are not only binding the hand that signs it. Some of Descartes' many contemporary opponents employed Thomistic reasoning to argue for a more delicate notion of the mind-body relation (Buchenau and Lo Presti 2017); but, by the eighteenth century and the pseudoscience of phrenology, mechanical dualism and efficient causality had already come to dominate medicine as it had dominated science as a whole. Rationality had also begun to exile moral reasoning to the realm of feeling and sensibility with all the denigration of the "animal" but none of the recourse to anatomy.

Nevertheless, a *patristic* approach to brain science should recognize that the prevailing fourth century, and eleventh century, theories of the linkage between brain anatomy and emotion, imagination, and behavior would have been enough by themselves to argue that there was no soul on the same grounds contemporary neuroscientists do. Such a view was not widely adopted at all because these figures, including those in Western and Islamic traditions, still had a realist philosophy, a coherent notion of the self, and a sense that the primary mark of the soul was its activity in life.[9]

---

of substance and the notion of the animal soul and vital spirits. In part it is because Descartes was employing a theory of nervous function that had been rejected even by the anatomists of his own day. But it is not Descartes' Aristotelianism or anatomy that makes him Cartesian, but the development of his method. The term Cartesian dualism suits numerous statements made by the philosopher in a number of times and places and represents how many of his contemporaries, along with subsequent generations, understood him. It is the aftermath of his position which is our object here.

9. There are significant divergences between Western, Islamic, and Orthodox psychologies. Stemming from different interpretations of Aristotle and St. Augustine, these involve both anatomy and physiology (the Arabic understanding of the heart [*qalb*] as the source of higher reason, for instance) and especially the view that signs as universals were perceived and processed only by the rational soul. Such differences deserve deeper examination in another work. The proponents of the Radical Orthodoxy movement

This caricature of Cartesian dualism has thus been an indispensable result of a long history of deracination. The body is a machine and the soul a rational and volitional agent that is notionally immaterial, but that exists and operates through accidents that are materialist—it moves in measurable ways, it occupies a particular space (such as the pineal gland), volume or mass, etc. Opponents to Cartesian dualism range from materialist monists that make nothing of the soul to Thomist dualists that take the soul to be the *eidos* of the body. We have shown in another work that the parody of dualism as it is currently held by most Christian scientists is inimical to the Orthodox tradition and thus disastrous in shaping our contemporary notion of the human (Trimble 2021). As Heidegger states in his *Grundbegriffe der Metaphysik* (Heidegger 2001, 208), Cartesian dualism was flawed in reducing the body to inert machinery and in reducing the primary mode of being to consciousness.

Rendering the animal and the body to a machine shattered them into mechanisms, processes, activities. True human action can only be a form of intellectual activity and living a mere set of continuous divisible processes or surfaces. As the phenomenologist and ethicist Max Scheler wrote: "The person is the concrete, autonomous, integral unity of acts of different kinds" (Scheler 1916, 397–98). However, the better we can explain the machinery that gives cause to action the smaller the realm of the integral becomes until it, like the Cartesian "ghost in the machine," is dismissed entirely. This is the state we are currently in.

While opposed to Cartesian reductionism, phenomenologists also pitted themselves against the positivist and "psychologism" of their day. Identifications of the brain, psyche, apperceptive inferences, and Kantian categories were, for Husserl, a μετάβασις εἰς ἄλλο γένος (*transition to another genus*), a category error. In his *Cartesian Meditations* he calls this "transcendental psychologism." To be brief, only a form of analysis that can define something subjectively can account for phenomena which are subjective by nature. The positivism which had "misled and paralyzed the whole of modern philosophy" (Husserl 2012, 144) attempted to give

---

(established in Milbank 2006) set the causes of this fissure in the development of thirteenth- and fourteenth-century nominalism, prime culprits being John Duns Scotus and William of Ockham. I would maintain that this change was gradual, influenced by Arab metaphysicians and their readings of Aristotle and his later neo-Platonic commentators. Nominalism plays an important role, but it is not until the sixteenth century that one can observe the full expression of mechanical causality and strictly supernatural theodicy. And even then there are exceptions.

objective accounts of phenomena which its own terms could not properly define.

Just like the debates between Aristotelians and atomists within metaphysics, or St. Gregory's implicit dispute with Plato's *Timaeus*, we can regard the history of neuroscience as made up of waves of reductionism and holism.[10] "Brain science" as we would now define it begins with Paul Broca's (1824–80) discovery, published in 1865, of the association between speech production and an area of the frontal temporal lobe, now called "Broca's Area." The pattern runs like this: a medical or technological development leads to the discovery that a patient with a lesion in this or that brain area is deficient in function for this or that behavior. This then leads to an identification of said anatomy or mechanism with said behavior. Upon this is built a reductionist argument that explains the behavior, faculty, and nature of the apperception. Later it is discovered that other patients have either the same lesion and do not exhibit said deficiency, or exhibit the deficiency with a lesion in a different place, or the behavior turns out to have a different basis, and the reduction of anatomy=function is replaced by another theoretical model. Thus Broca's anatomical discoveries were matched by Hermann von Helmholtz's (1821–94) brilliant experimental work, among others. These were then challenged from the 1880s by the holistic approaches of Gestalt experimentalists. The discovery of the anatomy and physiology of neurons by Santiago Ramón y Cajal (1852–1934) and Camillo Golgi (1843–1926) led to a new "digitization" of brain science near the beginning of the twentieth century that was matched with the growth of Pavlovian behaviorism. This continued to find its opponents in Gestalt psychology (see Ash 1998) and in the Darwinian focus of the American pragmatists.[11]

By the mid-twentieth century a new generation of phenomenologists and Gestalt theorists reversed what Husserl characterized as "transcendental positivism" by taking the results of experimental psychology and anatomy to form new categories, but ones that were effectively non-transcendental. These were then to form an adapted phenomenological method of perception led by Maurice Merleau-Ponty (1908–61).

Because this was a movement led by European philosophers that lay between the camps of empiricism and psychoanalysis, this generation had little influence on the birth of cognitive science that was shortly to

---

10. See the computationalist critique of holism in Fodor and LePore 1992.

11. Ramón y Cajal was, however, himself not reductionist and was influenced by James in his accounts of neural plasticity. See Ferreira 2014.

come. In a monumentally scathing review of B. F. Skinner's (1904–90) *Verbal Behavior* (1957), a young Noam Chomsky (1928–) correctly asserted that no form of stimulus-response mechanism, as behavioral psychology articulated it, could account for the acquisition of language, the categories of language or its generative abilities (Chomsky 1959). Chomsky (and others) were to advance a multidisciplinary approach that drew together fields such as linguistics, psychology, philosophy, information science, cybernetics, and artificial intelligence. While cognitive science was initially a "holistic" approach, unlike Husserl, it did not assert that logic or transcendental truths lay beyond psychology. Quite the contrary, they simply argued that different, multidisciplinary methods were needed to find their true location, function, and modes of operation in the brain. For his part, Chomsky has unwaveringly argued that universal grammar—his own extraordinary contribution to linguistics—was always there between the ears and would someday be confirmed as psychology (or brain science) advanced. Yet his approach has been to derive principles observed in the sign system and impute them to psychology, thus risking the same μετάβασις Husserl, Frege, and Kant before them had identified. At a sweep, the universals which were asserted by realists as being part of nature became physically encoded and existent only in the physical brain. Nominalism then took on physical rather than mental, or *ensouled*, properties. This new territory required its own currency, its own units of exchange. Neurophysiologists and cyberneticists, such as Warren McCullouch and Walter Pitts (1945), proposed a "psychon" as a single mental unit that corresponds to the activity of a neuron. Naturalist philosophers stepped in and proposed "qualia." These were the mental correspondences to things. While there has been a beastly rush to distinguish them from Descartes and Locke's "ideas," they have never shaken their half-semiotic and half-material position. The philosophy behind such a position has been hard going, and many have tried to conceive of qualia as subjective phenomena that were expected to occupy some objectively correspondent "spaces" in the brain,[12] whilst, at most, they could only be fixed as *orienteers* toward some physical entity or process. While some evidence shows certain features to occupy fairly discrete

---

12. Willard. V. O. Quine (1908–2000) struggled for decades to arrive at an epistemology where "neural connections" were an objective currency. He rejected qualia, and could not accept a common set of intersubjective neural connections; yet he could not have a naturalist epistemology without one or another version of it. See Quine 1969, ch. 6; Levine 1983.

representations, functional anatomy reveals a tremendous amount of flexibility and variety in the association between neural (and neural network) function and behavior (Anderson 2021). The final instantiation of this case can be seen in the philosopher Jerry Fodor's (1935–2017) "mentalese" (Fodor 1980). Though Fodor does not equate mentalese with a language, he says the correspondence between an object and its mental correspondent requires that it work like one. For this he offers no real recourse to biology.

Yet after nearly seventy years, and now three "decades of the brain" we would have expected long ago to have found a "language apparatus" that could anatomically account for universal rules in structures and pathways analogous to what we see in language and logic themselves. We know that language is mostly localized in the left hemisphere and can be anatomically and functionally accounted for by two very discretely organized systems of perception and production along with a much less discrete anatomy connecting them.[13] There are finer grained analyses that show general associations with lexical processes and syntax, yet we cannot take anatomical structures in the brain and find analogies to universal grammar or mental dictionaries as we can do with other functions such as mental maps or introception.[14] If we were to take our theory from brain to language, and not the reverse, then a word or phrase would have to be different if it were produced by the speaker than if it were received by a listener. This is not categorical and it is not universal. The progress made by Chomskyan syntax and phonology has been remarkable; but, like Husserl's ideas, language and logic are almost certainly not just "encoded" in the brain. Thus, the positivist claims to universal explanation have overstepped the modes of operation they purport to them and thus falsely characterize the nature of the human body. Much of what have been described as the "representation wars" of philosophy and cognitive science have circled round one version of reductionism or another. This is not just a problem for "neurophilosophy," or neuroscientific method. Explaining how the mind and body work, and work together, is an essential component in conceiving what thinking and living are for. No

---

13. This is primarily the arcuate fasciculus, which is also responsible for a number of other, non-linguistic functions related to attention and some sociality. For example, see Nakajima et al. 2018.

14. For example, there is ample evidence that mammals orient themselves using maps that are analogously represented by so-called "grid cells" and "place cells" in the hippocampus. See Horner et al. 2016. Discrete sections of the motor cortex coordinate afferent signals into a virtual map of the subject's body (Carlson and Birkett 2017, 256).

matter how sophisticated a machine, the reasons for its activity are always implied in its design and tend to have their aims lie outside of its operation. Having universals programmed in the brain and motivation programmed in the genes turns us into bundles of executed commands, activity and not agents in a living exchange with the world. In essence, these movements have not answered the objections Husserl brought to them some 130 years ago. By internalizing universalized sign systems they neglect the particular processes which involve the encoding of learned experience and behavior and which thus individuate higher-level processing. The presumption that everything is "encoded" in the brain as it would be encoded in a dictionary, or a card catalog is extremely destructive. Rather, we shall see that the only truly accessible qualia are those which are mediated subjectively.

The weaknesses of neuroscience come especially hard and fast in discussions of agency. In a classic experiment Benjamin Libet (1916–2007) noted that brain activity spikes before the subject recognizes that they have taken a decision.[15] From this many have concluded that free will does not exist. After all, following Hume's famous argument, if something determines a choice, it is not free. This argument is taken as so self-evident that later researchers have termed their investigations into choice not on "agency" but on the "sense of agency." Agency itself does not exist and research can only examine the illusion subjects have of it.[16]

Yet it is very difficult to imagine an experiment where it would be observed that a biological process came out of nowhere. Imagine a vial set in a vacuum where a protein, with no medium, with no addition or intervention, nor any time constraint, suddenly denatures itself. You set up impossible conditions for the behavior and then determine that, these conditions not being met, the phenomenon does not exist. Behind these suppositions (Hume's included) is a Cartesian notion of the will as a wholly non-physical entity with no mechanism or process composing it—the agent of the gaps. Should a mechanism associated with it

---

15. Libet asked participants to indicate when they felt the desire to perform an act and discovered that electric activity in certain brain areas preceded the movements participants made. He referred to this as readiness potential (RP) since it is registered before the activation of subjects' muscles representing the desired movement. Libet noted that RP was registered well in advance of movement and well before subjects become "aware of the wish or urge to act," which approximates at about 550 milliseconds prior to an act. Libet interpreted these results to mean that "the initiation of the voluntary act appears to begin in the brain unconsciously, well before the person consciously knows that he wants to act!" (Libet 1985, 51).

16. This is the principal argument of Dennett 2017.

be observed, it is not part of the will. Rather than considering that the subject makes choices on the basis of a number of internal processes, Cartesianism and reductionism do not dissolve the ghost in the machine, they insist upon it.

If we are to understand, in the spirit of St. Gregory, the meaning of brain science, and science in general, we must take terms, facts, and concepts foreign to theology, deracinating them from their materialist-positivist prejudices. We must not set the current positions on physical causes as arbiters of theology. In the terms of contemporary natural theology, this project must not be correlationist. This is not because we do not like the facts, but because we recognize, as any good scientist, that all facts are value-laden. And because we recognize, as unfortunately many good scientists do not, that these underlying values of modern empiricism are inimical to any coherent notion of the person as either an imminent or transcendent being. I maintain that behind such statements as "you are your brain," "consciousness" or "free will" "are illusions of the genes" is not a rigorous, empirically founded philosophy but an ideology that seems to have evolved to rob us of our native virtue and agency.

Along with these statements are sets of presuppositions, slippery metaphors, techno-gibberish, and popular myths, in short, as John Milbank put it, an ontology in the guise of a metaphysics (Milbank 2006, 279, 295). Many theologians, philosophers, and social scientists have followed the criticisms of positivist psychologism and argued that never the twain shall meet for brain science can tell us nothing about ourselves. This is an opinion highly irresponsible both to the rigorous work of science and scientists—many of whom are far more modest in their hypotheses than philosophers—and to the extraordinary thing that is the human body and brain, a thing divinely made.

Replacing Categories: Crypto-Cartesianism and Darwinist Teleology

The greatest achievement of the Orthodox theology of the person is that it grows out of and is constantly nourished by the theology of the Trinity and systematic reflection on the nature of the God-Man in Christ. This, as has often been noted, puts the human at an exalted position and shapes the particular and complex character of the Orthodox approach to original sin. It also grants speculation on the unknowable of God access to his much more knowable, but imperfect, reflections in the human.

The express humanity of Jesus in the Gospels impresses upon an impoverished human imagination the full scope and necessity of individual personhood for both the all-transcending Father and the life-giving and bodiless Spirit. This approach also keeps, again, questions about the human linked to fundamental questions of being itself.[17] This is, at times, a limitation on giving that greater moral and ethical resolution to human immanence that we see in figures such as St. Augustine of Hippo, but it never overextends the particular to cheat the human of its transcendent potential.[18]

Consider as an example St. Gregory the Theologian's argument on the personhood of the Holy Spirit in his *Fourth Catechetical Oration*.

> The Holy Spirit must be included either among those beings which exist in and of themselves, or among the things which are taken to be part of something else. Those who are skilled in such matters call the former a "substance" and the latter an "accident." Now if the Spirit were an "accident," He would be an activity of God. What else could He be, or from whom else could He come? Surely this is the best way to avoid taking him as something composite. And if He is an activity, He will be activated in the manifested result, will not be the one who activates, and will, once done with His activity, cease to exist. That is what activity is. But how is it that the Spirit *acts* [1 Cor 12.11], and *speaks thus*, and *sets apart* [Acts 13.12], and *becomes grieved* [Eph 4.30] and is *vexed* [Isa 63.10]? For anything between these two [categories] that might have nothing in common with either or be a composite of both is something that not even those who invented the [fantastical] goat-stag would dare imagine. (*Fifth Catechetical Oration* 6 [PG 36: 140])

Pure Aristotelian concepts here are set in plain application. An accident (συμβεβηκός) is an impermanent attribute of a permanent essence (οὐσία), an actuality-activity (ἐνέργεια) is dependent upon an essence. If the Holy Spirit is merely a mode of being of God, or an activity of God, as table-making is to a carpenter, then he exists only in that activity and has no independent being.

---

17. In this I would share the views of Christopher Knight (Knight 2021) that such a position can also be a basis for an "incarnational" foundation to scientific inquiry.

18. The examination of the questions behind moral reasoning is now termed "metaethics." However, such a term is only necessary once the foundations for agency and the good are already undermined.

St. Gregory has tipped his lance at an old, and unknown theological enemy (Radde-Gallwitz 2011) who regarded the Holy Spirit as a mere mode of God's activity and not a person. For this he makes use of Aristotle's ancient strategy of employing activity and agency as a means of arriving at the nature of discrete beings. To do is to be. That the Holy Spirit might only be activity would deny him agency; to grant him agency grants him personhood. Those who would deny the Holy Spirit (the Pneumatomachoi) are wrong.

Though the Church Fathers made good use of Aristotle's ethics (Bradshaw 2007), this passage asserts agency and personhood of an invisible and transcendent being on the basis of metaphysical terms. But neither Aristotle nor St. Gregory shared the disenchanted, "gray ontology" (Marion 1998) of the modern world as a flattened plane of being that divorced truth from value. As is often the case in Orthodox theology, doctrines of Trinitian metaphysics are relevant to metaphysics in general. The Holy Spirit has his *ousia* in the Father. Were we to know the Spirit by his works (John 3:8), we might conclude that he was only activity, that he was a "gerundive being" like "walking," "flying," or Eunomius' "being begotten." But doctrine shows us that personhood—hypostasis—is distinct from being. The person is something greater than its parts and qualitatively greater than any of its activities, and even greater than the sum of its activities. Such a notion of activity giving evidence to agency is lost on neuroscience.

The revolution in imaging techniques that allows us to observe brain activity is founded on a correlation between "activity" in a certain part of brain anatomy and a "stimulus" or "behavior" of the organism. From this "functions" are associated with "activity" which is associated with anatomy. This then translates motivations, objects, and actions into activity. The self then becomes a bundle of activities that are explained by functions attached to anatomy. As St. Gregory points out, an activity cannot be an agent by itself, it is reliant upon an agent of activity. For the heresy of the Pneumatomachi, the Holy Spirit was not a person and its activities were dependent upon the agency of the Father. For St. Gregory, and the Church, the nature of these activities was in itself justification for personhood. To act like a person makes you one. Personhood, on the other hand, did not presume an irreducible nature. The fact that one could see different activities in the person did not refute its existence, nor did the fact that it was dependent upon another being.

With its bundles of activities, neuroscience has no true understanding of agency for the human to fall back upon and so it builds up a set of anthropological myths. The most powerful of these comes out of the discovery of the very complexity of the brain itself, the "trillion cognitive handshakes" (Tallis 2012, 234)[19] of neural connections that represent the most complex place in the universe. It is believed that this cosmos is able to create the multiplicity of thought as if it were a matter of containment—like the wise men of the Grand Academy of Lagado in *Gulliver's Travels* who aim to carry the referents of the words they use on their backs. The trillion handshakes then suddenly become capable of encompassing a universe of ideas, sensations and imaginings. Even realists (in the medieval sense) now are called "meaning externalists" because they believe something like a universal might exist somewhere outside the head (Clark and Chalmers 1998). The complexity of matter then allows the brain to mystically transform into the immaterial agency of mind. This is a kind of sham holism that thrives upon the metaphysical trick of matter transforming into consciousness around a kind of critical point that is never defined. It is, in fact, a version of Vladimir Lenin's sham "theory of reflection."

As a myth it is based on a threefold set of presumptions, all interrelated. First, the world is a catalogue of entries—a basketball is one, basketball the sport is another, playing basketball is another. These are all reducible to signs where, as Saussure asserted, signifier and signified are two faces of the same coin. Sensations, feelings, introspection may phenomenologically have a different character, but these are also reducible. Second is the transducibility of these signs into neural signals. The already structured phenomena of the world are *encoded* into the cosmos of the brain and populate it. The structure of the encoding is the structure of the brain. The third component is desire. Once the calculating mechanism of the brain is filled there has to be some voluntaristic ghost to inhabit it. This role has been filled by the values and motivation of nineteenth-century Darwinism. The rational calculator is there to regulate the instinctual beast within, but the beast is that which gets the passive agent to act.

In a perceptive and wide-ranging essay, the great developmental psychologist Eleanor Gibson noted the anachronism of the "cognitive revolution," saying that was more of a return to an old-fashioned dualism. She wrote that figures such as Noam Chomsky and Jerry Fodor presume that

19. Actually reckoned at some 100 trillion (Zimmer 2011).

"the way the world is perceived must derive from preordained rules and concepts (an analogue of Descartes' innate ideas) that serve as premises for inferences about it" (Gibson 1987, 12). Thus Descartes' innate ideas have been replaced by computational theorists with "universal grammar," "mentalese." We can extend this to say that the Cartesian soul has likewise been replaced by encoded rules and instincts. This system purports to derive rules which it finds externally consistent and internalize them. They then become "the way the brain works" with little connection to anything that actually represents biological processes. While the brain does encode information, there is no reason why the structure of that information must analogically resemble principles of logic, grammar, or any other non-biological system. Following Gibson's insight, we will call this temptation Crypto-Cartesianism. This can be seen to have two modes of operation. The first takes brain anatomy and activity and reifies these mental correspondences to facts into pseudo-essences. The second takes brain activity and, like St. Gregory's opponent, makes it into a pseudo-agent. The processes and algorithms that can be observed or deduced are mapped onto the processes of making decisions. The algorithm, or "program" inside thus takes the place of the Cartesian soul—will and reason locked in a semiotic loop within the neural machinery.

A classic example of slippery pseudo-Platonism can be found in Jaime Villablanca's article "Why do we have a caudate nucleus." This paper correlates fMRI observations with "behavior associated with affection" in cats. The observations show regular increased activity in the caudate nucleus (Villablanca 2010; see also Acevedo et al. 2012). While the researchers associate behaviors (fixed action patterns) with brain activity, the leading argument is that "love is in the caudate nucleus."[20] This is, of itself, a rather trivial conclusion: the caudate nucleus is a large region that has long been functionally associated with emotions. There is no reason that the press that followed this research could not have put its conclusions differently: "you love *with* your caudate nucleus"—the brain is an *instrument* of the person. Yet, true to form, the position is that "it's not you that loves, it is your caudate nucleus." Things that the brain does become objects in the brain. On the analogy of a computer memory bank, objects are "encoded and stored" there. The brain's processes, its algorithms that formulate and issue commands to itself and the rest of the body, are then the self's activities. The sets of commands to secrete insulin, focus attention on a dinner plate and raise the knife and fork are

---

20. Antieu 2007 has also examined this reductive phenomenon.

each elements in these algorithms. Just as St. Gregory argues, the notion of agency is dependent on being, deny being to that which exhibits activity and it cannot be an agent.

Functional magnetic imaging (fMRI) research has resulted in extraordinary advances.[21] There is also strong data that very specific stimuli (primary substances, keeping with Aristotle) can map to quite similar brain activity.[22] Yet this does not mean that the quale of an individual object is an object in any form other than as a response to these stimuli.

It is impossible to theoretically arrive at a clear account of a stimulus from its so-called quale. A simple pain response in the skin may trigger nooreceptors to indicate something as unpleasant or painful, piercing, but it is not going to tell us what the object is—a pin or a twelve-gauge needle. One identifies the behavior from the object but not the object from the behavior. For this reason, and the diversity of higher brain functional anatomy between individuals, many neurosurgeons operate, if possible, on conscious patients. The patient then gives an intentional, interpretive tour of their own brain and consciously supplies the correlations themselves. This is an important, and oft-neglected, inter-subjective element which will offer us some theoretical promise.

One of the problems surrounding qualia is that they are, essentially, the subjective mental equivalents of words. Though philosophers use such clever ineffable examples as "the taste of lemon" there is no quale which cannot be accounted for by an existing or invented word or something else that acts like one. Acting like a word means that something functions as a sign and, as such, a part of communication. A representation as a sign is a message which is issued by its author and read by its recipient. This is not the way internally governed processes of the body work. For example, while signals associated with hunger and satiety are collected in the hypothalamus, the body has no need to "translate" the "message" of "hunger" from mentalese to (and from) the digestive system. Hunger is a subjective (or introceptive) appellation we give to discrete sets of behavior: the secretion of a neuropeptide by the stomach, the activity of glucose detectors in the liver, etc. (Carlson and Birkett 2017, 391). Hunger and satiety are in a regulatory continuum with the brain and body together. Saying that something "encodes" hunger is in no way contributive to understanding the phenomenon.

21. Though not without much overstepping, see Eklund et al. 2016.
22. Pontifical, "grandmother," or "Jennifer Aniston" cells. This is still an unsettled category. See the review in Quiroga 2013.

When we speak of messages, or representations, we mean some sort of mediation from one subject to another. While touch receptors in the skin, innervation of muscles, or the lining of the gut lead to actions which are neural in character, their electrochemical or mechanical nature is not mediated or translated like a message is. Even if we speak of what is called neural "crosstalk" as forms of communication, this is only useful on the basis of analogy and not description. Thinking otherwise opens you up, again, to Crypto-Cartesianism.

We know that the body operates on the basis of a number of chemical reactions which can be described and modeled as algorithms. Neural networks and neurochemical reactions together form sets of algorithms in varying layers of connectivity and complexity. The last two centuries of brain science have identified many similar behaviors that are associated with different algorithms in brain activity, and also many different behaviors that have similar algorithms. For example, a lesion in the right inferior parietal lobule can lead to the inability to write, do arithmetical calculations, point with or properly recognize one's fingers, confuse right and left, in addition to other linguistic and spatially related dysfunction (Kolb and Wishaw 2009, 392). While thinking of these activities with an eye toward a Merleau-Ponty-like approach to symbol, thought, and bodily comportment, one could trace some sort of reason that might bring these behaviors together; but would that reason be comparable to the logical or philosophical categories of Aristotle, Kant, Russell, Quine, or Chomsky? The physiology of such algorithms has little resemblance to the "laws" of behavior in a system of such complexity as the brain. Added to this, the subordination of desire to instinct guided by Darwinian and utilitarian praxis makes a hash of what it means for us to do and to be.

Though the language of "messages," "commands," and "representations" may be good terminological shorthand, it can render the relations between the nervous system and organs as one between individual subjects and not ὄργανα, instruments, working together both as and for the subject. This puts the functions of the body under many masters—your caudate nucleus loves—and dissolves the agency of the organism as a whole. We should not forget that reason as the full operation of the soul is νόημα (or νόησις), not a calculation or mere ratiocination (διάνοια, etc.), or fantasy (λογισμός), but a meaningful expression that is directed outward and, hopefully, upward. The transformation of reason into an algorithm has denied the subject its essentially discursive nature as an agent engaged with its environment.

Darwinian Voluntarism

Along with the injection of algorithms in the place of "innate ideas," Crypto-Cartesianism uses the operation of the algorithm to replace volition—you are programmed to write papers or eat your breakfast. To oppose her style of psychology to that of the computationalists, Gibson goes on to argue that her approach is: "a modern-day empirical one rooted in biological science, naturalistic, resting on evolutionary and ecological principles" (Gibson 1987, 12). Now, of course, these principles can themselves become algorithms inserted into the brain with no more confirmation than those of logic. Computationalists do just this when they claim that we are programmed by Darwinian principles of adaptation. Mentalese takes the place of biology and Darwinian instincts take the place of the will. Evolution has programmed your caudate nucleus to love (Dennett 1996). We should first recognize the difference between Gibson's criticism and this one. Crypto-Cartesianism presumes that the process adopted by a system outside of the brain is analogously mapped in the brain: that the way it works on paper is the way it must work in your head. This Darwinian presupposition is a functional explanation: it explains *why* you might love, but not *how* the caudate nucleus might do that among other things. As David Berlinski, among others, has pointed out, this type of reasoning conflates the operations of populations and species with those of an individual (Berlinski 1996). To argue that "the function of the brain is the preservation of the species" is absurd, a "distributive fallacy" as Fodor observed (Fodor 2000, 191). The heart is not there "to preserve the species" any more or less than another organ, its function is to circulate blood. The same confusion obtains for the relations between the individual and the species and how individual traits and the adaptational benefit of them coalesce into the emergence and persistence of a species—the problem of natural kinds is still a theoretical bugbear for biology (Ereshefsky 2016). We shall argue here that the ethical component of activity is precisely that which can render a notion of the kind and species, but this requires a great deal more preparation.

Most fundamentally, the problem with Darwinism for Christianity is that it is an ideology.[23] Rather than having the purpose of life be to exalt God and exult with God, it has us fulfilling a utilitarian, economic law of marginal utility. Uprooting this ideology frees up the individual living

---

23. With theological roots; see McGrath 2011.

being to ask "what am I doing?" and "what am I for at this moment in my life?"

The enactivist and ethical position we are putting forth asserts that setting the organism as the focal point of activity requires a particular relationship to agency. Agency, as St. Gregory points out, then requires there to be a cohesive, integral agent defined by its activity. Agency thus cannot be taken as being the particular organs that are part of the process of an act (your caudate nucleus is in love, Charles's stomach is eating). This requires an understanding of the boundaries of reductionism and the necessity of holism. As we shall see, the neuroscience of sociality is very important for understanding why we have such a complex being. How can we conceive of sociality without a conception of naturally interacting individuals that recognize one another in social relations? Orthodoxy has a number of possible contributions to this sensibility, ones that, again come from its rich incarnational theology.

In a wide-ranging article Fr. Methody (Zinkovsky) has argued that the patristic category of hypostasis may be used to resolve the difficulty of defining discrete entities. In classical debates, nature was taken to be either made up of individual elements or made up of continuities. Fr. Methody suggests that, in the light of contemporary debates on the subject, discontinuities can be best understood by the patristic notion of the hypostasis. Continuity is part of nature (φύσις) (Zinkovsky 2021). While Fr. Methody applies this notion metaphysically, we may also consider its value for defining the relationship of the individual and species. Hypostasis must always be conceived as a relative term. The hypostases of the members of the Holy Trinity depend on the *ousia* of God. The hypostases of the Son and Holy Spirit depend on the monarchy of the Father. Likewise the species depends on the individual and the individual on the species. We may conceive of elements which belong to our nature as a species as being part of that condition which has been formed by the generations which have preceded us and which shape part of our own nature. We are also products of the ethos of the whole of humanity that surrounds us and to which we contribute. The inherited conditions of our genetics, and the cultural conditions that shape us must have a role in how we are structured biologically and how we may act; yet we are not completely passive in the formation of our cultural environment, nor the legacy we would pass on to our children through parentage or education. Reexamining a different approach to natural kinds (one also distinct from Thomism) may be helpful in resolving the nature-nurture nexus in human development. Biology may also help us to understand some of the patristic uses of hypostases as referring to the human race, harmony, symmetry in form, as well as the relationship between an individual's moral actions and the conditions of humanity.

With respect to the division of will between nature and reason, the orthodox doctrines of the will may also be of assistance. In the Christological conflicts of the sixth century, St. Maximus Confessor defended, to his hurt and later glory, the two wills doctrine as the only one consistent with Christ's two natures. Those who argued for Christ's single will reasonably argued (on a logic akin to that presented above by St. Gregory the Theologian) that a reasonable agent could only have one will in order to act in accordance with that will. But St. Maximus, in his subtle distinctions, illustrated that one should not confuse the will and the possibility of choosing (McFarland 2007). The will is not the sum of the choices that have been and can be made, the will is a capacity that is part of the nature of rational beings. In fallen human nature, natural choices are hobbled by sin and the character of the will is distorted. Yet in the sinless Christ, the divine and human natures live in perfect accord. Christian moral action amounts to harmonizing our inclinations with our true nature as revealed in the freedom of the God-man. Just as we have seen with St. Gregory, the determination of the divine informs the nature of the human (Thunberg 1995, 226–30).[24] An account of the nature of God is also a general statement about rational nature. Our nature in the divine image is the nature of the whole hypostasis of mankind. The will guided by that nature is directed toward the final goal of life in God. The individual human nature may make choices in accordance with that specific (i.e., species-level, hypostatic) teleology, or it may not. As it is commonly formulated, the human will may act in synergy with the divine will. Defining freedom and volition is a question of defining the nature of beings that are capable of action and not a question of defining whether this or that action is or is not determined or constrained. For created beings, all acts are subject to levels of freedom and constraint. The question is whether that being is fulfilling the nature it has been given.

Typical of the culture it represents, with its Calvinist values, Darwinism possesses a negative notion of freedom. Freedom is the absence of restraint, and nature offers only restraints. Note that the question is not grounded in the agent but in the nature of individual acts. Similarly,

---

24. See also the quote from St. John Damascus above and a reasoned formulation of St. Maximus as a virtue ethicist in Blowers 2013.

God's will offers only restraint and you are free only to sin. A view which regards freedom as emerging from the flourishing of the divine life would say that nature offers the means by which to act in the world and be free. One is free to do what is in accordance with one's nature, one is free only to do good. A notion of the will which is based on the concordance of activity and nature might aid in understanding how a non-Cartesian notion of the instinct might emerge. The instinct would not be a program animating the zombie-like organism, but that to which the organism through its living aspires. Crucially, its aspirations are not expressed only in its own individual activities, they are part of the summation of mankind. We have inherited the conditions of sin, but our virtues, and God's mercy, love, and grace change our conditions as we change ourselves.

The Teleology of Flourishing

Once we have removed this crypto-teleology—this Darwinian voluntarism—from our actions, where is an empirical science to find the sources of activity? Where, after fight or flight, are we to locate our desires? Despite what the rampant libertinism of contemporary life would have us believe one of the great tragedies of the modern it that it removed us from genuine desire. This is first because an impassive will and a mechanical body have only room for an appetite. But, more profoundly, this is because grey ontology removes us from the *source* of our desire, from our natural entelechy (Taylor 2012, 249).

The replacement of motivation with innate and uncontrollable instincts (either Freudian or Darwinian) has helped precipitate this condition. It has also led to, as we have mentioned, the distributive fallacy that takes these motivations and sets them in the place of the functions of organs, and thus living processes. Both philosophy and morals would be enriched by a return to the concept of flourishing as an empirical, broad, and fundamental value for life and all living things. As the Thomistic ethicist Jane Porter writes: "Human morality in all its diverse forms reflects the goodness of the human creature and as such it is an expression of God's will that creatures should exist and flourish" (Porter 2004, 126–27).

The obvious function of any organism, and any organ within an organism, is to flourish. Flourishing is a gift of the Holy Spirit, the Giver of life. The heart flourishes by circulating blood, the lungs and digestive system by taking in nutrients and expelling waste, the skin by forming an interface between the interior and exterior. As part of the same epithelial developmental layer as skin, the brain may be said to have a similar function: to engage with and help govern the organism's internal and external condition. All of these organs flourish when they contribute to the overall flourishing of the organism. Flourishing is not just descriptive, it is also normative. A tumor may grow like mad, but hypertrophic proliferation is not flourishing. The entelechy of a cell is when it serves its purpose for the tissue, the tissue for the organ, the organ for the whole body, the body for the *nous*, the *nous* for the whole hypostasis of mankind and, individually and collectively, for God. Life is not only a being-with it is also a being-for.

Agency and Perception

The gap between the representation of phenomena in the world and the neurobiology that mediates the self's interaction has led many to a position of absolute skepticism. Yet I would argue that a brief examination of ways in which we can be certain of subjective experiences tells us something about the ensouled integrity of the Person as illumined by St. Gregory the Theologian's enactivist position.

Part and parcel of Descartes' dualism was a particular theory of retinal vision. I have argued in a recent article that an epistemology based on vision is prone to certain excluded middle terms (Trimble 2023). This is because light as a medium presumes an immateriality that chemical or mechanical perception does not.[25] An epistemology based on smell or touch is something we have yet to observe. Descartes' classical interpretation of vision understands the retina as a small chiaroscuro device that transfers pictures on a grid via the optic nerve so that they can be "viewed" by the soul. But neither the soul, nor the visual cortex is a "viewer" like the human spectator *looking* at a video screen. The projection from the retina is a set of already highly processed neural signals that are transferred in an *unmediated* fashion to the visual cortex and beyond.[26]

---

25. Of course, visual perception is also chemical and the source of this philosophical temptation comes more from the complexity of the "snapshot" of a dynamic environment than just the ethology of photons. It should be noted that nearly all of the major theories of cognition—from von Helmholtz to Broca to Chomsky—are based either on vision or language.

26. The ecological psychologist James Gibson (and husband to Eleanor) said as much in a debate with the art historian Ernst Gombrich: "I do not accept the eye-camera analogy, since I strongly disbelieve that the retinal image is an image in any proper sense of the term. It cannot be looked at, for there is no seer inside the head to

This realization is at once deeply disturbing, that there is no *watcher within*;[27] yet it also allows us to be freed from the notion of a soul that is materialist in orientation and passive in agency: occupying space and time, sitting on the sofa watching the world's television program roll by. Recognizing the soul as the prime agent of the body requires a model of it that is inexorably stitched to all the body's parts and lineaments to the extent that they have life in them. This is an ancient and radically different notion of the soul, and agency with it, than that to which we have become accustomed.

Subjectivity and Learning

If a qualia and ideas are not comparable to words, what form do subjective cognitions take? Perhaps a purely subjective experience as pain (Hardcastle 1997) or hunger might be understood as a significant part of a feedback loop of behaviors that, when needed, can be collected together and *phenomenologically* named not "hunger" but: "I am hungry."[28]

This is not as trivial a conclusion as one might think. Rather than attaching names to neural anatomy one can insert the agency of the subject into the process of identifying their own anatomy. Phenomenologists would argue that this radically changes the nature of these objects, and I would argue that contemporary neuroscience would have to agree. In a fascinating set of articles from the early 2000s, the neurosurgeon Hugues Duffau began to account for a new approach to the removal of glial cell tumors whilst operating on conscious patients. In the late 2010s, he began to announce what he defended as a new philosophy (in the sense surgeons use the term) of neurosurgery. In part this had to do with the nature of glial tumors which could grow threadlike along dendritic networks and so had to be removed in narrow channels over a wide area. Yet the philosophical part of his approach was that it was dependent on the functional mapping of the individual awake patient during or before resection. In this philosophy he juxtaposed operating on the basis of gross anatomy and preliminary brain imaging (MRI, fMRI, diffusion tensor imaging [DTI] scanning) with an individualized functional mapping of neural networks that was determined by tests on the awake patient.

---

see it" (Gombrich et al. 1971, 195).

27. On the uncanny and agency in neurosurgical intervention, see Trimble 2020.

28. Antieu 2007 also examines the inadequacy of lexicality for neural states.

Gross anatomy was inferior because of its lack of detail and the range of individual variation. Imaging was inferior because it used mathematical algorithms to generalize activity and did not accurately represent what was going on when and where. Duffau backed his arguments up with very strong quantitative and anecdotal data (Duffau 2018). His method used imaging to come up with a general picture, but then removed the tumor and surrounding tissue only when it was clear what the functional relationship was between that tissue and the patient's behavior. The brain has no pain receptors, so a local anesthetic is enough to block the pain of a local incision in the scalp. Since nerves work with an electrochemical current, an electrode placed on a particular brain area "short circuits" that area and "turns it off" only so long as the electrode is applied. Thus the surgeon can test the area they think might need to be removed and see what effect that might have on the patient. This allows for removing as much of the area of and around a tumor with as little iatrogenic damage as possible.

This practice is fascinating not only because of what it tells us about the individual nature of brains, the weaknesses of brain imaging techniques (and the hundreds of thousands of articles that have been based on them), but also because it does allow us to see how a quale in the brain can be actually defined.

First to consider is the battery of tests which are used. After all, if the patient is not tested for a relevant behavior, the part of the brain that would be stimulated would not be mapped and could be inadvertently removed. Thus a suitably rich set of stimuli must be given within the functional anatomical knowledge of the given area, and then some. This is an engaged, enactivist type of inventory. Another essential part of this "philosophy" is that anatomy is not defined by structures, but by networks. Networks are then determined by activity. Surgeon and patient move in a kind of gnosic-agnosic journey up and along the neural network.

The definition is given not by the physician but by the patient, who actively and consciously engages with the determination of the functions he or she is able to undertake. Some might quibble with the fact that you are consciously engaged with having part of your brain turned off, but that is a trivial objection. This is an eminently *rational* process where surgeon, patient, and a testing régime are all devoted to keeping as much of the organ intact as possible.

Thus subjective phenomena can be located in the brain—they must have a place there—but they are most reliably defined not by lexica or logical deduction on paper, but when the *subject his or herself* engages with them. The debates over representation persist because cognitive science and philosophy want to remove the subject and render it into a unit of semiotic exchange. This is probably not, structurally or functionally, how the neurophysical finds its correspondences with its supposed reference, nor with external phenomena in general.[29]

In this particular example we have the surgeon and the tests as mediators that help the patient define where his functions are. There are other striking examples of different sorts of mediation and how they illustrate the same process of agent-driven, enactive cognition.

Few examples of the neuro-physical connection are more compelling than watching amputees use neural-machine interfaces to manipulate prosthetic limbs. In some cases the lost arm or leg leaves some viable nervous tissue behind to which interfaces can be connected. In other cases, especially along with damage to the spine, neural interfaces are connected to nerves for other parts of the body and the patient is retrained to use these instead. The capacities of these interfaces have been gradually moving up the spinal cord as patients, some completely paralyzed, have been trained to manipulate objects on a computer screen using the stimulus of brain wave signals. This can gradually allow them to communicate and issue commands. In a recent case, a man suffering from ALS who had lost all motor control was able to issue some commands by an interface inserted in the motor control region of his brain (Chaudhary et al. 2022). In none of these cases is this merely hooking up nerves and wires. Many of these prostheses employ highly sophisticated computing to monitor and regulate movement. The data received from the body in artificial memory storage (such as in the famous artificial hippocampus [Berger et al. 2012]) is not mentalese—you cannot play it back and experience the patient's subjective memories—they are merely signals that are, by nature, already encoded by the body in a form the body can use. The patient is thus consciously trained by these interfaces

---

29. An interesting anticipation to our argument comes in Dennett 1993. There he mentions that biofeedback allows subjects to manipulate objects in a virtual interface: "What counts for an individual as the simple or atomic properties of experienced items is subject to variation with training" (309). However he does not accept that these could be qualia, although this observation itself is not a bad definition of them. Dennett's own, Darwinian brand of crypto-Cartesianism keeps him from accepting the existence of qualia as it is defined by computationalists and also from recognizing it when it is not in the static form he would wish it to be.

at various levels of awareness and trains the interfaces to respond to him or her.

Much attention was made of a study that was able to recreate images representing the "pictures in the brain" of cortical activity. Even fuzzy images of the experimental subjects" dreams, one with a ghostlike postman, were rendered. This has inspired a small field of literature that seeks to generate images by coordinating brain imaging sessions. There is even, in a gross crypto-Cartesian turn, a new word—the "voxel," the brain correspondent of a pixel on a computer screen (Beliy et al. 2019). But closer examination reveals that this is actually no more than the reverse of the prosthetic example. In these studies subjects are first monitored whilst watching sets of images that correspond to neural hierarchies of visual processing. The data collected are processed through variations of Bayesian deep-learning analysis so as to predict possible future images. Later activity without the stimuli (sleeping, awake and looking at images, imagining things) was then correlated with a signals analysis of training material. Thus the conscious patient trained the machine to read their brain by providing a corpus of digitized observations (Ren et al. 2021). A different patient would need to retrain the machine to inform it of their respective hierarchies at a similar level of resolution. The qualia identified in these fuzzy pictures have no claim to be universals and are generated by processes comparable to those used to anticipate a shopper's habits on a commercial website. The fact that neurally encoded interfaces move in and out of the brain seems more impressive than it is in fact. In the first case the patient consciously informs the surgeon of the connection between objects and their brain region, in the second the neural interface allows the patient to consciously monitor the connection and train themselves to manipulate it, in the third case a computer program records and statistically models brain behavior and then produces a representation of that behavior on the basis of the model. In each of these cases there is self-monitoring, regulating behavior that establishes, mediates, defines, and manipulates the correlation. Despite their overblown theoretical claims, the facts around these cases nonetheless do have philosophical significance. Science uses forms of human agency to ascertain the nature of its own contents. There are few things about neuroscience more inspiring than watching paralytics or amputees learn how to manipulate cursors on a computer monitor and then artificial arms, legs, and hands. But this shows us that the brain is not an encoded dictionary or manual at any integrated level of functioning—from motor control to visual processing to agency. Defining qualia is theoretically useless but *practically* possible with a dynamic organism that learns, responds, acts and is, as Scheler said, *among those things which exist in and of themselves* and determine their own activity. From this perspective, the soul adapts its subjective contents to suit these new parts of itself not by flipping switches in a machine but by living, active, engagement with them. That is the way, and perhaps the only way, any subjective content can be defined. Thus the science that actually *gets at* the brain through surgery or neural interfaces is much closer to the thought of Alfred N. Whitehead and the early pragmatists, who understood signification as an intentioned engagement with the world and not a mechanical act of encoding and decoding.

Indeed the identification of the brain with a digitized memory bank and its contents with signs is a slippage from analogy and metaphor to identification.[30] The agent that defines signs for itself is a conscious, living, dynamic, and *learning* being. Even many activities that take place outside of conscious control—brain waves and muscle movement—can be defined and determined through these dynamic processes. Thus we should not limit ourselves to a language which conceives learning behavior as the decoding and encoding of messages. It is also for us to concede that these processes—which offer the most precise correlations of brain activity and behavior—have a fundamentally ethical character because learning and choosing is precisely what they are about.

Anatomy

The evident empiricism of such a position might neglect that it is also a fundamentally *ethical* one. Again this seems contradictory: thriving in the Darwinian conception must take place at the expense of others, especially in the light of contemporary ecological concerns. Yet flourishing carries an ethical component because it involves activity and both facilitates and motivates choices. This is set against viewing the principal part of the person as rational, analytical, and passive while activity is mechanical and bestial. To the contrary, the flourishing human is that which thinks in order to do. What it does is to live virtuously.

---

30. It is also a historical fudge. Those who developed the first Monte Carlo computer programs in the 1940s speculated on neural networks. The resemblance is intentional. John von Neumann wrote: "anything that can be exhaustively and unambiguously described, anything that can be completely and unambiguously put into words, is ipso facto realisable by a suitable finite neural network" (Chrisley and Begeer 2000, 436).

Secondly, this position sets rational and biological activity along the same course. Superficially this might, again, be seen to facilitate libertinism, but it also views biological and human nature as something made with the same divine intention and destination.

Let us take an uncontroversial interpretation of brain function and development as a useful application. This cross section shows basic brain anatomy.

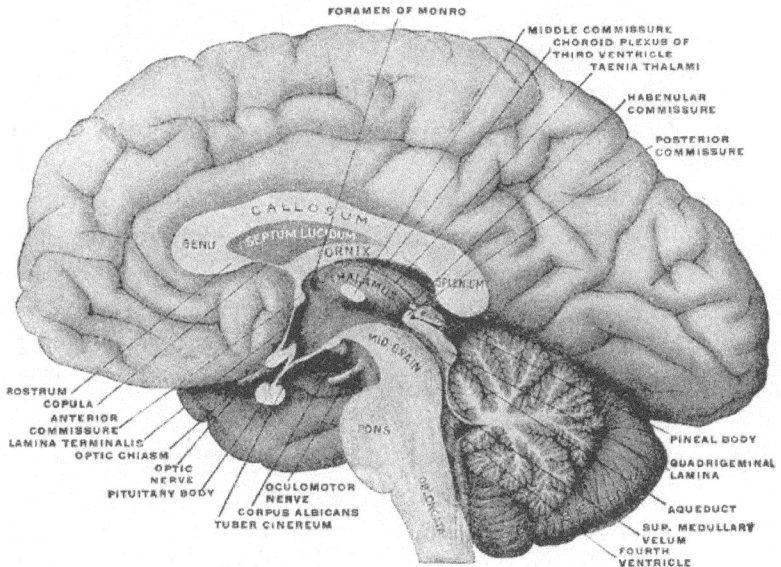

Figure 4: Sagittal cross section of the human brain. Source: *Gray's Anatomy* (1918) 2:715.

An obvious formal observation is that the nerves rising out of the brainstem have their core along the "deep brain," the limbic system up to the corpus callosum, a highway of connections. In simpler animals the analogues to these organs, the thalamus especially, are involved in decision-taking after the collection of sensory stimuli (Dragomir et al. 2020). In more complex animals, humans included, they are associated with emotion, mating, fight or flight reactions, and central aspects of memory. When a stimulus requires an immediate response, the parts of the limbic system, the thalamus and amygdala especially, send projections to the motor system. When the situation is not urgent, depending on the individual's neurological condition, which includes the results of long-standing behavioral conditioning, the cortical system involves itself in the response in various degrees of intensity. The best way to conceive of this structure dynamically is to imagine it both as it develops in an embryo and how it is theorized to have developed phylogenetically. The form unfolds from the end of the spinal cord and brainstem like a flower with the more "eloquent" brain," the cortical system, uncurling like the petals to the edge. In Darwinist explanations of evolution, it is argued that the primitive, "reptilian," parts of the brain are most essential and basic (Bp. Alexis's "center of the brain"), while the cortical system is an add-on for complex reasoning. The central is the animal and the human is an "illusional" addition.

Regarding flourishing as the center of life, and the best explanation of bodily forms, however, the cortical system could be interpreted as forming relations between parts of the brain and organism as a whole and funneling its activities into those things which inform it of the life within and about the organism and which direct it towards life. Just as a flower, the outer petals point to the inner functional organ of pollination—the outer gray matter of cell bodies points toward the inner white matter of axons guiding and forming connections. The cortex is not an alien rationality parked as an overgrowth on top of an animal brain. Nor is it a wrinkled schoolmaster repressing an impetuous subcortical rabble. It is an outgrowth designed to perfect the engagement with the self and world. Rather than the king reckoning and governing in his citadel, as Plato says of it in the *Timaeus* (70a), reason is an energy fed into the dynamic streams of living. This rather evident interpretation is nonetheless the reverse of the common picture we get from systemic explanations of the brain's anatomical functioning—explanations in which we can now see the Cartesian worldview. After all, if we consider reason not to be mere λογισμός, but the operation of the νοῦς, this is always a type of engagement with the inner and outer world, always directed, and not a mere internal calculation which says, with the psalm, "man returns to his dust . . . and on that very day his plans perish" (Ps 146:4).[31]

The Crypto-Cartesian temptation that would equate a set of steps in neural processing and a set of steps behind a choice is perhaps even more powerful than that of objective qualia. This is because behavior must result from a set of internal processes and rules can be a description of those processes. It seems natural to presume they are the same. But just as with words, rules are part of a communicative act. They convey a message

---

31. LXX: "ἐν ἐκείνῃ τῇ ἡμέρᾳ ἀπολοῦνται πάντες οἱ διαλογισμοὶ αὐτῶν."

and have a particular sphere of application. The conveyance of a message is not the same as the application of a rule, the application of a rule is not the same as the operation of a process. The algorithms that determine brain activity are like those that control the secretions of the liver. They are not applied, they merely *operate*. Since rules take place in the world of signs and their contexts and implications, they are always descriptive. The correlation of moral rules with the brain's algorithms is a form of Crypto-Cartesianism that is a process fallacy. Just because you have a comparable result doesn't mean you have comparable mechanisms that produced that result. This is especially evident when we consider that other intelligent animals, including cetaceans and some birds, have remarkably similar cognitive activity but radically different neural anatomy (Horik et al. 2012, 82). Form does not dictate activity.

The process fallacy is especially important because it characterizes the nature of moral behavior on the basis of a mechanism which can influence or alter the basis of moral claims. Kantian deontology becomes a program inside the brain which justifies its own categories.[32] Just as with other forms of Crypto-Cartesianism, the mechanical is always opposed to the volitional. Rather than belonging to the soul, the volitional is taken to be the engine of tooth-and-claw Darwinism, the limbic system, and the chemical operation of neurotransmitters. Thus if you operate rationally, and morally, you are employing the algorithms of your neocortex to inform your decisions. If you are enraged, or depressed, or ecstatic, your cortical system has given rein to the brews and juices of the lower brain bubbling up like Pythian smoke. Examining what makes this false shall illustrate to us the weaknesses of a strictly deontological system of morals.

There are four ways by which the contrast between deontology and aretology can be reconciled if conceived as having a relationship to what goes on in the brain: (1) rules for behavior are encoded in the brain (deontology), (2) the organism has a particular disposition that shapes its behavior (virtue ethics), (3) dispositions are the collective expressions of encoded rules occurring at various levels of functioning (deontology), (4) rules and dispositions together work to shape sets of habits and choices (virtue ethics). We maintain that empirical analysis of the body (brain included) points to 2, while observation of the self heuristically, which,

---

32. This is one of the reasons why nineteenth-century Neo-Kantians were so staunchly opposed to psychologism. They understood the erroneous application of this analogy.

as we observed, is a more accurate understanding of internal processes, points to 4.

Neurochemistry

To examine the wooly basics of neurobiology, neurotransmitters and hormones in the brain do not just operate with respect to emotions, they are fundamental elements in neural signaling itself. Furthermore Hebb's axiom that "neurons that fire together wire together" dictates complex network effects. To this are added the demonstrated influences of hormones (including those which have their own neurotransmitting effects), the immune system, blood sugar, oxygen and other elements of general health. Such an environment makes brain activity much more like a set of dials rather than algorithms of on-and-off switches. This is especially evident when we consider the chemical pathways behind how various neurotransmitters work. The famous serotonin has an uptake mechanism which reduces its effects, then there is an inhibition of the uptake which inhibits the inhibition. The neurotransmitter GABA inhibits, dopamine excites. GABA pathways can inhibit inhibition (Carlson and Birkett 2017, 115–17). A dopamine secreting pathway can excite the inhibition of excitation. A dopamine pathway directed over a GABA pathway can disinhibit the disinhibition of the disinhibition of the inhibitor. Which pathway the chemical reaction takes depends on the manner it branches and direction it follows. The "rules" which might be reflected in behavior do not operate in a system built according to the rule but by algorithms which might correspond to the behavior the rule *describes* but that themselves have a far different etiology.

Zooming out from neurotransmitters, a famous study examined the relationship between the decisions Israeli judges make and their physical satiety (Danziger et al. 2011). Relying on data which illustrate the well-known lack of compassion for those who are hungry, researchers argued that judges with a full stomach would be less harsh. Now a judge has criteria by which they make a decision, and those criteria are employed by the brain, but the rules that make up those criteria occur in the judge's person in a different way from which they would in a legal code. Here they are colored by the judge's internal condition. Research did not indicate what effect informing judges of the results of this study would have. Perhaps they would rearrange their schedule, or be more careful in examining their internal biases and to what extent their feelings affect decisions. Perhaps they would have a snack. Perhaps they would ignore the study all together as the law for them is a matter of belief and not subjective reflection. After all, once you start questioning your judgment on the basis of your diet, why not consider your other habits? Where will you stop? Any of these reactions would affect future outcomes for a certain number of individuals. Judgment, prudence, knowledge of one's weaknesses, flexible social institutions, inflexible individuals—a rich mix that over-emphasis on neural calculation can crudely oversimplify.

Thus deontology cuts both ways, like St. Paul's law and spirit: rules are put to use by a subjective individual who learns them, but their learning and employment are shaped by that individual's surrounding and underlying condition. It makes no sense from a cognitive point of view to say one is imposed upon the other, each is applied by the individual out of their behavior—much like the manner in which neural interfaces interact with and learn from their users.

In his popular book *Behave*, the neuroendocrinologist Robert Sapolsky has given broad and deep analyses of the conditions surrounding human behavior. A rabid atheist, Sapolsky is not taken seriously enough in theological circles, yet the conclusions we draw from his work are highly engaging for moral philosophy. He begins with the premise that there is no free will and all behavior is either already predictable on the basis of some statistical norm or someday will be. His notion of free will is, of course, Cartesian and he ventures into philosophical territory with a notable lack of sophistication. For him, rational moral choices are made by the cortical system suppressing the limbic system. He illustrates how childhood experiences, parenting, genetics, and general brain health contribute to conditions such as depression and violence. Physical trauma to the frontal cortex can be found in a significant percentage of the incarcerated. Emotional childhood trauma, physical and material adversity, and parental attachment issues also influence cortical development and enlarge the amygdala which is associated with quick emotional responses (Sapolsky 2017, 196-97). On the false basis that there is no free will, he quite legitimately questions the justice of imprisoning those whose behavior is associated with brain trauma.

Most interesting is that the chapters of his book are divided into "one second," "seconds to minutes," "hours to days before," "days to months before"—that is to say "before an act." The "seconds to minutes" before the organism does something are characterized by a certain set of processes that are already highly automatized. The "minutes to hours" by the conditions around that day, and days to "months" before set up broader and more deeply set conditions that help determine behavior. Before that, adolescence, childhood development, and inheritance shaped the functioning of large parts of brain anatomy, along with all the rest. A neuro-deontologist would argue that this means the basic rules of behavior were established over these periods and, as algorithms, they inform decisions made now. A set of rules of behavior for individual instances that could be collectively named "a sense of justice and fair play" was encoded in the growing frontal cortex at early stages of development. This informs decisions now at a deep level. But the ways in which fixed patterns of behavior grow and build upon one another, and how these must be linked with the establishment of fixed patterns of brain activity. Again, these are more like our sets of dials at which some responses are set at high, some at low. At other levels, these responses are limited, or intensified, by other settings with other sets of dials, and the choice is taken, at one level, on the momentary predominance of one position over another; but it is always taken against the background of other contexts which continually shade and influence the intensity of a particular choice and the likelihood of other choices being made around it.

Sapolsky has a certain pattern of argumentation which relishes in the baffling diversity and heterogeneity of what a particular neuroactive hormone or transmitter can do. He then exudes over the moral quandaries of how the same substance can result in both good and bad behaviors based on the right conditions. Oxytocin is part of inducing contractions during birth, but it is very important to brain activity. It creates feelings of attachment between couples, chumminess between friends of both sexes, and dogs and their masters. But it also induces the aggression of a mother defending her young, and, in turn makes people less fair to others outside of their peer group (Sapolsky 2017, 115–18). Testosterone is famously associated with aggressive behavior, but only if it is against the background of *patterns* of aggressive behavior (Sapolsky 2017, 115). Rather than a sense of blind fate and determinacy, one is astonished by the range of possibilities that a single set of neural and chemical pathways can yield. If we are willing to grant this organism agency, we might even call these *options*. One may not be aware of one's testosterone levels, but one might well make oneself aware of one's habits of anger and how they might breed upon each other. From this perspective, it is more reasonable to conclude that much moral behavior is not made up of internal rules, but that internal rules operate in the context of settled dispositions. A person does what he or she does because of the person he or she has been made into and, we would add, made herself into. This is indeed expressed by St. Augustine when he holds "the will is at fault in the case of the man of whom it is said, 'He is not inclined to understand, so as to do good'" (Augustine 2022, 5). The contribution of neuroethics would be to identify how the will is formed by patterns of actions and understanding that shape this man's inclinations.

Let us take a relevant example. Since the subject of racial discrimination is an important one for society, there is a great deal of research as to how it is inculcated into individual psychology. It has been shown that subjects from WEIRD societies[33] identify skin color at very basic neural levels and respond to it negatively. Studies have shown, for example, that a subject shown a dark-skinned person is more likely to believe that person is threatening them. When a policeman has to make a split-second decision as to whether that person is or is not reaching for a gun, the dark-skinned person is more likely to be shot. This is because, generally speaking, the limbic system (the thalamus and amygdala in particular) is giving an immediate order to preserve the organism before the processing of other parts of the brain can suppress it.

This can easily be put into a Darwinian ideology. Humans, like lions, recognise their group, outsiders are no good. The fight or flight mechanism of the lower brain is put into action to primitively neutralize the threat of the other.

However, no one would expect the same prejudices to inhere in, shall we say, Tanzania, where most everyone has dark skin. There would be other criteria. Nor would we expect someone who does not have or know how to use a gun to draw one and shoot it at short notice. Lions in Tanzania, at zoos and elsewhere, would not be expected to perform any of this behavior, nor would the unarmed human population. Complex behavior is learned, enforced, and reinforced. Set different conditions for shaping that behavior and you will have different results no matter at most any level of "instinct" or automaticity. As Sapolsky often iterates, and anyone familiar with the field attests, the dichotomy between nature and nurture is a false one.

---

33. Western, Educated, Industrialized, Rich and Democratic.

Nature and the Patristic Ethos

A set of principles for taking decisions based not on pre existing rules but established on the collective result of a set of dispositions is called virtue ethics. As Alasdair MacIntyre argued in his signal work, *After Virtue* (2007) the system of ethics one subscribes to, like one's epistemology and ontology, is dependent upon how one understands the human nature which takes the decision. Kant's deontological system marveled at "the moral law within me" because he believed that imperatives were both internal to the person and universal. We may consider that the biologically determinate processes Sapolsky describes can also arrive at a theoretical account of choice, but one that describes processes and behavior and not principles. For this reason, Sapolsky is, despite himself, a virtue ethicist.

A remarkable example comes in the case of Wesley Autrey, a construction worker who, on January 2, 2007, jumped onto the New York subway tracks to save a man who had been convulsed with a seizure. Autrey lay on top of the man and clasped him tight while five subway cars passed over before the train stopped. Neither were seriously injured. Autrey called out to the shocked bystanders, among whom were his two young daughters, that he and the man he saved were alive and well (Buckley 2007). Such acts have long been a challenge to the standard utilitarian and Darwinian explanations of behavior. While Darwin discussed altruism and what is termed group selection in his work, only recently has a principle of altruism entered the broader debate within biology (Nowak 2013).[34] Self sacrifice is simply an unacceptable argument for any system that has an atomic notion of self interest at its heart.

Sapolsky mentions such individuals as an illustration that this behavior cannot be rational: they tend to say "I didn't have time to think!" (Sapolsky 2017, 185, 474). But his own system does not imply this means their decision was not informed by conscious activity and prior behavior. Quite the opposite, the behavior such individuals undertook "months" and "years before" builds up the patterns of neural architecture, neurochemistry, and basic biology that made taking exceedingly moral decisions automatic. Autrey's case is a telling example. Reports at the time indicated that he had been to all around him not an exceptionally unusual, but still an exceptionally decent man. He also had worked for several years as a construction worker after service in the navy. Thus he had the

---

34. See the theological context of this critique in the excellent work of Coakley and Nowak 2013.

moral patterns of behavior that might result in such a truly saintly act, and he also might have had some acquired skills that gave him a sense of the space around the rails to shape the instinctual, but reasonable, set of behaviors he took. His own reports of his thoughts at the time,[35] and the amount of time he would have had to make such a decision, argue against the "rational"—if we consider rationality to be only a set of calculations, utilitarian or categorical.

If we take reason to be what St. Gregory the Theologian, Evagrius of Pontus, or St. Maximus the Confessor mean by it, Autrey drew his virtues together to perform a supremely rational act of love in the pattern of his Heavenly Father. Indeed, for contemporary Darwinists, Autrey's behavior was not only irrational—because for them all behavior is irrational—it was supremely *unnatural*, even perverse, which is why figures such as Steven Pinker and Richard Dawkins have addressed the introduction of altruism and group selection into theories of selection with contempt.[36]

Until the turn toward biblical literalism and rationalism, the cultivation of the virtues was one of the most important aspects of the Christian life. It was not just taken as a set of rules which one was to observe, but as a means of transforming the self into that which was nearer to God. As Evagrius says: "The way of prayer is also twofold: it comprises practice and contemplation" (Evagrius 1983, 29). It is the first that lays the ground for the second. The representatives of the ascetic tradition were extremely attentive to the fact that habits and behavior are determinative aspects of the person, hence the emphasis on discipline and abstinence as those things which reined in the mind and body together.

Patristic anthropology based its understanding of the operations of the body on contemporary medicine (Wright 2022), which they understood to be a developing science with a variety of explanations and opinions. In the ancient world medicine was based on an understanding of health as a balance of elements within the whole body. The fact that thoughts and dispositions had a material basis was generally presumed up into the seventeenth century (Paster 2014). For example, when defining the different types of choleric dispositions, St. John of Damascus says: "When it is initiated and awakened, anger is called 'initial bile.' A stubborn retention of anger is called resentment (μῆνις), because it remains (μένειν) in memory (μνήμη)" (*Expositio fide orthodoxa* 2.16 [PG

---

35. When asked what he was thinking at the time, he reportedly said: "I thought, "you better save him, *fool*. That man's going to die!"—humility and charity as instinct.

36. The debate can be summarized here in Nowak et al. 2011. See also Pinker 2012.

94.933A]). One could read this statement, like Libet's experiment, as a simple abrogation of free will. Bile, produced by the liver, builds up in the body and leads to anger. No matter how much one repents, if it remains you have resentment. You have no choice in the matter. Yet we should regard St. John as saying that *cholē* remains in the body because the soul has not repented. Bile is an index of the condition of body and soul together. As we noted, the fact that ancient and medieval philosophers thought that images could be located in the brain did not keep them from believing in the reins of the soul. Neither does the recognition of the effect of body chemistry on behavior here mean that we have no free will. While no one is advocating a return to the doctrine of the four humors, the foregoing description of the complexities of neurochemistry should at least support a return to the foundations of this idea.[37] It should also aid us in arriving at a more sensitive understanding of illness, especially mental illness.

Extending St. John's reasoning might also expose some of the foundations of St. Maximus dithelestic anthropology. Divine nature works within the human in cooperation with the rational forces of the individual will. Virtue and contemplation help to transform that image closer to its prototype in the divine. Psychological distress is not just a "chemical imbalance" at which one can toss antidepressants, it is a result of modes of thinking which then influence the manner in which we think. Nor is real mental illness merely the matter of a lack of willpower when a neurological condition has impeded one's ability to change behavior. How one views illness and health depends on how one views the relations of the body and soul. As St. Gregory of Nyssa says in his characteristic sensitivity:

> The rational nature is not seated in bodily voids, nor would the presence of flesh drive it out. For the body as a whole is constructed like a musical instrument. It is often the case that those who know the melody may not be able to show what they know owing to a fault in the instrument.... So the mind, acting upon the whole instrument, touching, as is usually the case, each member with reasoned activity, acts in accordance with its nature. Those parts which then refuse to accept the activity of its art fail and cease to be acted upon. (*De opificio hominis*. 12.8 [PG 44:160–61 Col. 351–53])

---

37. See also St. John Chrysostom, *Or. 10 Eph.* 4:4–7 (PG 62:73–74), and *Or. 13 1 Tim.* 4:11–14 (PG 62:568). For an examination of the patristic understanding of the humors, see Trimble 2021.

Is this not a finer account of the relation between soul and body, soul and disease, than any of those presented by the "humanists" we have examined, and more in keeping with the facts they themselves have presented? This is not because St. Gregory had a better understanding of oxytocin than Dr. Robert Sapolsky, it is because the saint understood material substances as being one of those things which contribute to the whole self. For St. Gregory the essence of that self was the soul, and for biology the self has no essence whatsoever. Sapolsky admits: "I can't imagine how to live your life as if there is no free will. It may never be possible to view ourselves as the sum of our biology." He concludes that "our homuncular myths"—Cartesianism, that is—at least should be "benign" (Sapolsky 2017, 613).[38] Such is the unenviable spirit of naturalism from Laplace onward—rejection of the transcendent then the grudging acceptance of normative myths for fear of the alternative. We can do better.

Metaphysics of the Person: Radical Ethics

With all the well-justified wonder at the complexity of the brain, biology is in a genuine quandary as to *why* we would have an organ which would allow us to speculate on the cosmos, and the moral law, when such things are unlikely to help one's individual fitness. One who believes that doing physics or theology makes one a better mate and thus more likely to produce a greater number of offspring is not well acquainted with the field. The best explanation biology has to offer is that we evolved our complex brains for the performance of complex tasks related to social interaction.

Recent neuroscience has given great weight to the influence of social factors in the evolution of the brain. The best evidence is anatomical and comparative. Despite the cart-before-the-horse world of crypto-Cartesianism, the function of language is communication. Cats do not need mentalese to find mice. When the brain anatomies of humans and other animals are compared, the greatest functional similarities are in centers related to vocalization. That human speech emerged from animal vocalization is a reasonable evolutionary conclusion. However many of these speech centers in humans, around the frontal and temporal medial lobes, are associated with social activity in animals. Naturally, most vocalization is social. You must determine who is screeching at you and why.

---

38. Sapolsky has given a book-length version of this pseudo-ethics in Sapolsky 2023.

Abstract thought, imagination, and ratiocination are all intimately associated with language. And, as we have seen, social activity overlaps with language centers in the human brain as well. This should point to some of the fundamental motivations behind reason—in all senses of the term—as something which makes us in the world. For some this is a lust for praise and status, for others this is an effort at collective progress.

Even more convincing are comparative analyses of social animals and their brains. The animals with the most complex brains—humans and other primates, cetaceans (dolphins and whales), corvids (crows, etc.), and some parrots—are highly social and highly dependent upon communication. In fact a famous study by Robin Dunbar demonstrated an association between the size of an animal's frontal cortex and the size of its social network (Dunbar 2009).[39]

While we should not succumb to that singularly nineteenth-century conflation of history and ontology, the importance of the social to the brain should extend beyond an interest in evolution. All of the abovementioned species have a highly developed theory of mind. That is to say, crow A knows that crow B has the same ability to perceive, remember, and pilfer that crow A does, crow B knows that crow A knows, and so on. Though in many social animals a theory of mind is absent, certainly its presence is the supreme mark of the social. It is also a fundamental mark of the ethical. Here we might be reminded of the radical ethics of Emmanuel Levinas who argued that we only have an existence as ourselves because of our absolute relationship to the other (Levinas 1969, 118–20), and the relational ontology of Bp. John Zizioulas. We could extend this to say that we only have a profound understanding of anything because we have acquired the understanding of the other. It is the ethical which has given us the capacity for absolute understanding. We are able to marvel at the starry law above us because we have the moral law (and disposition) within us.

Since it is impossible for the social to emerge without the recognition of the self and other, it is a pity that Sapolsky is unable to recognize that the very principle of the self he cannot accept is demonstrated by a field to which he is a major contributor. More than a third of *Behave* deals with social neuroscience. Perhaps the "homuncular myths" he wishes he could abandon keep him from recognizing the implications of his own discipline because they are more essential to his scientific outlook that he

---

39. Though generally persuasive, the strict correlation between sociality and the neocortex require more nuance. See Lindenfors et al. 2021.

is willing to admit. Once we set the ethical is at the heart of the rational, then certain facts about what we understand of the world also have an ethical dimension. This would seek to undermine the fact/value distinction that lies at the heart of the modern world-view. Better not to shake those foundations.

Unsettling the fact/value distinction requires a reassessment of what the nature of being a living, flourishing, organism, and agent, means. Just as in St. Gregory the Theologian's argument in the *Fourth Catechetical Oration* questions of ethics then become foundational for questions of metaphysics. Just as in Evagrius and St. Maximus, the movement toward truth in contemplation is founded on a movement toward virtue in action. That notion of the motion toward God as a fundamentally natural and ethical state is a cardinal feature of Orthodox metaphysics and anthropology. By reassessing the ethical element behind metaphysics we may be able to arrive at a notion of individual beings and natural kinds (species and hypostases) that can provide philosophical foundations for science as a whole. An extension of Fr. Methody's metaphysics of hypostatic discontinuities may also serve in reestablishing the fundamental notion of the good—the moral—as a truth in the world.[40]

If Richard Dawkins makes the unit of biological life the gene, Francis Galton the individual (and the "race"), and Charles Darwin the species, then patristics would take all units of life to be in sets of infinite relations. The first relation is infinite ("beyond infinite")[41] because it is God's relation to his creation. Our object is to realize the image of God as mediators between him and creation. Caught in death and sin, we restore our image through a filial relationship to our Creator and a loving relationship to others individually and corporately in the mystery of the Church. This is what affords the person, as hypostasis, its entelechy, its agency, and its reality.

In fact, the social is the only way to conceive of an answer to the Hard Problem of Consciousness as well as the emergence of the question itself. Under the values of nineteenth-century utilitarianism, advancement up the hierarchy of species means advancement in intellectual ability. Ironically this is evident in current "neuroethical" discussions over the recognition of animals as persons. We are to regard dolphins as persons because they have very advanced brains (AAAS 2012). But

---

40. This is also an element of Fr. Christopher Knight's (Knight 2021) incarnational focus in the theology of science.

41. "ὑγιηαπείρος" in St. Maximus the Confessor, *Ambigua* 5 (PG 91:1049C).

why should a brain be the only measure of relevance? Perhaps whales are more important because they are big, or tigers because they are strong. By its own system, Darwinism would only regard an organism as advanced if it is well-adapted to its environment, in which case very few creatures would be superior to viruses, bacteria, or fungi.

There is no particular utilitarian reason why we should be interested in the far reaches of the cosmos, the fantastical worlds of advanced mathematics, or the fantastical dimensions of art. The human body expends about a third of its energy[42] on brain activity. Reducing speculation on outer galaxies or multiple souls would conserve resources and improve the adaptive capacities of the species.

The only valid biological proposal is that the brain has evolved into such an expensive organ because complex social relations are important to individual survival, and such relations rely on complex reasoning ability. This view has a great deal of evidence behind it. First, the brain anatomy associated with language is closely related to vocalization and social activity in other species (Shepherd and Freiwald 2018; cf. Gavrilov and Nieder 2021). Second, comparative studies of animals have noted that complex social activity, social groups of a certain size, and certain reproductive strategies tend to go together with high levels of intelligence.[43] Third, genetics (Mozzi et al. 2016), comparative evolution of the mouth (Lieberman et al. 1972), and cognitive archaeology (Mithen 1996) show that culture has developed in tandem with human nature. Fourth, processes of language, distinctions between self and other, the determination of social groups (kin, kind, friend, foe), deception, imagination, and hypothetical reasoning are often shown to be closely related from the perspective of neuroscience and psychology in general. Finally, there seems to be no other reason to evolve a coherent notion of the self other than in relation to another. This is not an element of an oft-repeated philosophical dialectic, but a neuroscientific account of why cognition of the self would have evolved.

However, evolution is not essential to understanding the human. Why I do what I do at this moment plays only a bit part. Proponents of Noam Chomsky's merge hypothesis, as we have noted, argue that evolution led to a genetic mutation that gave humans the advantage of logical

---

42. Calculated by comparing metabolic expenditure per organ in proportion to average body mass at rest. See Wang et al. 2010.

43. The classic groups of comparison are birds of the parrot family, the crow family, cetaceans, and primates, including humans. See Horik 2012.

recursion prompting the development of language and abstract thinking. Yet I have not found any serious attempt in the literature to assess what this means as a system of communication—what merge would mean for the social—as if communication were not the function of language at all! The merge hypothesis is another historical fudge so etiologically specific as to be unlikely and so general as to have little scientific value.[44]

This is not an oversight, or a distaste for the unsettled trivialities of sociolinguistics, it is a symptom of the problem. Computationalists do not need language as a system of communication, they need it as a generator of platonic ideas, a generator of code to be injected in the Crypto-Cartesian machine between intention and denotation. Behind the very framing of the hard question is the notion that the function of the brain is about abstract thinking, solitary calculation and analysis. One is persuaded to think that such an approach is unlikely to lead to any explanation of the mind when it is divorced both from its morphology and the ways in which it is most often used on a daily basis by most of us.[45]

Needless to say, the ethical relation in the Abrahamic traditions is a completely different animal. As St. Gregory the Theologian said, "for man most takes after God when he does good" (*De pauperum amore* 27 [PG 35:892–93]). And thus, made in his image, we are an image able to do mercy through the energies of the love he has given us.

The theology of the icon might thus aid us in arriving at an alternative to that fragmented, isolated, Hobbesian subject that is no more than a bundle of activities. Rather we may see the hypostasis of the person as a whole which is demonstrated as such by its virtue to act. It also maintains its integrity by possessing marks of its identity. These marks do not operate as traditional signs, nor do they point to propositional, or modal, statements of identity (see Goncharko and Goncharko, 2017; Pfau, 2022; Schneider, 1993).

As is well known, the development of the doctrine of the icon chose to select portraits of the Lord, his mother, and the saints and not to rest on symbols or abstract signs. Unlike other signs which can be rendered in whole or in part, the face bears a highly subtle, and inexpressible, set of characteristics that convey the person behind them. Alter any of these, and the viewer has the sense that the person is not the same. Only

---

44. However, extensions of merge beyond Chomsky's etiology are very promising. See Yang et al. 2017. But this requires that we get out of the black box of the brain and into the world.

45. To make this point one has only to unhappily compare the volume of "scientific" communication with that of "social" media.

recently has artificial intelligence software attained human capabilities of facial recognition, and that by very complex means. In the brain a large section of the fusiform gyrus is associated with the recognition of faces (Kanwisher and Yovel 2006), a behavior essential to social function. It is possible that the flatness and (relative) hairlessness of the human face, along with large lips and well-marked eyebrows, exists as a "canvas" for expression and communication. This wholeness then must be taken as a self that is created to communicate with the other. The psychological, philosophical, and ethical aspects of the icon may have much to offer neuroscientific theory.

For example, assessments of beauty in the face have been associated with activity in the medial orbitofrontal cortex. This area is also active in the assessment of whether a set of behaviors is good (Sapolsky 2017, 88). On the surface this would be the kind of behavior that Sapolsky would call "depressing" as it would justify judging the book by its cover. Yet it also can be seen to show that we perceive the actions of another not by a set of arbitrary rules but by the person who is doing it. The Christ who "had no beauty or comeliness" was rejected by the world. The saint, wracked by fasting, disease, and old age, can radiate from within. While a certain majority will always judge things by a questionable set of values,[46] rules and values themselves are not determined by the majority. Wesley Autrey's heroic action was not biologically *wrong*, as some commentators would have us believe, because it was exceptional. What is true love or morality without a face?

Here we can see how a reading of neuroscience informed by a different set of principles should lead to a radically different understanding of the person. And we can also see that such principles do not resemble what we read in the works of leading neuroscientists, but, sadly, nor to they represent the principles of most theologians and "conservative" thinkers who oppose them relying on the same Cartesian presuppositions and a wilful ignorance of biology.

The iconicity of the person as a radical subject is especially relevant with respect to the ethical dimensions of neuroscience. Sapolsky very rightly raises the issue of the spectrum between neurological types and neurological disease. Should diseases such as obsessive compulsive disorder be diagnosed by a brain scan, or a blood test, will we gradually be able to diagnose our own individual ticks and eccentricities as some deviation

---

46. Notions of physical facial beauty are fairly standard across the world. See Rhodes et al. 2001.

form the norm. The dubious specter of "designer neurosurgery" comes to the fore. For Sapolsky, this is "very disturbing" because it breaks down that homuncular myth that "I am what I am" by an account of my own neural machinery which describes why I write books or tug at my ear. I venture that this troubles Sapolsky because his myths are vacuous ones.

Yet a response to these fears has already come from those engaged with autism activism and research. They argue that those "on the spectrum" are not necessarily subject to a diagnosis. We all represent a range of neurological types. Unfortunately, they couch this argument in typical Darwinist utilitarianism: we have evolved "neurodiversity" because the species needs people with a variety of talents to persist (Silberman 2016, 15). Liberal values are, presumably, not sufficient in themselves. If we regard the person as an icon, a being of uniqueness and value for and of itself—by nature, by experience, by agency—the importance of "neurodiversity" is self-evident. But, unlike the argument behind identity politics, that icon itself is tarnished by the condition of sin. The person is of value for what it is as an image of God, but it is even more important for what it must become. Orthodox ethics has a great tradition of recognizing identity, but it must reject a politics that turns our iconic individuality into a brand, a fetish, an idol, and not that which has as part of its nature the ability and necessity to move forward and upward.

Conclusion

Essentially, the foregoing returns us to an old question: "Is love a faculty of reason?" We are now, with the help of neuroscience, in a position to answer this question. For the bulk of pre-modern humanity, virtue was reasonable and virtuous desire was reasoned desire. Thus the sensation of joy, the racing heart, the dilation of the pupils, the secretion of oxytocin, could be marks of this virtuous state. The Piercean *indexation* of these signs of love was as unproblematic as any other physical disposition.

Modern love became sundered. Rational desire was segregated to the will, expressed in the body with insignificant Piercean *icons* (i.e., in the doctrine of the sentiments). As natural philosophy in the guise of Darwinian utilitarianism changed the nature of the human (Hanby 2003, 676), love returned to the position of index, but of a complex, collective, and undetermined set of instincts for survival and reproduction. The love for the good of mankind, for God and country, was either (for nineteenth-century utilitarians) an evolutionary advantage that set the human at the pinnacle of creation or (for twentieth and twenty-first century liberal utilitarians) a perversion of the hypertrophic appendage attached socially (or, more rarely, genetically) onto the encoded instincts for survival, mutual altruism, and reproduction. In this icy atmosphere, Christian love and Sapolsky's "homuncular myth" were allowed to exist so long as they assumed the teleology of science, empire, and state.

Yet if reason is inextricably linked with the social, then the abstract thought that leads us to speculate on the outer reaches of mathematics, or the cosmos, or the vaulting heights of abstract art must also have some ethical content. I would argue that only theology can show us the connection.

In his *Second Theological Oration*, St. Gregory of Nazianzen provides theology with a rich introduction to its principles with a long and characteristically eloquent summary of the knowledge of the natural world from the "microcosm" of man to the ranks of angels. Rather, his cosmological prolegomenon is a summary of the ignorance of imminent creation that can only lead us to wonder at how we could presume to rationally approach the transcendent Creator. For us St. Gregory's selection of details and transitions between various objects of contemplation is strange, a bit like the categories of animals in Jorge Luis Borges' story of the Chinese Encyclopedia. Gregory, following the Psalmist, marvels at mankind, at the mixture of the immortal and mortal within us, then at the ability of the mind to fly from one end of the universe to another, then how we were made by the principles of nature. Then parentage, inherited traits: "the nature of the bond and that condition between parents and children, and the charm of love between them."[47] This leads to a consideration of the differences between species, which then leads to the differences in the modes of perception. Later, he curiously mentions that scripture marvels at how God instilled the wisdom that women show in their skill of weaving (see Job 38.36 LXX), and then continues:

> But I would have you marvel at the natural knowledge even of irrational creatures and if you can, explain its cause. How is it that birds have for nests rocks and trees and roofs, and adapt them both for safety and beauty and for the comfort of their little ones? From where do bees and spiders get their love of work and art? Bees plan their honeycombs and join them together by hexagonal cells set one beside the other, and secure

---

47. "Τίς ἡ τῆς φύσεως ὁλκὴ, καὶ πρὸς ἄλληλα σχέσις τοῖς γεννῶσι καὶ τοῖς γεννωμένοις, ἵνα τῷ φίλτρῳ συνέχηται" (*Oration* 28:22 [PG 36:56]).

the fabric by means of the dividing wall and the alternation of angles with straight lines—and this is done in such dark hives, that the structure itself is invisible. And spiders weave their intricate webs by such light and almost airy threads stretched in various ways from almost invisible beginnings . . . ? (Gregory 2011, 34–35)

It would seem St. Gregory occupies a position of wonderment not at intelligent but at *epiphenomenological design*. We observe elements of creation related to one another not by causality but by how the interconnectedness of their existence links them to God as their Beginning and End. The observations of mankind are also elements in that chain of existence. Like God's revelation to Job (ch. 38), of which this passage is a partial commentary, we see what he makes before us and stand in bafflement. Yet the fulsome iteration of all these facts and relations begins itself to accumulate a different sense of order. Euclid could not make shapes like the spider, Phidias the sculptor and Zeuxis the painter could not capture the beauties of the movements of cranes. Science, art, knowledge examine things as they are. There is nothing in St. Gregory's works that suggests a *distrust* of empirical observation and scientific deduction in relation to any other human pursuit, quite the opposite. But the reality that is expressed by establishing general principles of relations—the theory that comes of science—is never to be taken as a complete account.

Because being is not complete without recourse to the One who bestows it, science that does not address that transcendent Being, at least apophatically, is not a pursuit of truth. In this, St. Gregory's long survey of natural philosophy finds a deeper sense. We understand that scaling the heights of theology is like Job calling to the whirlwind. But the living act of understanding the world in our ignorance is a praise of those deepest principles which lie beyond it.

The wonders of the brain which can attain to the extraordinary heights of these natural and artificial marvels are an expression of that capacity to reach toward continuities and discontinuities, orders and hierarchies, sameness and difference, as part of what it means for the natural organism to thrive. To do this in an evidently scientific way—through observation, testing, enquiry—is to approach through praise that transcendent Font of Being to whose essence no amount of enquiry can attain.

Many of the mysteries St. Gregory mentions have been answered by science, those of the architecture of birds and bees not so long ago (Frisch

1974). The aforementioned oxytocin can explain much of the bond between parent and child in the human as well as many non-humans. The presence of an explanation does not limit Gregory's exhortation. His is not a God of the gaps. Nor is he the God who intelligently designed the rules of Newton so Newton could find them for us. Induction and deduction aid in defining the nature of an entity but they in no way reduce its being because the Source of that being is not reduced by any distinction. Science looks at nature not to define God's absence, but to thrive in his Presence because that is what it means to be rational. We can read the function of St. Gregory's rational inquiry into the vast mysteries of the world as a call to the sublime, but over its expanse the rhetorical function of his oration becomes laudatory. Science can become an art of praise.

We would maintain that arriving at an acceptable scientific account of the nature of the human person requires a reassessment of the foundations of natural philosophy, science as a whole. This is because we have misunderstood how being is shaped in relation to action and we have misunderstood how distinctions can be theorized both psychologically and in an explanation of reality. It is no wonder that figures such as Scheler and the Gestalt theorists confronted the atomism of the self with a full defense of the natural instinct to find harmony and beauty in our activity as a living, perceiving organism.

Furthermore, this is because crypto-Cartesianism has, so it seems, exhausted its ability to explain such phenomena as direct environmental influences on the development of the organisms and species, group selection and the influence of cooperation on evolution, communication, and a range of other "epiphenomenal" issues. Many theological questions for neuroethics, bioethics, and general science remain. Firstly, while the distinction between *ousia* and *hypostasis* can help arrive at a theory of continuities, regularities, and natural kinds, the relationship between hypostases and species is complex in the patristic tradition. On some occasions, the Fathers speak of the hypostasis of the person as the whole species of mankind and, at others, focus on the person as an individual. Closer examination of the role of autonomy and activity in this respect may help to shape categories to be useful for theoretical biology, not to mention the theology of history and politics.

Another particularly vexing question regards the place of semiotics outside the brain. If the critique of Crypto-Cartesianism is valid, then the structures behind sign systems must come from some other source. This would include logic and mathematics. If we assert that God created sign systems we make ourselves susceptible to the idolatrous excesses of Eunomianism and the Name Worshippers (*Imyaslavtsy*). If God did not make signs and they do not reside solely in the brains that use them, then what is their ontological status? A reasonable position would be to understand signs as phenomena that statistically emerge in matrices between what is encoded in the head and regularities in the world. These regularities bear some correspondence to inner principles as the *logoi* of St. Maximus Confessor. The *degree of correspondence* represents the degree of truth value in a metaphysical sense.[48] Just as an amputee learns in tandem with their neural interface the neural signals that are going to govern a prosthetic limb, a crippled rationality finds truth heuristically. We are not going to find a dictionary or a quantum key to the *logoi*. Natural laws—quantum interference, thermodynamics—are not *logoi*. Natural laws are our own creation. But our struggles to define reality get us closer to the Truth and Life (John 14:6). Theology may be able to address fundamental questions as to the nature and origins of information by setting our scientific laws in *relation* to the principles of created nature (Maximus' "λόγοι ὑπαρκτικοί"),[49] but not as identical with them. I would argue that this approach is significantly different from medieval notions of realism (Thomist, Scotist, Baconian, etc.), but such a hypothesis needs examination from the positions of cognitive ethology, information science, and theoretical physics. In some respects, this sense is already receiving some attention as is amply evidenced in these pages (see also Tsvelik and Aksenov-Meerson 2021; Knight 2021).

An equally important question persists in the reformulation of neuroethics through incarnational ontology. If we define the person in relation to health as we would define the person in relation to Christ, where are the boundaries of disease? All sin is disease, the *cholē* that makes one resentful also makes one ill. But where is that boundary of illness that marks one as insane? Neuroscience and psychology have long ago lost the image of the person that would properly inform this definition

---

48. Evagrius of Pontus, one of St. Maximus' sources here, gives a concise account of this heuristics: "We practice the virtues in order to achieve contemplation of the *logoi* of created things, and from this we pass to contemplation of the Logos who gives them their being; and He manifests Himself when we are in the state of prayer" (Evagrius of Pontus 1983, 52). The parallels between moral reasoning and contemplation were later systematized by St. Maximus in *Mystagogia* 4 and *Ambigua* 10. See Louth 2023, 337–40.

49. *Ambigua* 42.15 (PG 1329A–B): "Πάντων οὖν τῶν κατ' οὐσίαν ὑπαρκτικῶς ὄντων τε καὶ ἐσομένων, ἢ γενομένων, ἢ γενοσομένων ἢ φαινομένων, ἢ φανσομένων, ἐν τῷ Θεῷ προϋπάρχουσι παγίως ὄντες οἱ λόγοι."

and thus commercial norms define health and morals are a "lifestyle choice." Doctors liberally distribute antidepressants and tranquilizers as if one had no more control over one's brain chemistry than one does in the composition of one's bone marrow. This is because they accord *no sanction* to the will and fundamentally do not understand the bipartite nature of the person. But true madness *does* negate the operation of the will. How do patristic principles aid in defining that point at which madness merits medical intervention? On one side, we have the aid of neuroscience to help us determine degrees of brain damage, deficiency, or malfunction. On the other side we have the deontological definitions of personal responsibility that reside in the legal system. While the practical bioethics of figures such as Tristram Engelhardt made significant progress in moving toward the latter, legal position, we still must define the boundary where "he is not inclined to understand, so as to do good" becomes "he is incapable of understanding that he does evil." The dynamic, enactive understanding of the person gives us an opportunity to arrive at an evidentiary answer to the problem, but not a simple one. The foregoing should have demonstrated to us that neuroscience needs a new anthropology to determine that boundary, a boundary that, thankfully, still matters for the law and society as a whole.[50] Orthodox ethics argues that freedom comes in the exercise of the virtues, and not in the exercise of sin, for virtue is our natural state. How should this change approaches to definitions of agency, disease and treatment in a neurological context? Furthermore, the iconic core of Orthodox anthropology can, and must, also resist the normative utilitarianism which defines mental health as that which makes a good worker or consumer. Those who argue for the value of "neurodiversity" are in this at least temporary allies.

We have set forth the argument that patristic anthropology is in a position to aid in determining the boundaries of the human, but only once the fundamental principles of science are redefined. We have shown that the philosophy of the Modern creates false metaphysical categories which are then used to create a model of realism. So long as this model affords a place to a supernatural will, it can allow a nominally "conservative" Christian anthropology to fill the gaps with what cannot be explained materially. However, because it is incapable of demonstrating a living,

---

50. Sapolsky notes with laudable horror two cases where a positive test for a gene experimentally associated with aggression (low-activity MAO-A) was used to lessen the prison sentences of convicted murderers. The data surrounding genetic expression does not support such pat eitiology in the least (Sapolsky 2017, 253).

active, autonomous subject, this model eventually transforms the self into a machine controlled by algorithms as laws of behavior. The inability to define a subject means that there is no understanding of what a species or class of beings is supposed to do or be. We have argued that ecological and enactive theories that reject this approach better correspond to an empirical understanding of brain science. Paradoxically, they better suit a proper theological position because they do not impose categories outside the system save the thriving of the organism itself. Flourishing, an ethics based on the virtues, the striving toward a pre-ordained conception of perfection at the level of the organism and the species, and a conception of the self based on a dynamic, progressive, relation to that perfection in the other—all stem from a notion of the person which can be illumined by the patristic tradition and to which the facts, as well as the prejudices, of contemporary science call us to return. The stakes are high: what it means to be, to do, to think, to strive toward the good.

Bibliography

AAAS. 2012. "Declaration of Rights for Cetaceans: Ethical and Policy Implications of Intelligence." https://aaas.confex.com/aaas/2012/webprogram/Session4617.html.

Abadía, Oscar Moro. 2008. "Beyond the Whig History Interpretation of History: Lessons on 'Presentism' from Hélène Metzger." *Studies in History and Philosophy of Science Part A* 39(2): 194–201. https://doi.org/10.1016/j.shpsa.2008.03.005.

Acevedo, Bianca P., et al. "Neural Correlates of Long-Term Intense Romantic Love." *Social Cognitive and Affective Neuroscience* 7(2): 145–59. https://doi.org/10.1093/scan/nsq092.

Anderson, Michael L. 2021. *After Phrenology: Neural Reuse and the Interactive Brain*. Cambridge: MIT Press.

Antieu, Bernard. 2007. *La neurophilosophie*. Paris: Qui Sais-je?

Ash, Mitchell G. 1998. *Gestalt Psychology in German Culture, 1890–1967: Holism and the Quest for Objectivity*. Cambridge: Cambridge University Press.

Augustine, St. *On Grace and Free Will*. 2022. Edited by Benjamin B. Warfield. Translated by Peter Holmes and Robert Earnest Wallace. https://www.newadvent.org/fathers/1510.htm.

Beliy, Roman, et al. 2019. "From Voxels to Pixels and Back: Self-Supervision in Natural-Image Reconstruction from FMRI." *Advances in Neural Information Processing Systems* 32. https://proceedings.neurips.cc/paper/2019/hash/7d2be41b1bde6ff8fe45150c37488ebb-Abstract.html.

Berger, Theodore W., et al. 2012. "A Hippocampal Cognitive Prosthesis: Multi-input, Multi-output Nonlinear Modelling and VLSI Implementation." *IEEE Transactions on Neural Systems and Rehabilitation Engineering* 20(2): 198–211. https://doi.org/10.1109/TNSRE.2012.2189133.

Berlinski, David. 1996. "The Deniable Darwin." *Commentary Magazine*. https://www.commentary.org/articles/david-berlinski/the-deniable-darwin/.

Blowers, Paul M. 2013. "Aligning and Reorienting the Passible Self: Maximus the Confessor's Virtue Ethics." *Studies in Christian Ethics* 26(3): 333–50. https://doi.org/10.1177/0953946813484409.

Bradshaw, David. 2007. *Aristotle East and West: Metaphysics and the Division of Christendom*. Cambridge: Cambridge University Press.

Buchenau, Stefanie, and Roberto Lo Presti. 2017. *Human and Animal Cognition in Early Modern Philosophy and Medicine*. Pittsburgh: University of Pittsburgh Press.

Buckley, Cara. 2007. "Man Is Rescued by Stranger on Subway Tracks." *New York Times*, January 3. https://www.nytimes.com/2007/01/03/nyregion/03life.html.

Carlson, Neil R., and Melissa A. Birkett. 2017. *Physiology of Behavior*. Global ed. Boston: Pearson.

Chalmers, David J., ed. 2002. *Philosophy of Mind: Classical and Contemporary Readings*. New York: Oxford University Press.

Chaudhary, Ujwal, et al. 2022. "Spelling Interface Using Intracortical Signals in a Completely Locked-in Patient Enabled via Auditory Neurofeedback Training." *Nature Communications* 13(1): 1236. https://doi.org/10.1038/s41467-022-28859-8.

Chomsky, Noam. 1959. "A Review of Skinner's Verbal Behavior." *Language* 35(1): 26–58.

Chrisley, Ronald, and Sander Begeer. 2000. *Artificial Intelligence: Critical Concepts*. London: Routledge.

Clark, Andy, and David J. Chalmers. 1998. "The Extended Mind." *Analysis* 58(1): 7–19.

Collins, Jack. 2003. "Miracles, Intelligent Design, and God-of-the-Gaps." *Perspectives in Science and Christian Faith* 55(1): 22–29.

Damasio, Antonio. 2008. *Descartes' Error: Emotion, Reason, and the Human Brain*. London: Vintage Digital.

Danziger, Shai, et al. 2011. "Extraneous Factors in Judicial Decisions." *Proceedings of the National Academy of Sciences of the United States of America* 108(17): 6889–92. https://doi.org/10.1073/pnas.1018033108.

Dennett, Daniel C. 1993. "Quining Qualia." In *Readings in Philosophy and Cognitive Science*, edited by Alvin I. Goldman, 381–414. Cambridge: MIT Press.

———. 1996. *Darwin's Dangerous Idea: Evolution and the Meanings of Life*. New York: Simon & Schuster.

———. 2017. *Consciousness Explained*. Boston: Little, Brown, and Company.

Dragomir, Elena, I., et al. 2020. "Evidence Accumulation during a Sensorimotor Decision Task Revealed by Whole-Brain Imaging." *Nature Neuroscience* 23(1): 85–93. https://doi.org/10.1038/s41593-019-0535-8.

Duffau, Hugues. 2018. "Awake Mapping Is Not an Additional Surgical Technique but an Alternative Philosophy in the Management of Low-Grade Glioma Patients." *Neurosurgical Review* 41(2): 689–91. https://doi.org/10.1007/s10143-017-0937-6.

Dunbar, R. I. M. 2009. "The Social Brain Hypothesis and Its Implications for Social Evolution." *Annals of Human Biology* 36(5): 562–72. https://doi.org/10.1080/03014460902960289.

Eijk, Philip van der. 2008. "Nemesius of Emesa and Early Brain Mapping." *Lancet* 372(9637) 440–41. https://doi.org/10.1016/s0140-6736(08)61183-6.

Eklund, Anders, et al. 2016. "Cluster Failure: Why FMRI Inferences for Spatial Extent Have Inflated False-Positive Rates." *Proceedings of the National Academy of Sciences* 113(28): 7900–7905. https://doi.org/10.1073/pnas.1602413113.

Engelhardt, Tristram, Jr. 2000. *The Foundations of Christian Bioethics*. Exton, PA: Swets & Zeitlinger.

Ereshefsky, Marc. 2016. "Natural Kinds in Biology." In *Routledge Encyclopedia of Philosophy*. https://www.rep.routledge.com/articles/thematic/natural-kinds-in-biology/v-1.

Erickson, Paul, et al. 2013. *How Reason Almost Lost Its Mind: The Strange Career of Cold War Rationality*. Chicago: University of Chicago Press.

Evagrius of Pontus. 1983. *153 Chapters on Prayer*. In *The Philokalia: The Complete Text*, translated by G. E. H. Palmer et al. http://orthodox.altervista.org/philokalia.html.

Ferreira, Francisco R. M., et al. 2014. "The Influence of James and Darwin on Cajal and His Research into the Neuron Theory and Evolution of the Nervous System." *Frontiers in Neuroanatomy* 8. https://www.frontiersin.org/articles/10.3389/fnana.2014.00001.

Fodor, Jerry A. 1980. *The Language of Thought*. Cambridge: Harvard University Press.

———. 2000. *In Critical Condition: Polemical Essays on Cognitive Science and the Philosophy of Mind*. Cambridge: MIT Press.

Fodor, Jerry A., and Ernest LePore. 1992. *Holism: A Shopper's Guide*. Cambridge: Blackwell.

Frisch, Karl von. 1974. *Animal Architecture*. New York: Harcourt.

Friston, Karl J., et al. 2020. "Sentience and the Origins of Consciousness: From Cartesian Duality to Markovian Monism." *Entropy* 22(5): 516. https://doi.org/10.3390/e22050516.

Gavrilova, Natalia, and Andreas Nieder. 2021. "Distinct Neural Networks for the Volitional Control of Vocal and Manual Actions in the Monkey Homologue of Broca's Area." *ELife* 10: e62797. https://doi.org/10.7554/eLife.62797.

Gavrilyuk, Paul L., and Sarah Coakley, eds. 2011. *The Spiritual Senses: Perceiving God in Western Christianity*. Cambridge: Cambridge University Press.

Gibson, Eleanor J. 1987. "Introductory Essay: What Does Infant Perception Tell Us about Theories of Perception?" *Journal of Experimental Psychology: Human Perception and Performance* 13(4): 515–23.

Gombrich, Ernst, et al. 1971. "On Information Available in Pictures." *Leonardo* 4(2): 195. https://doi.org/10.2307/1572214.

Goncharko, Oksana, and Dmitry Goncharko. 2017. "A Byzantine Logician's 'Image' within the Second Iconoclastic Controversy. Nikephoros of Constantinople." *Scrinium* 13: 291–308. https://www.academia.edu/85055102/A_Byzantine_Logician_s_Image_within_the_Second_Iconoclastic_Controversy_Nikephoros_of_Constantinople.

Gregory of Nazianzus. N.d. *Theological Orations*. http://users.uoa.gr/~nektar/orthodoxy/paterikon/grhgorios_8eologos_logoi.htm.

———. 2011. *Five Theological Orations*. Translated by Steven Reynolds. Toronto: Estate of Steven Reynolds.

Hanby, Michael. 2003. *Augustine and Modernity*. London: Routledge.

Hardcastle, Valerie Gray. 1997. "When a Pain Is Not." *Journal of Philosophy* 94(8): 381–409. https://doi.org/jphil199794828.

Heidegger, Martin. 2001. *The Fundamental Concepts of Metaphysics: World, Finitude, Solitude*. Bloomington: Indiana University Press.

Hierotheos. 2000. *Orthodox Psychotherapy: The Science of the Fathers*. Translated by Esther Williams. Bethlehem, PA: St. Nikodemos.

Horik, Jayden van, et al. 2012. "Convergent Evolution of Cognition in Corvids, Apes, and Other Animals." In *Oxford Handbook of Comparative Evolutionary Psychology*, edited by Todd K. Shackelford and Jennifer Vonk, 80–101. https://doi.org/10.1093/oxfordhb/9780199738182.013.0005.

Horner, Aidan J., et al. 2016. "Grid-like Processing of Imagined Navigation." *Current Biology* 26(6): 842–47. https://doi.org/10.1016/j.cub.2016.01.042.

Husserl, Edmund. 2012. *Cartesian Meditations: An Introduction to Phenomenology*. Translated by Dorion Cairns. Berlin: Springer.

Kanwisher, Nancy, and Galit Yovel. 2006. "The Fusiform Face Area: A Cortical Region Specialized for the Perception of Faces." *Philosophical Transactions of the Royal Society B: Biological Sciences* 361(1476): 2109–28. https://doi.org/10.1098/rstb.2006.1934.

Kemp, Simon, and Garth J. O. Fletcher. 1993. "The Medieval Theory of the Inner Senses." *American Journal of Psychology* 106(4): 559–76.

Knight, Christopher C. 2018. "The Human Mind in This World and the Next: Scientific and Early Theological Perspectives." *Theology and Science* 16(2): 151–65.

———. 2021. *Science and the Christian Faith: A Guide for the Perplexed*. Crestwood, NY: Saint Vladimir's Seminary Press.

Kolb, Bryan, and Ian Q. Wishaw. 2009. *Fundamentals of Human Neuropsychology*. New York: Worth.

Levinas, Emmanuel. 1969. *Totality and Infinity: An Essay on Exteriority*. Translated by Alphonso Lingis. Pittsburgh: Duquesne University Press.

Levine, Joseph. 1983. "Materialism and Qualia: The Explanatory Gap." *Pacific Philosophical Quarterly* 64: 354–61.

Libet, Benjamin. 1985. "Unconscious Cerebral Initiative and the Role of Conscious Will in Voluntary Action." *Behavioral and Brain Sciences* 8(4): 529. https://doi.org/10.1017/s0140525x00044903.

Lieberman, Philip, et al. 1972. "Phonetic Ability and Related Anatomy of the Newborn and Adult Human, Neanderthal Man, and the Chimpanzee." *American Anthropologist* 74(3): 287–307. https://doi.org/10.1525/aa.1972.74.3.02a00020.

Lindenfors, Patrik, et al. 2021. "Dunbar's Number' Deconstructed." *Biology Letters* 17(5): 20210158. https://doi.org/10.1098/rsbl.2021.0158.

Linson, Adam, et al. 2018. "The Active Inference Approach to Ecological Perception: General Information Dynamics for Natural and Artificial Embodied Cognition." *Frontiers in Robotics and AI* 5. https://www.frontiersin.org/articles/10.3389/frobt.2018.00021.

Louth, Andrew. 2023. *Selected Essays*. Vol. 1, *Studies in Patristics*. Oxford: Oxford University Press.

MacIntyre, Alasdair. 2007. *After Virtue: A Study in Moral Theory*. Notre Dame: University of Notre Dame Press.

Macken, John. 1990. *The Autonomy Theme in the Church Dogmatics: Karl Barth and His Critics*. Cambridge: Cambridge University Press.

Marion, Jean-Luc. 1998. "Descartes and Onto-Theology." In *Post-Secular Philosophy: Between Philosophy and Theology*, edited by Philip Blond, 67–106. London: Routledge.

———. 2018. *On Descartes' Passive Thought: The Myth of Cartesian Dualism*. Translated by Christina M. Gschwandtner. Chicago: University of Chicago Press.

Maximus the Confessor. 1985. *Selected Writings*. Edited by George C. Berthold. New York: Paulist.

———. 2014. *On Difficulties in the Church Fathers: The Ambigua*. Translated by Nicholas Constas. Cambridge: Harvard University Press.

McCulloch, Warren S., and Walter Pitts. 1943. "A Logical Calculus of the Ideas Immanent in Nervous Activity." *Bulletin of Mathematical Biology* 5: 115–33.

McFarland, Ian A. 2007. "'Willing Is Not Choosing': Some Anthropological Implications of Dyothelite Christology." *International Journal of Systematic Theology* 9(1): 3–23. DOI:10.1111/j.1468-2400.2006.00227.x.

McGilchrist, Iain. 2021. *The Matter with Things: Our Brains, Our Delusions, and the Unmaking of the World*. London: Perspectiva.

McGrath, Alister E. 2011. *Darwinism and the Divine: Evolutionary Thought and Natural Theology*. Oxford: Wiley-Blackwell.

Mehta, Arpan R., et al. 2020. "Etymology and the Neuron(e)." *Brain* 143(1): 374–79. https://doi.org/10.1093/brain/awz367.

Migne, J.-P., ed. 1857–86. *Patrologia Graeca*. Paris.

Milbank, John. 2006. *Theology and Social Theory: Beyond Secular Reason*. Oxford: Wiley-Blackwell, 2006.

Mithen, Steven. 1996. *The Prehistory of the Mind: The Cognitive Origins of Art, Religion, and Science*. New York: Thames and Hudson.

Mozzi, Alessandra, et al. 2016. "The Evolutionary History of Genes Involved in Spoken and Written Language: Beyond FOXP2." *Scientific Reports* 6(22157). https://doi.org/10.1038/srep22157.

Nakajima, Riho, et al. 2018. "Neuropsychological Evidence for the Crucial Role of the Right Arcuate Fasciculus in the Face-Based Mentalizing Network: A Disconnection Analysis." *Neuropsychologia* 115: 179–87. https://doi.org/10.1016/j.neuropsychologia.2018.01.024.

Nemesius. 2008. *On the Nature of Man*. 2008. Translated by Philip Van Der Eijk and R. W. Sharples. Liverpool: Liverpool University Press.

Nowak, Martin A. 2006. "Five Rules for the Evolution of Cooperation." *Science* 314: 1560–63. https://doi.org/10.1126/science.1133755.

Nowak, Martin A., et al. 2011. "Nowak et al. Reply." *Nature* 471(7339): E9–10. https://doi.org/10.1038/nature09836.

Nowak, Martin, and Sarah Coakley, eds. 2013. *Evolution, Games, and God: The Principle of Cooperation*. Cambridge: Harvard University Press.

Oliver, Simon. 2001. "Motion according to Aquinas and Newton." *Modern Theology* 17(2): 163–99. https://doi.org/10.1111/1468-0025.00156.

———. 2019. "Physics without Physis: On Form and Teleology in Modern Science." *Communio: International Catholic Review* 46(3–4): 442–69.

Paster, Gail Kern. 2014. *Humoring the Body: Emotions and the Shakespearean Stage*. Chicago: University of Chicago Press.

Pfau, Thomas. 2022. *Incomprehensible Certainty: Metaphysics and Hermeneutics of the Image*. Notre Dame: University of Notre Dame Press.

Pinker, Steven. 2012. "The False Allure of Group Selection." *Edge*, June 18. https://www.edge.org/conversation/the-false-allure-of-group-selection.

Porter, Jean. 2004. *Nature as Reason: A Thomistic Theory of the Natural Law*. Grand Rapids: Eerdmans.

Quine, Willard V. O. 1969. *Ontological Relativity & Other Essays*. New York: Columbia University Press.
Quiroga, Rodrigo Quian. 2013. "Gnostic Cells in the 21st Century." *Acta Neurobiologiae Experimentalis* 73(4): 463–71.
Radde-Gallwitz, Andrew. 2011. "The Holy Spirit as Agent, Not Activity: Origen's Argument with Modalism and Its Afterlife in Didymus, Eunomius, and Gregory of Nazianzus." *Vigiliae Christianae* 65: 227–48.
Ren, Ziqi, et al. 2021. "Reconstructing Seen Image from Brain Activity by Visually-Guided Cognitive Representation and Adversarial Learning." *NeuroImage* 228(2): 117602. https://doi.org/10.1016/j.neuroimage.2020.117602.
Rhodes, Gillian, et al. 2001. "Attractiveness of Facial Averageness and Symmetry in Non-western Cultures: In Search of Biologically Based Standards of Beauty." *Perception* 30(5): 611–25. https://doi.org/10.1068/p3123.
Rocca, Julius. 2003. "Galen on the Brain: Anatomical Knowledge and Physiological Speculation in the Second Century AD." *Studies in Ancient Medicine* 26: 1–313.
Rossi, Albert. 2019. "Overcoming Impulse through Relaxation and Prayer: An Interview with Fr. Alexis Trader." *Becoming a Healing Presence, Ancient Faith Ministries*, April 9. https://www.ancientfaith.com/podcasts/healingpresence/overcoming_impulse_through_relaxation_and_prayer_an_interview_with_fr_alex.
Ryle, Gilbert. 2009. *The Concept of Mind: 60th Anniversary Edition*. London: Routledge.
Sapolsky, Robert M. 2017. *Behave: The Biology of Humans at Our Best and Worst*. New York: Penguin.
———. 2023. *Determined: A Science of Life without Free Will*. New York: Penguin.
Scheler, Max. 1916. *Formalismus in Der Ethik und Die Materiale Wertethik*. Vol. 2. Halle: Niemeyer.
Schneider, Helmut. 1993. "Prototyp - Ikone - Relation. Zur Bildertheorie Des Theodoros Studites." *Hermeneia: Zeitschrift Für Ostkirchliche Kunst* 9(4): 206–14.
Shapiro, Lawrence, ed. 2014. *The Routledge Handbook of Embodied Cognition*. London: Routledge.
Shepherd, Stephen V., and Winrich A. Freiwald. 2018. "Functional Networks for Social Communication in the Macaque Monkey." *Neuron* 99(2): 413–420.e3. https://doi.org/10.1016/j.neuron.2018.06.027.
Silberman, Steve. 2016. *Neurotribes: The Legacy of Autism and the Future of Neurodiversity*. New York: Penguin.
Smith, James K. A. 2005. *Introducing Radical Orthodoxy: Mapping a Post-Secular Theology*. Grand Rapids: Baker Academic.
Swinburne, Richard, and David Bradshaw, eds. 2021. *Natural Theology in the Eastern Orthodox Tradition*. St. Paul: IOTA.
Tallis, Raymond. 2012. *Aping Mankind: Neuromania, Darwinitis, and the Misrepresentation of Humanity*. Durham: Acumen.
Taylor, Charles. 2012. *Sources of the Self: The Making of the Modern Identity*. Cambridge: Cambridge University Press.
Thunberg, Lars. 1995. *Microcosm and Mediator: The Theological Anthropology of Maximus the Confessor*. Chicago: Open Court.
Trader, Alexis. 2012. "Patristic Embroidery on a Cognitive Pattern and Other Uses of the Fathers' Yarn: Introducing the Evidence of Early Christian Texts into Therapeutic Practice." *Edification: The Transdisciplinary Journal of Christian Psychology* 6(2): 85–96.

Trimble, Walker. 2020. "Brains Situated, Active, and Strange: Neurosurgical Magnification and Physicalism's Aesthetic Consequences." *Autonomie und Unheimlichkeit*. https://doi.org/10.5771/9783748904861-101.

———. 2021. "'Species Specierum': Late Scholastic Eucharistic Theology and the Origins of Post-humanism. Pt. 1: Soul-Body Dualism and the Doctrine of the Four Humors." *Trudy Kafedry Bogosloviya Sankt-Peterburgskoi Duhovnoi Akademii* 1(9): 58–83. https://doi.org/10.47132/2541-9587_2021_1_58.

———. 2023. "From Function to Surface: Phenomenology of the Thinking Organ." *Iranian Yearbook of Phenomenology* 1(1). https://doi.org/10.22034/IYP.2021.1402 10.1026.

Tsvelik, Aleksei, and Mikhail Aksenov-Meerson. 2021. *Six Days of Creation: Mind as a Cosmic Phenomenon: The Meeting of Nous and Logos in the Wisdom of Science*. Mosow: Praktika.

Wang, ZiMian, et al. 2010. "Specific Metabolic Rates of Major Organs and Tissues across Adulthood: Evaluation by Mechanistic Model of Resting Energy Expenditure." *American Journal of Clinical Nutrition* 92(6): 1369–77. https://doi.org/10.3945/ajcn.2010.29885.

Weber, Meletios. 2003. *Steps of Transformation: An Orthodox Priest Explores the Twelve Steps of Alcoholics Anonymous*. Chesterton, IN: Conciliar.

Whitfield, William. 2003. "Towards a Neurotheology?" *International Journal of Psychiatric Nursing Research* 8(3): 941.

Wright, Jessica L. 2022. *The Care of the Brain in Early Christianity*. Oakland: University of California Press.

Villablanca, Jaime R. 2010. "Why Do We Have a Caudate Nucleus?" *Acta Neurobiologiae Experimentalis* 70(1): 95–105.

Yang, Charles, et al. 2017. "The Growth of Language: Universal Grammar, Experience, and Principles of Computation." *Neuroscience and Biobehavioral Reviews* 81(B): 103–19. https://doi.org/10.1016/j.neubiorev.2016.12.023.

Zimmer, Carl. 2011. "100 Trillion Connections: New Efforts Probe and Map the Brain's Detailed Architecture." *Scientific American* 304(1): 58–63. https://doi.org/10.1038/scientificamerican0111-58.

Zinkovsky, Methody. 2021. "Variegated Unity: On the Discrepancy and Overlapping of the Semantic Fields of the Terms 'Atom' and 'Hypostasis' in Patristic Thought." *Studia Patristica* 123(20): 249–57.

Index of Names

Anokhin, Konstantin, 2
Anokhin, Peter, 31
Aristotle, 162, 170–73, 180, 183–84
Ashbrook, James, 146
Ashby, William, 123
Augustine of Hippo, 78, 113, 172, 179, 201
Autrey, Wesley, 202–3, 210
Ayala, Francisco, 13

Bacon, Francis, xvii, 117
Badiou, Alain, 106
Bakh, Aleksei, 123
Baker, Mark, 22
Barbour, Ian, 20
Behe, Michael, 129
Berdyaev, Nikolai, 71
Berlinski, David, 185
Bernstein, Nikolai, 31
Bitbol, Michel, 48
Blake, William, 137
Block, Ned, 136
Bohr, Niels, 89
Borges, Jorge, 111, 212
Broca, Paul, 174, 189
Brodsky, Joseph, 1, 5, 7

Campbell, Donald, 16
Cantor, Georg, 106
Carroll, Sean, xviii–xix
Chalmers, David, xxiv, 6, 17, 55, 147, 155
Chernigovskaya, Tatyana, xxiv
Chomsky, Noam, 175, 181, 184, 189, 209
Clayton, Phillip, 15–19, 21

Coecke, Bob, 100–102
Collins, Robin, 19, 23
Conway, John, 151
Crick, Francis, 14, 134

Damasio, Antonio, 162
d'Aquili, Eugene, 147
Darwin, Charles, 202, 207
Daston, Lorraine, 162
Dawkins, Richard, 203, 207
Deacon, Terrence, 5
Dennett, Daniel, 22, 192
Dembski, William, 129
Descartes, René, 20, 22, 29–30, 33, 55, 154, 171–72, 175, 182, 189
Dobzhansky, Theodosius, 14
Donne, John, 155
Duffau, Hugues, 190–91
Dunbar, Robin, 206

Eccles, John, 129, 147
Eco, Umberto, 4
Einstein, Albert, 97, 149
Ellis, George, 14–17, 21
Elsasser, Walter, 120
Engelhardt, Tristram, 167, 216
Evagrius of Pontus, 203, 207, 215

Faist, Sofia, 122
Fludd, Robert, 153, 154
Fodor, Jerry, 18, 176, 182, 185
Forman, Paul, xvii
Franck, Semen, 114
Frankl, Viktor, 36
Franz, von, Maria-Louise, 153

226   INDEX OF NAMES

Frege, Gottlob, 175
Friston, Karl, xxviii
Fröhlich, Herbert, 120
Frumkin, Alexander, 123

Galen, 171
Galilei, Galileo, xv, 87
Gavrilyuk, Paul, 162
Gibson, Eleanor, 182, 185,
Gibson, James, 189
Gide, André, 110
Giotto di Bondone, 111
Goetz, Stewart, 22
Golgi, Camillo, 174
Gombrich, Ernst, 190
Gregory of Nyssa, 24, 168–70, 174,
    178–80, 182–83, 186, 204–5
Gregory Palamas, 114
Gregory the Theologian, 179, 187,
    189, 203, 207, 209, 212–14

Haldane, John, 17
Halvorson, Hans, 22
Hartshorne, Charles, 114
Hasker, William, 18–20
Hebb, Donald, 198
Heidegger, Martin, 173
Heisenberg, Werner, 88, 130
Helmholtz, von, Hermann, 174, 189
Henry, Michel, 47, 55, 66, 72–73
Hewlett, Martinez, 15
Hippocrates, 134, 170
Hoffman, Donald, 105
Hopfield, John, 39
Hume, David, 177
Husserl, Edmund, 47, 51–52, 54,
    173–77

Ibn Sīnā (Avicenna), 172

James, William, 155, 174
Jie, Ke, 3
John Chrysostom, 204
John Duns Scotus, 173
John of Damascus, 24, 168, 187, 204
Jung, Carl Gustav, 152–55

Kant, Immanuel, 66, 71, 80, 175,
    184, 202
Kapitsa, Sergei, 6

Kaplan, Alexeander, xxv, xxix–xxx
Kavokin Alexey, xxv, xxx
Kepler, Johannes, 152–54
Kierkegaard, Søren, 89
Kiryanov, Dmitry, xxiv–xxv
Knight, Christopher, 23–25, 179,
    207
Kobozev, Ivan, 122
Kobozev, Nikolai, xviii, 120–30
Kochen, Simon, 151
Kopeikin, Kirill, xxvii–xxiii, xxx–
    xxxi
Krause, Karl, 113
Krivovichev, Sergey, xxviii, xxx
Kurnakov, Nikolai, 123

Lanza, Robert, 105

Laplace, de, Pierre-Simon, 205
Laughlin, Charles, 147
Lenin, Vladimir, 181
Libet, Benjamin, 177, 204
Linde, Andrei, 109–10
Locke, John, 175
Lotman, Yuri, 6
Lyotard, Jean-Francois, 78

Macaulay, Thomas, xvi
MacIntyre, Alasdair, 202
Macrina, 168–69
Mamardashvili, Merab, 6
Marion, Jean-Luc, 171
Maximus the Confessor, xxii, 24,
    170, 187, 203–4, 207, 215
McCulloch, Warren, 129, 175
McGilchrist, Iain, 166
McGinn, Colin, 134–35
McGrath, Alister, 13
Meillassoux, Quentin, 60
Merleau-Ponty, Maurice, 71, 81,
    174, 184
Moser, Edward, 32
Moser, May-Britt, 32
Milbank, John, 178
Murphy, Nancey, 15–19

Nagel, Thomas, 6, 45, 54
Nemesius of Emesa, 170
Nesteruk, Alexei V., xxvi, xxx

Neumann, von, John, xxxi, 88, 90, 194
Newton, Isaac, xv–xvii, 114, 122, 172, 214

Paller, Ken, 135–36
Pauli, Wolfgang, 152–55
Pavlov, Ivan, 29, 30, 174
Peacocke, Arthur, 114
Phidias, 213
Philo of Alexandria, 87
Pierce, Charles, 5
Pinker, Steven, 203
Pitts, Walter, 129, 175
Plato, 161–62, 165, 170, 174, 196
Polkinghorne, John, 12–13, 15, 19–20, 24–25
Popov, Ivan, 116
Popper, Karl, 147
Porter, Jane, 188
Pyatigorsky, Alexander, 6

Quine, Willard, 175, 184

Ramón y Cajal, 174
Ramsey, Ian, 108–9
Redi, Francesco, 128
Reshetovskaya, Natalia, 121
Reznik, Oleg, xxviii, xxx
Rose, Nicholas, 138
Roskies, Adina, 134
Russell, Bertrand, 155, 184
Ryle, Gilbert, 161

Safire, William, 133
Sapolsky, Robert, 199–202, 205–6, 210–12, 216
Saussure, de, Ferdinand, 181
Searle, John, 2, 134, 148, 155
Sechenov, Ivan, 29, 32
Sedol, Lee, 3
Seraphim of Sarov, 155
Seth, Anil, 136
Scheler, Max, 173, 194, 214

Schrödinger, Erwin, xix, xxviii, 41, 97, 101, 114–16, 120, 124, 128
Shpitalsky, Eugene, 122
Skinner, Burrhus, 175
Snow, Charles, 111
Solzhenitsyn, Alexander, 121
Specker, Ernst, 151
Spinoza, Baruch, 28, 37, 155
Stăniloae, Dumitru, 24
Stefaneschi, Giacomo, 111
Stoeger, William, 21
Suzuki, Satoru, 135–36
Swaab, Dick, 31

Taliaferro, Charles, 22
Thomas Aquinas, 170
Trader, Alexis, 165, 167
Trimble, Walker, xxix–xxxi
Trincher, Karl, 120
Trubetskoy, Sergei, 116–17

Vasiliev, Sergey, 122
Vavilov, Sergey, 120–21
Vernadsky, Vladimir, 120, 126–27
Vesalius, Andreas, 171
Villablanca, Jaime, 182
Virchow, Rudolf, 128

Ware, Kallistos, 114
Ward, Keith, 20, 22
Watson, James, 134
Wheeler, John, 49–50, 104
Wiener, Norbert, 31, 123
Wigner, Eugene, 120
William of Ockham, 173
Whitehead, Alfred, 194
Wolf, Francis, 57

Zeilinger, Anton, 104
Zelinsky, Nikolay, 123
Zeuxis, 213
Zinkovsky, Methody, 186, 207
Zizioulas, John, 206

www.ingramcontent.com/pod-product-compliance
Lightning Source LLC
Chambersburg PA
CBHW050847230426
43667CB00012B/2183